# THE GIRL FROM CAIRO

## A Memoir

## Peggy Hinaekian

To my parents Araxie and Haryo Hinaekian for their unconditional love and their unflinching faith in me.

# MEET THE GIRL FROM CAIRO

The Girl from Cairo is a memoir of the author's early life in Cairo, Montreal, Boston and Manhattan, from 1940 to 1960.

It is a riveting story of an Armenian girl born and raised in Egypt, her trials and tribulations, her anxieties and desires. She describes her life in Cairo through WWII and two Middle Eastern wars that brought uncertainty and insecurity to her cushy life.

Her father having worked with the U.S. Army during WWII, Peggy was accustomed to meeting Americans and reading American comics and magazines as a child. American movies were the biggest entertainment of the family and this ignited a desire in her to go to the U.S. She focuses wholeheartedly on this venture and strives to make it happen.

In her boy-crazy youth, she yearns for a fairy tale life of marrying the man of her dreams. She finally meets K—as he is called in the Memoir—her first boyfriend, and they plan to get married against his parents' will, who think he is too young, only nineteen, and she eighteen.

They finally get married and go to the U.S. as university students with no financial means of support as that was the only way out of Egypt. Their future is nebulous but they are both young, naive and full of dreams.

Married life has its ups and downs. Peggy is restless. She has confused feelings about marriage. She falls out of love with her husband and looks at other pastures.

How does a young woman from Egypt, where working women were looked down upon, avoid becoming a *hausfrau*, dependent on a man for her support?

This is the story of a young rebel, trapped in age-old cultural stereotypes, who escaped the life planned for her. The story of a young woman creating her own world and achieving an impossible dream.

**To order additional copies of this book, contact:**
Xlibris
844-714-8691
www.Xlibris.com
Orders@Xlibris.com
819493

# CONTENTS

Chapter 1   The Apartment ...........................................................1
Chapter 2   Word War II ..............................................................5
Chapter 3   The War Years in Egypt ........................................... 14
Chapter 4   Heliopolis..................................................................20
Chapter 5   The Family.................................................................32
Chapter 6   School........................................................................45
Chapter 7   Everyday Life ............................................................54
Chapter 8   The Neighbors ...........................................................68
Chapter 9   The End of the War....................................................77
Chapter 10 The Arab–Israeli War ................................................85
Chapter 11 St. Clare's College .....................................................88
Chapter 12 Teenage Years............................................................94
Chapter 13 The Armenian Social Club ........................................98
Chapter 14 My First Boyfriend................................................... 103
Chapter 15 Political Upheaval..................................................... 115
Chapter 16 The New Boyfriend .................................................. 123
Chapter 17 Life with Kourken.................................................... 136
Chapter 18 Back to School.......................................................... 144
Chapter 19 Parties and Fun ........................................................ 147
Chapter 20 Alexandria................................................................ 154
Chapter 21 Same Everyday Life ................................................. 157
Chapter 22 My Jobs ................................................................... 167
Chapter 23 Our Engagement...................................................... 174
Chapter 24 Wedding Plans ......................................................... 185
Chapter 25 Getting Out of Egypt .............................................. 190
Chapter 26 United States and Canada ........................................ 195
Chapter 27 A Great Calamity......................................................208

Chapter 28 Life without a Husband ............................. 212
Chapter 29 Return to Cairo ....................................... 215
Chapter 30 Return to Montreal .................................. 221
Chapter 31 Boston .................................................. 227
Chapter 32 Manhattan ............................................. 231
Chapter 33 Ma and Judy in New York ......................... 235
Chapter 34 Separation Papers from K .......................... 241
Chapter 35 Single Life in Manhattan ........................... 247

Note from The Author ............................................. 253

# CHAPTER I

---

# The Apartment

It has been a couple of weeks now that I have been having a recurrent dream—dreaming about our ten-room apartment in Heliopolis, an affluent suburb of Cairo. It is a vivid dream, and I wake up having strange feelings of nostalgia, going back into time, really way back, to another lifetime. In the dream, I am about six years old, and I scamper from room to room, trying to find something, but I don't exactly know what. My dream feels very real.

When I wake up, I am sweaty and stay in bed, trying to visualize the apartment and remember all the details of its configuration, the fun times and the not-so-fun times I had there. That apartment was my cocoon. I played hide-and-seek there with friends, I danced in the north hall, I played hopscotch in the south balcony, and I sang in the north balcony. What a comforting place it was. It sheltered me from harm and infused me with joy. It enveloped me with love. It was my stronghold, my sanctuary.

Why I am dreaming about it now, after more than half a century, is beyond me. Am I subconsciously homesick? I feel I don't have roots. I was born in Egypt, but I am not Egyptian. I am Armenian, but I have never been to Armenia. My roots are supposed to be in Egypt, but that Egypt is no longer there. Yes, it is the country of my birth, but I don't feel as though it is my country. I don't feel Armenia is my country either. A different Armenian language is spoken there, and life in a previously Communist country is so different from our life in Egypt. The people have been brought up differently.

I feel in limbo living in the United States after having lived in Switzerland for forty-five years. I am just like the wandering Jew going from country to country, seeking shelter. Shelter from what? I just want roots. Just plain roots. I want to belong. Wherever I have lived, I have been considered a foreigner, although I have made myself very much at home, working and mingling with the locals and taking part in the life of the community. However, I am often asked, "Where are you from?" People detect an accent in my spoken English.

Sometimes I have a strong desire and longing to find myself in that apartment again. Just fly there for one day and recapture my childhood and youth, if that is at all possible. But alas, nothing can be recaptured. Time does not stop. It is the most elusive escape artist.

I have often tried to visualize the layout of the apartment and have tried to draw it several times but have not managed to do so. I do have a good memory, and I am an artist, so why can't I do it? "Mystère et boule de gomme" as the French say. It means "some unknown thing"—"a mystery to be discovered." Even the French do not know where that expression came from. There are several theories.

The apartment building was owned by Pa. Ma told me that Pa was a gambler and that he lost it in gambling debts. Actually, he lost everything in gambling—his buildings, his car, his horses (that was what he gambled on). He also sold Ma's jewelry—the ones she had not managed to hide from him. His explanation was that *he* had given them to her, and he would buy her other jewelry when he came in the money again. He was the perpetual optimistic gambler and dreamer. A very kind and generous man. Everybody loved him. He had an undeniable charisma and humor and was affectionate toward his family. It was easy to forgive him.

Unfortunately, I do not remember our affluent times. My memory only goes back to when I was four years old.

⌒

My first recollection from early childhood in that apartment is my tonsils operation at around that age. I was told nothing about it beforehand.

One day I saw a doctor coming in our apartment with an assistant, a doctor's examining chair and table, and some other strange equipment. The equipment was installed in one of our bedrooms. We had five bedrooms, which we always changed around. My sister and I sometimes took over our parents' bedroom. My parents sometimes shared a bedroom, and sometimes they slept in separate rooms when Pa had irregular hours, which he most often did.

"Who are these people, Ma, and what's going on?" I asked, tugging at her skirt, when I saw them going around installing strange equipment in one of the bedrooms. I was perplexed.

"The man in the white coat is my doctor and the other two, his assistants. The doctor is going to examine my throat and fix something. No big deal," she said casually. "By the way, will you please sit on the doctor's chair so that he can also look at your throat?"

I sat obediently on the doctor's chair, not suspecting what was about to take place. One of the assistants approached me with a smile and quickly put a kind of a mask on my face, and I was out. Out cold.

When I woke up, I was in my bed. I did not know what had happened to me. Ma was seated next to me, caressing my hair. I looked up at her with wide, inquiring eyes.

"The doctor removed your tonsils because they were bothersome, and they would have caused problems when you got older. Nothing to worry about," she said soothingly, continuing to caress my hair.

I started to tell her something, and a little bit of blood came out of my mouth. I got frightened at the sight of this and glared at Ma. Since then, I can't stand the sight of blood. Even a little nosebleed

Peggy Hinaekian

makes me go into panic mode. I even look away when a needle is poked in my vein, not that there is ever any blood in the poked hole.

I made some frantic motions with my hands, asking for pencil and paper. Ma fetched them for me. I wrote one sentence.

"You lied to me."

And I did not speak to her for a week, fearing that more blood would spurt out of my mouth. Ma reassured me that it was okay and that it would not happen again. She gave me a treat—ice cream—which I appreciated, but I was still mad at her. All my communications were on paper. She cajoled me to speak, promising me a gift of some drawing pencils and paper, and I finally managed a weak "Okay."

No more blood.

I snatched the paper and drawing pencils and drew a picture of my younger sister, Judy, a face with very little hair on her head.

"Excellent," Ma and Pa cooed over me.

But I was still angry and glared at them.

"If I had informed you of the operation, you would have run away, and there would have been a scuffle, and we would not have been able to go through with it," Ma said.

"You lied to me," I repeated.

4

# CHAPTER II

---

## Word War II

The second traumatizing experience I remember is World War II and the bombing of Egypt. This memory has stayed with me forever. I can never forget it. It is not a happy time in my life. I think the insecurities I felt later in life all stemmed from the war years.

It was 1940. I knew very little about this war. After all, I was only a child. To answer my innumerable questions, I was just told that the Germans and Italians were waging a war against some countries and that they were also attacking Egypt. The details I learned later when I was older. Part of the Allied forces—the British, the Australians, and all other troops from the Commonwealth countries—were trying to defend their positions in Egypt, to prevent the two armies of the Axis powers (Germany and Italy) of gaining control of it and, most importantly, control of the Suez Canal. This seemed to be the only topic of conversation my parents had with their relatives and friends, day and night. It was not comforting at all. I was on edge lest something bad would happen to us and did not want to sleep alone in my bed.

Our windows were painted in the color violet, and at nights, when the sirens would blast, we would shut off all lights. We could hear distant bombing. We could hear people shouting in the street

---

"Edfi'l Nour" (shut off the light in Arabic). Some neighbors were being stubborn and were not following orders.

I did not understand much of what was going on, but I felt the tension in everybody around me. I was scared, of course. My sister was not aware of much. She was too young.

The war was all over the news. It was a really big war. It seemed there had been another one, which was called World War I, but I was not born then. My parents and their friends compared the two wars in their conversations.

I heard that the Italian troops had entered Egypt and were occupying Sidi Barrani. Where on earth was Sidi Barrani?

"Ma, do we live close to Sidi Barrani?" I asked her, interrupting her while she was talking on the phone with a friend about this calamitous event.

"Don't worry, it is far away," she said, trying to reassure me. But that did not pacify me. I was an extremely curious and precautious child, and I wanted to know more. Ma then showed the location to me on an atlas. It was a coastal Mediterranean town on the Egyptian border with Libya, quite far from Heliopolis. I was somewhat relieved. The British then managed to recapture Sidi Barrani, and people felt safer. Me too.

"You see," said Ma, "there is nothing to worry about. We are safe."

One of the most frightful days of my life during the war was when, in 1940, still in kindergarten, the sirens started blaring in the morning. That was rather strange. Usually, they went on at night when we were home, tucked comfortably in bed. The people never knew whether it was the Germans or the Italians bombing us. They both came from Libya. I knew where Libya was. I had looked it up on the atlas already when the Italians had entered Sidi Barrani.

When the sirens blasted that particular morning, there was pandemonium in school—children screaming, vomiting, crying for their mothers, not their fathers. (Soldiers do that too, it seems—they ask for their moms.) We were ushered helter-skelter down to the basement of the school. It was half a basement. It had windows. I don't know why they thought we were safer there. Almost every child wanted to go to the restroom; they were peeing in their pants. I was in shock, crying for Ma, and I also peed in my pants. I hated that. I felt dirty and smelly. I took off my panties and threw them in the garbage. I hoped Ma would not be mad at me. I did have other panties at home.

"I want to go home! I want to go home!" I yelled over and over, sitting on a bench in the basement. One pretty teacher, whom I especially liked, tried to calm me down.

"Don't worry, dear, it will be over soon, and we can all go home," she said.

Don't worry—was she kidding?

Then there was an ear-shattering loud noise, which seemed to be coming from right next to the school. *My god,* I thought, *we have been hit by something, and we would surely die, and Ma is not here, and Pa is at work, and where is the cat?* I hoped he was safe. Teachers were running back and forth, trying frantically to calm us and assuage our fears, but to no avail. They were looking at each other, and I heard them, in hushed voices, utter the word "bomb."

"We have been hit by a bomb," one teacher said to another. I heard it distinctly. They did not know I was hiding behind a door, listening in on their conversation.

"There is a bomb! There is a bomb!" I screamed out loud, running to the restroom once again to puke and do number 2.

"Please, children, be quiet" was all the teachers said.

How can a child be quiet when the word "bomb" is uttered? Luckily, no other bomb fell on that day, just that one. But one was enough to scare us to death.

After the all clear sounded, parents came and retrieved their children. Pa came to get me from school. Some people were going to the bomb site, which was within walking distance. I insisted on going, so Pa took me along. I was curious to see what had actually happened and held on tightly to Pa's hand.

"Don't get scared, dear. The bomb has already fallen," he said.

People were shouting in the streets, "This way! This way!" The site was only one kilometer away from the school, so close it could have hit us, for sure. When I saw the site, it was one mighty huge hole in the middle of a beautiful park, a park where we often went with friends and family to play. The grass around the hole was scorched. I gasped, my eyes almost flew out of their sockets, and I was speechless. We had no iPhones to take pictures then, and we had not thought of bringing our cameras. We were told not to approach too close for fear of shrapnel. I'll never forget that incident as long as I live. I have never seen another bomb site since.

"I don't want to go to school today," I told Ma when she woke me up the next day. "I want to be home if ever another bomb falls. I am frightened. I want to be with you."

Ma allowed me to stay home one day, but the day after, she insisted that I go to school. Luckily, no other bombs fell during the daytime from that day on.

When the sirens would go on at nights, all the neighbors, including us—except for Pa—would rush down to the basement of our building.

"If I am going to die, I prefer dying in my own bed," Pa would say, and he stayed in bed. He was fatalistic, and he continued on sleeping without a care in the world until the next morning. Nothing bothered him. Sandy, our cat, also stayed with him, hidden somewhere. He came out of his hiding place when we regained our apartment after the all clear sounded.

The basement was the living quarters of the *bawab* (Arabic word for doorman). The doorman's job was not really that of a doorman. There was no door to guard. He was the cleaner/caretaker of the building when he felt like it. But he almost never moved his *derrière* to clean. He was paid a miserly sum by the owner who did not care less about the cleanliness of the building and did not heed the complaints of the tenants. Ma told me that when Pa owned the building, the entrance was clean and sparkling. Sometimes the tenants gave extra money to the *bawab* for services rendered.

Most of the time, Hassan, that was his name, sat in his quarters with his *galabeya* (Arabic word for robe), yoga style, at the entrance of the building, watching people come and go. He did notice a lot of things. He knew exactly who was visiting whom and at what hour. You couldn't escape his beady, vigilant eyes. If you wanted to know a neighbor's secret, you just asked him. He would gladly give it to you in return for a *baksheesh* (Arabic word for tip).

One thing I distinctly remember about the basement; it had stone walls, and it was damp and cool. Not very clean. The walls were gray, the floor was gray, and people's faces were gray in that gloomy light. There were no chairs, just a bench made with gray stone in the form of a U on which everyone sat down, children clutching their mothers, peeing in their pants and crying nonstop, when they heard the sirens or an occasional bomb drop in the distance. We had candles for light, and I remember the lizards on the walls. I had never seen one before and was scared of them at first. I thought they were some kind of a cockroach—there were plenty of those big brown ugly insects in Cairo.

In our apartment, Sandy, our cat, would stand vigil day and night, daring a cockroach to come out of its hiding hole, whereupon he would crush it to smithereens with his paw. In the morning, we would see them scattered, upside down in some corners. He never ate the damn things though. He was a sophisticated cat. Snobby-looking and aloof, very regal. I adored him.

"Don't be scared of them. They are harmless," Ma would say about the lizards. "And don't ever kill them. It's bad luck."

Ma believed in the evil eye and everything that would bring bad luck—examples being not to walk under a ladder or cross a black cat.

Up to this day, I remember Ma's advice and look at lizards with compassion and hate it when kids try to catch them. This happens often on the beach patio of our Fort Lauderdale condo, where kids run around with their nets, the parents just oblivious and not reprimanding them.

I have written a children's picture book about a child talking to a lizard. It needs to be illustrated. One of these days, I will take it up.

~

Then bam, another calamity happened, and people did not stop talking about that.

It was now 1942. I was a little older. People were talking about Rommel's troops being only one hundred kilometers away from Alexandria, the second largest city in Egypt. They had already crossed El Alamein, and the Battle of El Alamein had just started.

Where on earth was El Alamein? Another place to look up on the map.

People were uneasy, of course, but that did not prevent us from going to the movies two or three times a week. It was our favorite pastime, war or no war. News of the war was all over the Movietone newsreel. It was scary. Judy and I would listen to the grown-ups talk about it, and we were frightened to death. We asked questions, but most of them remained unanswered. Our parents did not want us to get involved in these conversations, especially regarding the war. This was serious stuff. Not for children. Ma always shooed us away to "go and play" when we asked who Rommel was and whether Rommel was a good guy or a bad guy. It turned out that he was a really bad guy.

"Everything is fine," she would say to pacify us, and we believed her.

Hitler, an ugly fellow with a stupid-looking mustache and his hair plastered on his forehead, was in the Movietone News a lot, yelling absurdities in German and the German audience saluting him with "Heil Hitler!" like he was God or something.

People were wondering whether the Germans would be occupying Egypt. There seemed to be some pro-German sentiment in the country. The future looked dismal.

"Not likely," Pa said. "The British won't ever let that happen."

There was a rumor going around that some factions in the government would welcome the Germans because the British had been occupying their land since a long time. Egypt was not a colony but a protectorate from 1882 to 1922, when the British conquered Egypt from the Ottomans. Then Egypt got her independence, I later learned. However, it was still considered an occupation because the British still ruled Egypt with certain clauses, although there was a king, King Farouk—a puppet king, I was told. Ma explained the basics of Egyptian history to me.

So, the Germans and the Italians seemed to be the bad guys, and the Allied powers were trying to protect us. Would they succeed? I asked my parents innumerable questions. I wanted to know details.

"Not for your age. Don't worry, nothing bad is going to happen. Egypt is safe," I was told time and time again. When was I going to be of age? Childhood seemed to drag on forever.

I wanted to grow up fast to be part of the real world. If I only knew then that childhood would be the best time in my life—without any responsibility—I would never have wished to grow up.

All these questions about names of places and people they were talking about left me perplexed, and I wanted to know more. It was so frustrating being a child and not understanding the events and circumstances surrounding me.

"What's happening, Ma?" I asked several times. She gave me some offhand explanation here and there.

The British soldiers and those of the Commonwealth (Ma explained what that word meant)—I saw Indian soldiers too—were all over Cairo, in hotels, in bars, and in movie theaters. Then the Americans joined the war because of the Japanese bombing of Pearl Harbor in Hawaii. They were also around the Cairo hot spots. People welcomed them with open arms. After all, they had helped in winning the First World War. There was a lot of commotion and chaos in Cairo in those days. It was exciting for me to see all these different soldiers around town.

After pestering Ma ad infinitum to tell me more about the situation, she sometimes explained stuff in an offhand manner. I imagine she did not wish to frighten me. She didn't think I was old enough for elaborate explanations. My questions to Ma were unending. I was being a pest, I was told.

Then it was rumored that some Italian troops were captured by the British, and photos of their march through Alexandria were in the newspapers. Some Italian civilian men were arrested in our neighborhood. This was too much for us children to understand. What was happening to our cushy lives? People would speak in hushed tones not to alarm us, but we could feel the concern in their voices. Of course, we were alarmed. We were not morons. They always told us "go and play." But, how could we? The news was all over the streets.

"Damn Hitler and that bellicose Mussolini," I always heard my parents and friends tell each other.

"Why are the British not stopping Rommel? He is almost next door. He is in El Alamein." The conversation would go on and on.

"Ma, are we going to die?" I asked Ma one evening after seeing the Movietone News at the movies, showing a battlefield with dead people lying around.

"No, dear, we are not going to die. These are photos of far-off places."

The damn coincidence was that on October 23 (my birthday) 1942, Field Marshal Montgomery, a good guy from the British side, launched the Second Battle of El Alamein. So now I have a memorable birthday. Ma explained to me who Montgomery was.

"Who are all these other people in the news?" I always asked Ma, and she gave me some vague explanations.

"Too complicated to explain it to you now. You'll learn in history class when the time comes."

"Are our Italian neighbors, bad people, Ma?" I asked.

In the building next door, some apartments were occupied by Italian families. They were friendly and held a lot of parties. I loved the Italian songs they played. They were so romantic.

"No, dear, they are okay. It's the Italian government that is bad."

"What does government mean?" I asked Ma, but she repeated that I was too young to grasp the logistics of politics. I was sick and tired of hearing that I was too young. I wanted to grow up fast and be part of the grown-up world. That prospect seemed so far away.

# CHAPTER III

## The War Years in Egypt

When the Americans joined the war, they had a camp at Huckstep, near Suez, a town close to the canal. Pa went to work as a contractor for the American army. We would vacation in Suez during the summer to be close to him. The hotel was on the beach, and crabbing was our pastime when the tide was low. Ma taught me how to catch crabs, gigantic ones, and hold them by their belly so that they wouldn't pinch my fingers. We also collected starfish. So many of them were left behind and could not make it to the water when the tide was low. We dried them in the sun and put them up on the walls of our apartment upon our return from vacation.

I remember distinctly that the restaurant of the hotel smelled of DDT (an insecticide) to ward off flies. Flies were rampant everywhere in Egypt, and food had to be kept safe; therefore, the restaurant was sprayed before the clients would set foot in there. But how safe was DDT? Considered poison now. Well, we did not die, but the flies certainly did.

Life in Egypt was quasi normal during the war. We were rationed for flour and sugar, but the quantity was more than enough. The parties and outings would go on every day, and people generally had fun, mostly going to the movies and visiting one another.

In the summer months—more than six months of the year—the movies were in the open air. They were not the drive-in types. They had regular rattan armchairs lined up in rows. There was also a stage in one cinema, the Roxy Cinema in Heliopolis, where there would be dancing with a live orchestra during intermission. The Movietone News was shown first, and that was where we got the news of the war and saw the heads of state—Roosevelt, Churchill, de Gaulle, Hitler, and Mussolini—in all their splendor, their propaganda speeches and planes bombing whole countryside. We saw the devastation in Europe, and we oohed and ahed. We considered ourselves relatively safe as only one bomb had fallen in Cairo. More had fallen in Alexandria. Surely the British and Americans would protect us, people thought.

I felt extremely proud when Pa would get up and dance with me on stage at the Roxy Cinema, me being only six or seven years old at the time. This was the only cinema that had a dance floor. He taught me how to dance the tango—my all-time favorite dance. In fact, my first husband and I used to participate in tango contests in Cairo. We always won first prize. I have not found a better dancer than him to this day. I therefore dance alone whenever the occasion arises. I refuse to follow men who are trying to learn this sensual dance. Either you have the rhythm and the moves or you don't. And he had them. Nobody had taught him. It was just inborn like in myself. I always thought that I might have been a dancer in a previous life.

When an air raid went on in the middle of the movie screening, everybody would rush to the restrooms or take cover under trees—as though a tree would prevent a bomb falling on you. The restrooms were packed with screaming children peeing all over the place. It was one stinking mess. I always felt like puking and had diarrhea. Ma said not to worry that this happened because I was frightened. At the end of the all clear, if it was still too early, we would resume watching the show. If the all clear sounded too late, then we were given tickets to come the next day to continue watching where we left off.

Yes, life was good despite the war.

I have lived in nine other apartments in different countries since 1956, but those other apartments all seemed like vacation homes to me. The apartment in Heliopolis was my real home. I grew up there. I knew every nook and cranny. It had a soul. I belonged there. I knew that Pa had hidden a handgun under one of the tiles in the sitting room. I am sure it is still there unless subsequent renters have replaced the tiles, which I doubt very much. People in Egypt are not that much into remodeling unless they are wealthy. No wealthy person ever lived in our building.

I lived all of WWII in that apartment. As I said before, it was home, my real home, where I experienced my first taste of war. I was only a kid then and terribly frightened of the air raids and the sound of bombs. Sometimes the piercing sound of sirens would go on all night, and there would be shouting in the streets.

There was a lot of shouting in Cairo whether during wartime or peacetime. People shouted at one another from balcony to balcony, from balcony into the street, from one end of the house to the other. The conversation at lunch and dinner tables was loud. People in the Middle East generally speak in loud voices and are very animated, gesticulating with their arms and hands. Others may think they are arguing or are angry. Not so, it is just their normal way of talking. We did not speak in low voices. The elderly did not need hearing aids. Shouting and gesturing were livelier—our preferred modes of communication.

Up to now, when Middle Eastern people come together, there are a lot of loud discussions, and even my husband, an American, who should be used to it by now, thinks we are fighting. He does not understand Armenian or Arabic. That's why.

The Armenians in Egypt spoke Armenian sprinkled with Turkish, Arabic, Italian, English and French words and expressions. These foreign words describe exactly what one is trying to convey. The translation into pure Armenian would not have the same impact. In mixing the languages, the conversation is more expressive and meaningful. Other diasporic Armenians, in the United States or in Iran, for instance, do not quite understand us when we speak. I, therefore, always try to eliminate all these foreign words to speak a pure Armenian when communicating with them, which is quite difficult for me. Pa was very good at it. Actually, Pa was good at almost everything except at making money.

We, the children, were often warned to beware of strangers approaching us in parks or wherever. A group of us, comprising of my aunties and cousins, used to go to the zoo and the lemon garden, and we, the children, wanted to play away from parents. We had strict orders not to listen or follow anyone who told us our mothers were calling or that they would take us to them. We were told to scream if an unknown person ever touched us. I was rather a mischievous child and wanted something to happen so that I could scream.

In fact, one such occasion arose at the movies during the war years. My sister and I were seated in front of our parents in an open-air movie theater. An English soldier was seated next to me. I was wearing a short skirt and, at one point, he put his hand on my thigh. I sprang up from my chair, turned around, and hollered, "Pa, the soldier next to me touched my thigh!"

Instantly, Pa got up from his seat, grabbed the soldier by his shirt neck, and slapped him around, calling him a pervert, whereupon the people seated in the vicinity of this scuffle got up and also shouted at this poor fellow.

"Why don't you pick up a prostitute!" one person yelled, breaking a soda bottle on ground to hit him with. Pa stopped him on time. He was shooed out of the cinema. There was no calling the police in Egypt when there were such incidents. We did not have cell phones, and there were no available phones anywhere. People took care of the problem themselves with fists and insults.

Typical insults were *kous ommak* (Arabic for your mother's cunt) or *Ibn sharmouta* (Arabic for son of a whore) and more often *khawal* (Arabic for fag), the greatest of all insults.

When we got home, I asked Ma, "What is a prostitute?"

"It is difficult to explain. You'll find out when you are older."

Always the same answer, "when you're older." I was fed up from being a child.

Pa taught me how to play backgammon when I was five. I admired the way he played. He mesmerized his opponent with his rapid movements almost as though he was playing with four hands. He would bang his fist on the table when he performed a good move and would declare, "I gotcha, there and there."

I also learned to play poker when I was six. My parents had poker parties with friends and relatives, and us kids would play among ourselves. We would have a ball, playing poker like grown-ups. Instead of money, we used plastic chips.

There was always a lot of laughter and good food, especially pastries. Middle Eastern pastries, of course. Ma was known to be the best *baklava* and *khadaif* (names of oriental pastries) maker in the community. She was proud of her reputation, but it caused her a lot of anxiety when she prepared them because she was a perfectionist. She liked receiving compliments. She wanted to retain her title till death do her part.

Sometimes, I was allowed to sit next to Pa while he was playing poker and was careful to be as quiet as a mouse; otherwise, I would be banished. I learned a lot of his tricks and his way of bluffing. Pa was a really good actor; he would fool his opponents with his discreet facial expressions. Too much would be too obvious. And he was fantastic. It was like watching a play. I was mesmerized by his play and tried to copy him when I played with friends. He always won at poker and backgammon, but, alas, those meager winnings did not bring his fortune back. These winnings were peanuts compared with the thousands he had lost. He lived his life always believing that one day he would get it all back and offer us the same lifestyle as before.

I remember we had a washerwoman, Fawzia, of Gargantuan proportions, who would come once a week to wash our sheets and towels in two huge basins in the big bathroom. She was an enormous woman with a double chin, dressed in a *milaya* (Arabic word for a shapeless black coverall) draped around her body. All *fellah* (Arabic word for Egyptian peasant) women covered themselves with this garment. Fawzia had sparse hair and small sunken, myopic eyes. I don't know how she could see stains with those eyes since her eyelids almost covered half of them. She used two gigantic basins. One was for boiling hot water and the other filled with cold water for rinsing. She used a Primus stove. This stove was imported from Sweden by the father of a schoolmate, who made millions during the war, selling them. He could later afford to send his three children to university in the United States.

Fawzia had the strength of a bull and arms like those of a wrestler. She would sit on the floor, yoga style—despite her weight and girth, she was agile—and attack the laundry with bare hands with thick sausage fingers, twisting and turning the fabric and singing or rather making wailing sounds.

We never gave her our clothes to be washed, only the towels and sheets. Otherwise, she would have torn them apart. That was how strong she was. We washed the delicate stuff ourselves. Egyptian cotton sheets could withstand her vigorous wrestling with them. She spent all day long washing, and then the wet stuff was strung up on ropes outside the balcony to dry in the sun. If there was too much laundry, it was taken up to the rooftop, where a maid had her quarters, and strung up there.

One day I wanted to use the bathroom and asked her to leave so that I would have some privacy.

"Don't you think I have seen girls' private parts?" she snickered. "I have work to do, so go ahead, do your business. I won't look."

I was aghast. I was a shy girl and ran to Ma, complaining.

Ma cajoled her into leaving the bathroom, giving the walrus some lame excuse. She obeyed reluctantly, complaining under her breath. When she came back in, she remarked with a smirk that I had stunk the bathroom to high heaven.

# CHAPTER IV

## Heliopolis

As I said earlier, we lived in Heliopolis. The word means City of the Sun in Greek. I learned in Armenian elementary school that it had been established in 1905 by Baron Edouard Empain, a Belgian industrialist, and Boghos Nubar Pasha, an Armenian, son of the first Egyptian prime minister, Nubar Pasha.

The teachers were proud to say that Egypt had a long history with Armenians.

"It dates back to the times of the pharaohs. An Armenian temple discovered in 982 was called *Deir Al Arman*" (temple of the Armenians), they taught us in between regular history lessons.

Both Baron Empain and Boghos Nubar Pasha had discovered the site in the desert. Baron Empain had a palace built for himself—on the way to Cairo airport, which is in Heliopolis. Boghos Nubar Pasha became the first prime minister of Egypt. His son founded the Armenian elementary school, Nubarian, in Heliopolis. That is the school I went to and where my step-grandfather was the principal.

Much later, when I was in my teens, we went to a party in the palace, hosted by the baron's great-nephew, who happened to be a friend of a guy in our group. We were so lucky to see this palace in all its glory. We danced under the stars on the gigantic terrace with exotic potted plants and marble statues.

Ma told me a lot of things about Heliopolis. It was advertised as having *"ni poussiere, ni moustique"*—no dust or mosquitoes. Most of the wealthy people from Cairo moved there to create this beautiful suburb of Cairo, with luscious parks, charming villas, and grandiose apartment buildings and hotels in a unique architectural style— mixture of Byzantium and Egyptian. Each ethnic origin built its own school, sporting club, social club, and church. The imposing Basilica, a Catholic cathedral, was also built right smack in the middle of Al Ahram square, where Baron Empain is buried. I often visited the Basilica, especially on hot days as it was so cool inside, and it had a solemn heavenly atmosphere. I was quite religious when I was young, and going to church gave me solace. I always lit some candles for the health of my family.

When Google came into existence, I found out that this cathedral had preserved a pipe organ, composed of 1,407 pipes, since 1914. Fortunately, up to this day, it has not been vandalized or destroyed after all the problems that have plagued Egypt—the uprising in 1952, the 1956 war, the Six-Day War, and lately, the burning of the Coptic churches. I also found out that the Egyptian government has converted it into some kind of a museum now.

Ma related to me that Pa had bought real estate in Heliopolis in the 1930s when he inherited his vast fortune at age twenty-one. His father had died at age sixty when Pa was one year old, bequeathing all his estate to his only son. After living a royal life for a few years with yearly six months trips to Europe, where my sister was born, Pa had little by little squandered all his money in gambling. Judy and I do not remember our parents' lavish lifestyle. I wish I did, but I was too young.

Before the disappearance of Pa's fortune, my parents had moved in one of the buildings in Heliopolis, owned by him. It was a four-storied, U-shaped building with three floors and only two apartments on each floor. Pa had joined two apartments on the second floor to make one larger dwelling. That was how we happened to have ten rooms.

I lived in this apartment until I got married and left Egypt in 1956, before the start of the Suez Canal War. That was my sanctuary. I'll always remember it with nostalgia.

We were the only family who owned a mailbox. It was a rickety thing, and the flap remained open as it had been broken a long time ago. Nobody stole our mail anyway, so why fix it? We were the only ones receiving any mail—mostly from our U.S. relatives and friends, away on vacation.

Our apartment was spacious and airy and did not have a proper rectangular shape. It was decorated in Art Deco style. The decorating was done when Pa had his money. After that, nothing was done. It had five bedrooms, two dining rooms—one formal and the other informal—and two salons—one formal and the other not. We called that one the sitting room. We had two large halls, in one of which Pa had installed our huge electric train. We loved playing with it. We would all sit on the floor and watch the train wagons go around and around. It made one hell of a noise. Our cat would watch from under an armchair. He was too scared to do anything about it. He would sometimes hiss to express his displeasure.

The only room I did not like was the kitchen. Kitchens in those days were not regarded as rooms to be decorated. They were there simply to cook the meals. It was bleak and gloomy. It had two windows above the enormous old-fashioned sink. These two windows offered interaction between close neighbors. Ma never talked loud in the kitchen. She did not wish the neighbors to hear our conversations or arguments—there were many of those. When I came into the kitchen to complain about one thing or the other, Ma always put her forefinger to her lips.

"Speak in a low voice or rather whisper," she always warned us, "lest the neighbors hear and gossip about us."

Ma was very conscious of what others would think or say.

The kitchen did not have a sitting area. Ma was always in there with the maid and prepared every meal from scratch. I wanted no part in it, but sometimes I was given the task of cleaning string beans or separating the black stones from the rice and lentils. They were rather tedious tasks, which I did not particularly care for.

We only had two bathrooms, both with large windows, one of them overlooking the building next door. We had to close the window every time we wanted to use the bathroom because the neighbors in the building across the yard had a good view of what was happening inside. It was about fifty yards away, but people could still see us sitting on the john.

The apartment had four sides—south, north, west, and east with windows and balconies on all sides, which provided our entertainment if we stayed home in the evenings. That was quite rare though. Middle Easterners like going out. Pa was almost never home in the evenings. He was out with his cronies in a café, playing backgammon. This was the case with most Middle Eastern men.

The windows had green wooden shutters on all four sides, and therefore, the apartment was very airy. We did not need air-conditioning or fans. It was situated on Sharia Salah-El-Dine (which still exists), the main street going to the metro station.

From the north oversized balcony, we watched all the people walk by going to the metro station. We especially liked watching the women in their trendy clothes. Clothes were a big thing in Cairo. People liked being dressed fashionably, some more than others. They had matching shoes and handbags. The fashion in those days was flared skirts below the knee, some with crinolines underneath. We gossiped about the people, the way they were dressed, the way they walked, who they were with. The men always had their shirts freshly ironed. They wore custom-made shirts and suits. There was no ready-to-wear. Everything had to fit just so. I remember sometimes going to the tailor with my father and was in awe at the time he took to get the sleeves of the vest sewed on just right. He would adjust and readjust. When I watch movies now, my discerning eyes look at the sleeves of men's suits and see some bad tailoring there.

We had a biannual ritual of moving furniture from one side of the apartment to the other when the seasons changed. We would hire two people—one being the floor cleaner, Ali, and the other, his friend—to move the two main bedrooms furniture to the north side in summer, where it was cooler, and in winter, it was moved back to the south side.

On the east side, there was a building full of Italians—a few good-looking young men with whom my sister and I flirted now and again (when we were teenagers), if you call looking at each other and smiling, making hand signs, flirting. Those were the days of innocent glances and encounters. Teenagers don't know how to flirt nowadays; it is all about getting laid. Romance has evaporated into thin air. I am so glad I lived during that era of romance and romantic music, not like the rave parties that teenagers go to now, where they gesticulate like monkeys in a trance, with no emotion, under the influence of drugs.

From the west side of the apartment building, we would watch the Armenian Boy Scouts' meeting grounds. It was a small yard separating our building from the one across. As children, we annoyed the Boy Scouts during their activities by throwing water on them, drenching them, and then hiding. So silly to hide, they knew it was us.

I fancied their leader when I was thirteen. His name was Aram, and he was eighteen. I thought I was in love with him. Actually, he was the nephew of Ma's ex-fiancé. I never learned the true story of her breakup with this ex-fiancé of hers. I don't know why I never asked. I suppose I did not like the idea of Ma having been close to another man other than Pa. This leader of the Boy Scouts was rather a serious fellow and never laughed. He pretended we did not exist and never looked up when we drenched them.

Our apartment had two huge balconies, one on the north and the other on the south side. The south side one was as big as a ballroom. We played and entertained there. The one on the north side was divided into two sections. One section was like a rotunda with arches for windows and where we slept on very hot nights by putting mattresses on the floor. It was an adventure for us kids. We loved it. It was like a private hideaway; no one could see us. We sang songs and then fell asleep. There were no bugs or mosquitoes ever. This was Heliopolis, the town advertised as having "neither dust nor mosquitoes." That was one huge advantage of living in Heliopolis.

Summers are extremely hot in Cairo but winter mornings, quite nippy. In winter, we never wanted to get out of bed to get dressed for school. We had no electric heaters to keep us warm. We sometimes used hot water bottles and somehow managed to put our uniforms on under the cover of the thick eiderdown, after a lot of coaxing from Ma. We would pretend our teeth were chattering just to annoy her.

From the south-side balcony, we had the view of a sumptuous villa with a well-manicured garden owned by a wealthy Muslim family. I used to love lying down on the couch in this balcony and watch the serenity of the scenery and the chirping of the birds. This calm was shattered one day when a new building was coming up next door, and the laborers would haul bricks up gangplanks on their shoulders, chanting monotonous tunes. They built it quickly though. It was done within six months. Chanting while working is very common in Egypt. I suppose it helps in not getting bored doing the same task day in day out.

When I was eight years old, I wanted my hair to be braided like my classmates'. Ma never had the time; she was always too busy, too harassed, too stressed. She wanted everything done perfectly and got frustrated when it was not. So, I learned to do it myself. After that, I became the family hairdresser. No kidding. I did my sister's hair, my auntie's hair, and some of my friends' hair. Later on, when I was a teenager and went to a hairdresser for the first time, I hated how he fashioned it. I came home and did the whole thing myself. Waste of money. Never went to a hairdresser since. I became a do-it-yourself person.

"Do you want to be a hairdresser when you grow up?" I was often asked.

"Of course, not" was my reply. "I want to do something much more glamorous than that." *Like be a movie star maybe?* I saw American films and envied the movie stars. How little I knew of their miserable personal lives, which came out later in biographies. Being a movie star was too far-fetched though. I would be content in being a fashion designer.

I liked to do things on my own but only the stuff I really liked. That certainly did not include housework or cooking. I learned to sew my own clothes at the age of twelve. We had sewing class in Armenian elementary school and also an embroidery class. I still use the napkins I have embroidered when I was eleven. They are timeless. Most things I have kept, being a hoarder, remind me of my youth. Some people tell me I am living in the past. Well, my past was exciting. Why should I not relive it? My present is exciting too. As for my future, I wish I knew something about that, only good things though. I don't want to know when death will overcome me, for instance.

The well-to-do women had their clothes made by dressmakers. We made our own clothes. Ma was an expert seamstress and extremely capable, and she taught us. We sometimes hired a dressmaker for a few days and had our wardrobe done for the whole summer or winter. We would work alongside the seamstress to finish up faster and pay less, of course. I was a fast learner and managed to do all my clothes from then on. We used an old Pfaff sewing machine inherited from my grandmother. I was so attached to this peddle machine that, when I lived in Geneva much later, I found one just like it at the flea market and bought it and used it as a piece of furniture in the living room. I put potted plants on top. Every time I looked at it, it reminded of my sewing days in Heliopolis, rattling away on the sewing wheel.

There were several fabric shops in Cairo. It was an expedition and a treat to go there and choose fabric. The rolls would be laid out for us, and we would drape a fabric on our shoulders and look in the gigantic mirror to see how it looked on us. The employees were mostly Europeans.

I remember one time I chose a pink cotton fabric with white polka dots. Ma was against buying it because the dots were not woven but kind of painted on. She said they would come out in the washing. For once, she was wrong. I still wear that dress after many, many washings, and not one dot has worn off. I have done some alterations to it to fit my mature figure. We usually chose imported French or Italian fabrics, but this one fabric happened to be of Egyptian cotton, famous for its endurance.

Wrinkles in clothes were a no-no. We had the ironer's shop next door to our building, and our dresses and shirts were sent to him to be ironed. We never did any ironing. His assistant would then bring them back on clothes hangers (even men's shirts), and if Ma's discerning eyes would see one wrinkle, they would be sent back. After wearing a dress once, it was sent to the ironer to be ironed again before wearing it a second time. We would wear cotton clothes only three times before they were washed and pressed.

When I went to Montreal, after getting married, it surprised me to see all these badly dressed people with their synthetic clothes. No synthetic clothes in Egypt. Everything was made of cotton or silk. Egypt was one of the foremost cotton-exporting countries. In fact, my maternal grandfather exported them to his family's Lancashire cotton mills in England.

When the furniture was moved from one side of the house to other, everything was moved except the voluminous Art Deco wardrobes. One was full of winter clothes and the other of summer ones. I loved the south-side wardrobe; it had three full-length mirrors that would open up, enabling me to scrutinize myself from every angle. I was very critical of myself as I was very skinny and hated it. I often wondered whether I would ever put on weight so that when I became a teenager, boys would like me. Middle Eastern girls were amply endowed, and I was the skinny one, "flat as an ironing board," they called me, and I hated it.

Looking at myself in this three-paned mirror, I also realized that I did not like my nose. It looked Armenian, and I definitely did not want to look Armenian. I wanted to look like an American or a European. My nose had a slight bump on the bridge, and I tried to pull it this way and that to see how it would look if I had a nose job.

"Ma, when I grow up, I think I will have plastic surgery done to my nose, like Diane did." Diane was one of Ma's friends. "I don't like this tiny bump on it."

"You always come up with crazy ideas," Ma said. "You would be stupid if you fiddle with your nose, and you're not stupid, are you? Diane had a ghastly hooked nose, so it was necessary for her. Otherwise, she would not have found a husband."

It seemed to me that in the Middle East, things were always done with the objective of finding a husband.

Well, I thought if I go to the United States, and I certainly intended in doing so, I would earn my own money and could have a nose job. When I finally got to Montreal (almost the United States), much later on with my husband, I told him I wanted a nose job.

"Never will you do that," he barked, looking at me threateningly. "If you ever touch your nose, I'll leave you, you understand? I can't stand looking at women who have had plastic surgery done to their faces. You know how many I photograph every week?" He was a photographer working in the swankiest photographer's shop in Montreal. "These women look ghastly and phony. This one woman in our shop had some stuff pumped in her face, and her cheeks looked like they are inflated with golf balls."

"Yes, sir," I retorted sarcastically, not liking his authoritative tone one bit. Well, he was Middle Eastern.

I got rid of the nose job idea soon, though, because after I left my husband and began dating other men, I received compliments about my profile. One thought I had a Nefertiti profile, another, that I had an ancient Grecian one, this from a top lung specialist in Montreal who was lascivious and was coming on to me. I was very uncomfortable lying on the examination table in my bra and panties and him ogling me. Patients did not wear robes in those days. You just lay there with your undies and pretended not to be self-conscious.

"I like your lace panties," this doctor said.

I didn't look at him and didn't utter a word. I wanted to get off that examination table fast.

He persisted on commenting on my looks.

The next time I had to visit him, I went with my sister.

Speaking about the kitchen again. There were two old-fashioned Primus stoves—Swedish-made stoves imported by the father of a classmate. He made millions importing these stoves to Egypt. They lived in a part of Cairo called Maadi—a posh neighborhood—and had four villas on their grounds plus a building that housed an enormous kitchen and a dining room. All the family members, who lived in the separate villas, joined together for the meals. It was a great idea, I thought, not to have to cook separately. I have always wished to have that kind of life with my extended family.

Ma did not like me to handle those stoves. They were lit by kerosene and were dangerous, she said. Whenever I wanted to wash my hair, a cauldron full of water would have to be heated on one of them. Ma always said, "Not now. Don't you see I am busy in the kitchen?" She was always busy in the kitchen. So, I learned to do it by myself, disregarding her objections. I was very careful though. I did not wish to burn myself.

We had a small oven in the kitchen. When Ma prepared a large oven dish, it was sent to the Armenian baker, around the corner, to be baked in his large oven. All the neighbors did likewise. The youngest son of this baker used to sit at the cash register since he was twelve years old. Later on, when he immigrated to the States, he became a millionaire with his pita bread, sold nationwide. He never graduated from high school. He wanted to be in business, and he succeeded without a business degree. He had brains and just hired the required personnel.

The metro, which joined Heliopolis to Cairo, was above ground. It was built by the French in 1890, Pa told me. It was superfast and had few stops until it reached Cairo. There was a special compartment for women in the first class. Women were allowed to sit in the general carriage, but men were not allowed in the women's compartment. We always tried to sit in first class, even if we had to stand, rather than in second class, where some fellah women would fling their black coveralls left and right, trying to fix them just so, and have their lice spewing onto our hair. Yes, we had been de-loused once or twice already, and it was not very pleasant. The way it was done in Cairo was with gasoline combed through our hair.

It seems that now most of the metro and tram rails have been removed, and an underground metro transportation system is in place.

There were also buses, but the metro was cleaner, and it was our preferred mode of transportation. The buses were generally overcrowded with *fellahs* and smelled foul, and we did not trust the bus drivers. They did not have a good view of the street as people would often hang on to the bus from the sides. It is a wonder that they did not topple over.

Pa had owned a cream Ford convertible, with white leather interior, but I don't remember it. I have only seen photos of it. No cars were needed in Heliopolis. We walked everywhere—walk to the movies, walk to school, walk to the stores, walk to friends' houses. In any case, few people had cars then; therefore, there were few streetlights. There was no car insurance either. If there was ever an accident, it would be settled with insults and fists, and the strongest would win, rarely monetarily though. The police seldom intervened.

There were none around anyway. I remember there being only one dressed in white in the largest square in Cairo, who directed traffic with his arms and a whistle, just like in Italy.

There were three distinct classes of people in Egypt: the very wealthy upper class, which is composed of Muslim landowners, Europeans, Armenian, and Jewish merchants and traders; the middle class, which is composed of all Europeans—almost no Muslims—who worked in offices, stores, and schools; and the lower class, which is composed of the Egyptian *fellah*, the uneducated peasant, servants, and street vendors.

# CHAPTER V

---

## The Family

Ma told me that Pa lost his fortune gradually in the span of five years after he inherited it through gambling on horses. He lost all the buildings and his horses as well. Pa had been an extremely wealthy man, but my sister and I do not remember those years. We were much too young. He had lost it all by the time we were aware of the circumstances. My pa was a multitalented, fun-loving, and generous man but had one big vice, and that was gambling at the races. Everybody loved him and liked his company. He sparked up life wherever he went. I don't know how Ma put up with his gambling vice. She was stressed all the time. Maybe that was why she developed asthma.

Women did not divorce their husbands in Egypt in those days. Who would marry a woman with kids? And in any case, Ma never thought of divorce. She wanted to get the marriage and the family going.

Not many people knew that Pa had lost his fortune because Ma kept up a good front. She knew how to save money. She dressed up and us in the latest style. She would sew all our dresses herself with fine, imported fabrics, styles copied from French and Italian magazines. Ma paid a lot of attention to "what will people think."

---

"People have to respect you," she always said. "If you go around shoddily dressed, nobody will look at you or pay attention to you. We have to keep up appearances. We don't have much money, but we don't want to look like paupers."

We were always well dressed. No chance that we would ever go around in outmoded clothes and tarnish our reputation of the "nice-looking Hinaekian sisters."

Ours was not a conventional Armenian family in Egypt. We did not act like typical Armenian families. We were not clannish or traditional and did not go to church often. The Armenian Mass was much too long, and it bored me. Not very religious were we, although we did believe in God. Ma had taught me to say a prayer before going to sleep, about our health and Pa's job—that was of the utmost importance. I still do this every night; otherwise, I can't fall asleep.

Ma was half-British, and encouraged by her British father, she worked outside the home before getting married. Usually, a girl from a good family did not seek employment outside. She waited for a "nice" and, hopefully, wealthy husband to materialize. But Ma rebelled against this custom. She was a beautiful, tall young woman, speaking and writing several languages, and went to work at Kodak, where she met a number of men who courted her. She got engaged to an Armenian guy.

Ma was approached by the head of British intelligence in Cairo, an acquaintance of her father, who asked her to work for them. There were not many British women in Egypt, so being British born, she was considered a most eligible candidate. Ma declined, however, saying that she was getting married soon and did not intend to work after marriage. But she did not get married soon. She found out her fiancé was a liar. (I don't know the details.) She broke off the engagement when he went to Lebanon on business.

It seems her great-aunts had been ladies in waiting to the queen. I don't remember which queen, although Ma had told me all about it.

I never failed to tell everyone that my mother was half-British. I just did not want to be considered an Armenian for as far back as I can remember. It sounded more sophisticated to be a quarter British.

It made me stand out. I always wanted to be different from the other girls anyway, and I was. I was the only Armenian girl in the whole of Cairo who had freckles. My grandfather, from Ma's side, had reddish hair, some freckles, and green eyes. I wish I had also inherited the green eyes. That would have made me really stand out.

My grandfather, from Pa's side, was from an old Armenian town called Yerzenga (in Turkey now). Half of Armenia is in Turkey, and the consensus is that the Turks will never give back conquered land, even if they recognized the Genocide of 1915. Actually, I heard that the main reason for not recognizing it is restitution of the lands. The Turkish history books don't even mention that shameful horrific period as though it never existed, I was told by a couple of Turkish friends. Yes, I do have Turkish friends. We were not even taught about the Armenian Genocide in our history class, nor did our families talk about it. Later on, I was informed by Ma that it was felt children would be too traumatized by learning of such a horrific event at a young age.

My paternal grandfather came to Egypt and opened up a tobacco factory. A total of ninety percent of the tobacco in Egypt was processed by Armenians. He was sixty years old and extremely wealthy. The Armenian priest (who, besides being a conventional priest, acted as psychologist, marriage counselor, wife finder, teacher, you name it) advised him to bring a nice young Armenian woman from Yerzenga and marry her to beget children so that he could have heirs to his vast fortune. My grandfather agreed. He was a tall, good-looking man who wore a *tarboush* (the red cylindrical hat made of felt with a tassel on top) and had an imposing mustache, like most men did during that period. Almost all Turks and Egyptians wore this *tarboush*. A young girl came over with her younger brother. The twin of this brother could not undertake the journey at that time as he was sick. He died during the Armenian Genocide. He would have been better off traveling to Egypt in a sickly state than remaining in Turkey and getting killed. That's fate. This young girl, who was brought over, turned out to be only sixteen years old. She was introduced to my grandfather.

"I can't possibly marry a sixteen-year-old girl. I am almost sixty," he was reported to have told the priest.

"We can't send her back. People in Yerzenga will think that she is not good enough, and it would tarnish her reputation, and she'll never find a husband," the priest had said to convince Grandpa.

This conversation took place in the presence of the priest's wife, who later reported it to our family in one of her ramblings about the past. After much insistence, my grandfather agreed to marry this pretty, uneducated peasant Armenian girl from Yerzenga.

They bought a villa in the suburb of Zeitoun (means olive in Arabic, although the town was not known for any olives—not one olive tree in sight) and my father was born. Zeitoun is also the name of a town in Turkish Armenia, where a fierce battle took place during the genocide. There is even a song praising the Armenian fighters called Zeitountsiner (people from Zeitoun). I can still sing this song, learned in Armenian kindergarten in Egypt. It is a marching song and is quite a catchy tune.

It seems my grandfather, I don't even know his first name—how ignorant can I be?—would bring home gold coins from his daily dealings in his tobacco business and dump them in my grandmother's lap. I was told that he was a shrewd businessman. The gold was then converted into paper money to be spent.

When Pa was one year old, his father died of a heart attack at sixty-two years old, leaving his fortune in trust to his son to be given to him when he was twenty-one years old.

In the meantime, my grandmother, still being only eighteen years old, was approached by the same priest, and another husband was found for her—a distinguished, highly educated scholar and lawyer (educated in France and Italy) who spoke and wrote five languages and was younger than her. He was penniless, however. The priest thought it was a good match—a beautiful wealthy widow and an educated man who would bring up her son in the best manner possible.

My grandmother was not educated. She just knew how to read and write, keep house, and cook—badly. It did not matter because they had maids. In those days, marriages were arranged according to circumstance and not according to compatibility. I suppose that is the reason they lasted. Husband and wife knew their roles and duties and did not expect much other stuff that would make them go to psychiatrists or therapists, or what have you, to "fix" their marriage. The man was the breadwinner and the woman the *hausfrau*, taking care of home and children. The only problem, a big problem, was that the husband almost always died young, leaving behind a widow. I suppose that did not leave them enough time to grow old together, bickering ad infinitum. Divorce was thus avoided and was a rare phenomenon. The misfortune was that divorced women—the very few who existed—were pointed out with scorn as though it was their fault.

Besides having their villa in Zeitoun, my step-grandfather had another building built on the premises of their garden (with Pa's money, no doubt), which he converted into a library. He had the largest private library in Egypt, with books stacked on dark brown bookshelves all around the room up to the ceiling. The books were all leather-bound—in English, French, Italian, and Armenian. In his spare time, he categorized them in a handwritten ledger.

"You can come to my library and read if you want," he would tell my sister and me. "I will give you the appropriate books to read, but you cannot take them out of my library."

He took great care of his books and wanted to keep them in pristine condition.

"Okay, Grandpa," was all we said.

"And I want you to be quiet because I like to listen to classical music when I am working on my ledger."

"Okay, Grandpa."

After he died, his books were given to the Armenian diocese, and they are still sitting there in the basement. No benefactor has come forward to have them donated to Armenia. They are going to rot there as the Armenian population in Egypt is depleting year after year by departures to other countries and interracial marriages.

Grandma had two children from the second husband, a son and a daughter. The son was sent to France to study chemistry (with Pa's money, of course) and the daughter, Shamiram, my only aunt, whom I loved dearly because she was outrageous just like Pa. Eventually, she became a piano teacher and made oodles of money. She was a generous person and would always give us jewelry for our birthdays and for Christmas. Jewelry is the preferred gift in the Middle East. Women collect jewelry; even the *fellah* woman wears 18 kt. or 22 kt. bangles on her wrists.

I wanted to learn the piano, and my auntie offered to give me lessons whenever we visited her weekly. However, after I tried it for a couple of weeks, I found it too difficult and time-consuming. It was too much work for me. I wanted to grasp things fast and easily. I had no patience to practice, so I gave up the idea after a few lessons.

When I was older, Ma told me that her mother-in-law had confided in her that her "older husband had been more virile sexually than the young one." She had imparted this fact to Ma after the young one had died on her also.

The wife of the priest, who had arranged Grandma's marriages, was called Yeretsguin (meaning priest's wife) and lived with my grandmother's family for as long as I remember.

There are two types of Armenian priests, the married ones and the unmarried ones, the former being the family priest and the latter rising in hierarchy to become bishop, cardinal, and head of the church.

Yeretsguin had an extremely wrinkled face and skin like tissue paper. She had her snow-white hair in a thick braid and sat yoga style on the couch all day long and told tales of the past. I remember she had long droopy ears that almost touched her shoulders.

"Why are your ears so long, Yeretsguin?" I was a very cheeky and curious child.

"When I was younger, I wore heavy dangling gold earrings, and my earlobes got pulled down. You see, even the holes are elongated."

That is the reason I never had my ears pierced because I did like dangling earrings but did not want my earlobes going down to my shoulders. I, therefore, stuck to clip-ons.

My maternal grandmother was Armenian, born in Chios, Greece, and was well-educated—had gone to college in Istanbul—a pretty woman and certainly not a homebody. She read books in four languages and was reclusive, wanted to be left alone. She was a gentle soul and an introvert. She was badly matched to her husband, who, it seemed, was a sex maniac and wanted to have sex every day. This was told to us by her younger sister much later on, after Grandma and Grandpa had died. I never knew Grandpa because he had gone to England just before the war and died there before the war ended.

They had five children, Ma being the eldest. Two of the four boys died from a contagious disease—probably typhoid—when they were infants. Two remained. One was a crazy genius. He had enlisted in the British Army but was let go for insubordination. He played the piano without having been taught. He did not finish high school but spoke six languages, learned them just by listening. The other brother died in his twenties in a motor cycle accident. My grandmother was devastated with the fate of her four boys, and she did not want anything to do with sex or her demanding, brutal husband, the British guy. Lucky for her that he never returned from England. She was left penniless, however, and moved in with us. She did not mourn her husband as she had never loved him in the first place. It had been an arranged marriage, like most marriages in those days.

Ma's friends usually went out together in a group. One person among them was Pa, who, unbeknownst to Ma, had a secret crush on her. Upon hearing that Ma had broken her engagement, he asked his stepfather to go and ask for her hand in marriage. This was the way things were done then. One rarely asked the intended person outright. One went through the parents. Grandpa thought he would take a short cut and go directly to the young woman instead of the parents.

So, one day Karekin—Grandpa's name—showed up at the Kodak store. It seemed Ma was quite surprised seeing him, and after the preliminary salutation, she asked the reason for his visit.

"I have come to ask your hand in marriage. My son, Hayro, is in love with you and would like to marry you if you accept." Hayro was Pa's nick name. His real name was Hayrabed.

Ma was speechless and stared at him wide-eyed. She had no inkling that Hayro had any sentiments toward her. He had kept his feelings well under control, was what he told us.

"But he is younger than I am," she managed to say, being at a loss for words.

Women in the Middle East always married men much older than them.

"That's not a problem. I am also younger than my wife. I don't know whether you are aware that Hayro is an extremely wealthy man, having inherited a large sum of money from his father. You don't ever have to work, and you will live royally with servants galore. I will, of course, be there to be his mentor and guardian."

Ma did not care about the money that much. Her reticence was Hayro's age—too young. He was only twenty-one, and she was twenty-three. She admitted to us that she was attracted to him as he was extremely good-looking with movie star looks and had great charisma.

Karekin was quite persuasive, and Ma finally agreed.

Pa was much in demand as husband material because of his money and looks. He had gone to the best schools in Cairo. In fact, it was rumored that lots of Armenian families were virtually throwing their daughters at his feet, but he refused them all. He was fixated on Ma because she was different. She was not a typical Armenian girl. She was tall—inherited from her British father—and had a most engaging, flirtatious look. She did not show a great deal of enthusiasm and did not offer herself to him too willingly like all the other girls who wanted to grab him. The Armenian girls who were after him were all stay-at-home, wealthy, eager-to-get-married girls. Pa liked the chase, it seemed. Their marriage created quite a commotion among the Armenian community—an extremely wealthy, most sought-after handsome bachelor marrying a working girl.

They got married and lived an enviable life for a few years. They made several extended trips to Europe with big metal shipping trunks, and when I was born, there was also an Italian nanny who went along. Her name was Pepina. It seemed she washed the diapers by hand on the boat crossing the Mediterranean. She boiled water in a huge aluminum pot on a portable stove. There was ample space in the two cabins that my parents occupied—first-class cabins. Those were the days of grandeur, traveling in luxury.

Italian was the first language I spoke being with the nanny most of the time.

Ma told me a funny story about Pa's wardrobe. It seemed he had innumerable ties. In fact, he had so many that one suitcase was used for his ties only and, on one occasion, a customs official in France asked him whether he was a tie merchant. Ma thought it was ridiculous to travel with so much stuff, but Pa insisted that they dress up elegantly and be *à la mode*. He even sometimes chose Ma's clothes. I have kept some of them. They are gorgeous, made with taffeta and silk and lace imported from France. My parents were always well-dressed until they passed away. Clothes were important to them.

I had the bright idea, much later on, during my life in Geneva, to sell Ma's evening gowns to the Geneva Museum of Art and History. At least they would be exhibited from time to time.

That luxurious lifestyle soon came to an end when Pa lost his fortune. He lost his real estate and his horses and his car. He then started a couple of businesses, one was of interior design called Le Foyer d'Art (the Home of Art). Pa had impeccable taste in home design and in everything else, for that matter. The other business was in handmade shoe manufacturing. They both went under after a couple of years because of mismanagement and untrustworthy employees. He did not know how to manage them as he was too young and inexperienced and certainly not a businessman. He was a born artist, and his stepfather, although he had promised to guide him, never lifted a finger. His family blamed Ma for the loss of his fortune and thought she should have reigned him in.

"How can you control a gambler?" Ma argued.

She had been powerless.

I regret that I never asked Ma for details of her life when she was young. I never asked Pa either because I never saw him. He was always in a hurry, coming in or going out. He did not have specific hours.

Cairo had a fabulous social life, and my parents often went out in the evening when they were still wealthy. Ma would kiss us good night. She smelled so nice—she had perfume bottles galore on her dressing table—and looked so chic in her Parisian designer evening clothes. Pa looked ever so dashing in his black tie—they looked just like movie stars. Those were the days of grandeur and elegance and maybe of decadence also. I was so proud of my parents. Ma would later relate to us that the women were all dressed to kill, and the men donned their handmade sharkskin suits made by expert Egyptian tailors. I often asked Ma to draw me the women's clothes. I was hungry for ideas already then.

That was when I decided to become a fashion designer. And I was determined to do this in the United States one way or another. Conclusion being that when one wants something badly enough, one somehow manages to get it. That has always been my motto. I had big dreams in those days, and they did materialize. I focused on them, and I did become a fashion designer first in Boston and then in Manhattan. Getting out of Egypt was a complicated hurdle, but, somehow, I managed it via Montreal, with my first husband. It is a very circumvoluted story that will come later on.

When my parents went out in the evenings, we were left with the maid, who would put us to bed and was given instructions to call them if anything out of the ordinary happened. She was taught how to use the telephone to call the number of the venue given to her on a piece of paper. We were one of the few families who had a telephone—a remnant of our wealthy days. On the maid's day off, our turbaned doorman, the *bawab*, would be summoned upstairs and to be our guardian. We preferred the doorman because we were treated to a *baboula* (boogeyman in Arabic and Greek) story. He was a trustworthy fellow who slept on the floor outside our bedroom door—seemingly to protect us from home invaders, although there never were any. Maybe a cockroach or two.

Before he took his position outside the door, we implored him to tell us a story.

"You promise to fall asleep after the story, okay?"

"Yes, yes, we promise," we said and looked at him wide-eyed.

Why on earth did we ever want to be told a scary story before going to bed is beyond my comprehension. But we insisted. He would then sit cross-legged on the floor next to our king-size bed (Judy and I always slept in the same bed while we were young and even in our teens), and in a low, melodious voice, he would relate a story. Judy would often close her ears and did not want him to continue if she got too scared.

"Don't continue. It's too scary," she often told him.

"No, don't listen to her. Please continue," I would urge him on.

Judy then closed her eyes and ears and went deep under the covers. The *bawab* would then finish the story just for me.

It always ended well.

Judy was born in Switzerland, in a remote village called Sentier, during one of my parents' trips to Europe. We did visit this village when we were all living in Geneva in the 1970s, and it was a "nothing" town. I could not understand what sophisticated people like my parents would be doing there. Ma said, "it was tranquil and had a good maternity clinic." Pa said, "I did a lot of writing there." He wrote poetry. I have kept some of them. In fact, I have kept all my father's school notebooks—he had a calligraphic handwriting. I personally think his notebooks belong in a museum.

These lengthy European trips ended, of course, when Pa lost all his money.

After Pa's unsuccessful businesses, he finally worked as a contractor for the American army during WWII. He was stationed in Suez, a coastal town on the canal.

Pa would bring home American GIs as guests. I was about six when I fell in love with one of them. He was my first crush. I still remember his name, Johnny Pendergast. He was a tall blond guy with blue-gray eyes and had a whimsical smile. He had a girlfriend, a South African WAC (Women's Auxiliary Corps), an attractive young woman who looked like Ava Gardner. I have a photo of the family with the couple. I saw that guy a few times, and my heart would go pitter-patter each time. How I wished I were older to take him away from his girlfriend and make him fall in love with me. My parents did not know of my premature feelings of love and lust. It was my secret. I liked the girlfriend though.

During Pa's U.S. Army days, I had another traumatizing experience. I woke up one morning and heard Ma talking in French to her aunt, Nevart (who was Ma's closest relative—only eight years older than her). Her daughter, Anoush, who was supposed to be Ma's first cousin, was about my age. Ma was talking about Pa. She sounded worried sick and was talking fast in an agitated manner. Ma became easily freaked out as far as I can remember. I think she was born that way. Anxious. Every time Ma did not want us to understand what she was talking about, she spoke French to Pa and to everyone else. By that time, I had picked up enough French to understand almost everything she said. I did not divulge my secret, though, so that she would continue doing it, and I would continue to eavesdrop.

"Hayro has not called in three days," she was telling Tante Nevart. She sounded frantic. "Something bad must have happened. I had a nightmare last night and dreamt that he died in a car accident. I am very psychic. My dreams always come true."

Ma fell silent when she saw me.

"What has happened to Pa?" I inquired, interrupting her phone conversation.

"Nothing. Go back to your room."

"You're lying. Something has happened to Pa. What is it?" I insisted, stomping my feet.

"Go ask the maid to prepare you breakfast," she ordered, ignoring my question.

I went away reluctantly, glaring at her and shouting, "You better tell me, if not . . ." If not, what? What would I do? Nothing. I hated so much being a child and being ordered around. When would I ever grow up? I had visions of never attaining that status.

Ma was irritable all day long and would hardly speak with us until Pa finally called in the evening. Actually, I answered the phone.

"Pa is on the phone!" I shouted. "He is not dead!"

Ma glared at me. She guessed I had heard her talk to Tante Nevart. She snatched the phone from my hand and sat on the trunk, where the phone was located, to talk to Pa. She was relieved and cried of joy. She immediately called Tante Nevart to impart the good news.

It seemed Pa was driving an army truck and got hit by a local train that had disregarded the signals. The car had catapulted three times and was in flames, but he came out of it unscathed except for a jagged cut on his forehead. The wound poorly healed. The medic at the army clinic did not patch it too well—I guess he lacked the touch of a plastic surgeon—because up to the day he died, he had a big welt on his forehead, an ugly scar. It did not take away from his looks though. He was still a very handsome man. I have a photo with my parents and a few American GIs in front of our Art Deco bar with Pa at the back, holding his hand up to his forehead, trying to hide the scar.

# CHAPTER VI

## School

I attended Nubarian Armenian Elementary School in Heliopolis at age five. It was a couple of short blocks from our building.

The teachers were competent and strict and the curriculum, excellent. My step-grandfather was the headmaster and was quite strict with me, stricter than warranted, so as to show no favoritism toward me. I did not know at the time he was a step-grandfather. Ma had not told me. I learned about it from bitchy female classmates. They kept throwing offhand remarks like "Your grandfather is only a step-grandfather, ha ha." I did not understand what they were implying. I went crying to Ma one day, and she explained to me the story of how my real grandfather had died when Pa was one year old, and his mother had then married this man. I don't know why she had kept that a secret. I suppose not too many Armenian children had step-grandparents. Did she think it was shameful?

Parents often hid facts from their children to protect them. When an elderly person died, for instance, they would talk to each other in hushed voices. Children were not supposed to know about death or go to funerals. We grew up protected from grief and calamities.

We wore uniforms in school. They were made of a bluish-gray cotton fabric. The girls' style was different from that of the boys. The uniforms were sewn by the mothers or seamstresses. Almost all women in Cairo knew how to sew—some better than others. Being eager to learn everything, I always took part in the sewing of mine. Learn everything so as not to rely on others.

We were taught four languages in elementary school: Armenian, English, French, and Arabic. The reason being that Egypt was such a cosmopolitan country, and several languages were spoken in everyday life.

"Languages are most important," repeated our schoolteachers time and time again. "When you become adults, you can get a job anywhere if you know languages."

This proved to be absolutely true. When I landed in Montreal as an illegal immigrant in 1956, I got a job as a secretary the third day after my arrival. I had learned shorthand and typing in English in Cairo and had worked there as a secretary.

In second grade, I fell for a boy in my class. He had black hair and impish black eyes and was a daredevil. Whether he was conscious of me was hard to tell. He teased me a lot. I always managed to sit next to him and loved to watch him. He had a mischievous look in his eyes and was often contradicting the teacher. I don't think he cared for girls at that age, but I certainly was aware of him. He went to Armenia during the first exodus from Egypt. Stalin had decreed that all Armenians could repatriate to Armenia if they so wished, promising them all good things. More of this later.

In fifth grade, I shifted my attention to another boy, who was the most intelligent of the boys in the class. In Armenian school, girls were always brighter than the boys, but Chris stood out. The other boys did not have a chance against him. He was special. He was smart, cute, and quick-witted, and we would swap answers during tests, behind the teacher's back. We always managed to sit across from each other to facilitate this task. His parents were friends of my own parents, and they would socialize together to play poker. I had visions of marrying him when I grew up. However, when I saw him thirty years later in Geneva, I was disappointed and wondered how on earth I even thought of taking him on as a husband. He was just an ordinary fellow and rather short. I liked tall guys.

I knew nothing about sex as I was growing up. The first encounter with a man's private parts occurred on my way to school when I was about ten years old, and my sister was eight. School was three short blocks away, and we were old enough then to go on our own. One day while walking to school, I noticed a *fellah*, a kid of about fifteen, wearing a *galabeya*, on a bicycle, brandishing something long and fleshy, that looked like a sausage, between his thighs. I realized it was part of himself, an organ. I was shocked and immediately looked away.

"Don't look at him," I told Judy, who was staring at him wide-eyed.

That afternoon, I told Ma about our encounter. She told us that these teenage *fellahs* were rather harmless and wanted to shock young girls. They never exhibited themselves in front of adults because they would be shooed away.

"All you have to do is not look at them, and if they do not get your attention, they will go away," she said. She was right.

The second encounter about sex—also when I was about ten—happened when an Arab Christian family moved in the building next to us. One side of our north balcony overlooked one of their bedrooms on a lower floor. It was only about twelve feet away. One day, as I was looking out from the balcony, I noticed that a young guy, completely naked, was playing with his penis—by that time I knew the name of that organ—in front of the mirror in that bedroom, with the windows wide open. At the time, I did not know the movement he was making was called masturbation. I did not even know the meaning of the word. I called Ma and showed him to her. She immediately pulled me away.

"Don't ever look at him again."

"What is he doing, Ma?"

"I'll explain when you are older, but just don't look, okay?"

"Well, why does he have the window wide open?"

"Just go away and do as I say."

I obeyed Ma, but I secretly looked the next time he was doing it. What he was doing looked disgusting to me, but I was curious. I wanted to understand it, and I asked Alice, a girl in our class who was one year older but who seemed to know about such things. She asked her male cousin, and we learned about masturbation. It seemed girls did this act also, but how they did it was beyond my understanding.

Another thing I did not know was about men and women having sex until I was twelve. It never occurred to me that my parents would have to do something in bed to beget children. I never wondered how we were born. I never even asked. I took it for granted, that a woman just fell pregnant. Ma never talked to us about sex. There was no sex in the movies. There were amorous scenes of embracing and kissing but no actual sex acts like today. We learned everything about sex from our peers.

One day, during recess, Alice told, a few of us clustered around her, what sex was about and how it was done. Her older male cousin had explained it to her. Her older cousin was fifteen, and he knew stuff. She took a piece of paper and drew a couple of figures, a man and a woman.

"The man lies on top of the woman, and his penis goes into the woman's hole, not the pee hole, it seems there is another hole, and moves it back and forth until it produces some kind of liquid, which is called sperm. This then causes the woman to become pregnant."

"That cannot happen," I said. "When a man lies on a woman, his thingamajig (I was too shy to say the word "penis") is pointing downward. How can it go upwards in the hole?"

"Well, it seems when a man gets excited, the penis gets erect and flips upward, and then it can go in."

"That's awful. It must hurt terribly," was my remark. "This thing is too big and wide. I have seen it on a *fellah* and on a neighbor of ours. It cannot possibly fit in the hole of the woman. How big is this hole anyway? Does every girl have one?"

"Of course, everyone does, you silly girl. Haven't you tried to examine yourself in the mirror? Babies come out of that hole. And also, it seems that both the man and the woman take a lot of pleasure out of this act."

"What? Impossible. What kind of pleasure is that?" I asked. I had never looked at myself in the mirror. I had never needed to do it, so I kept silent lest I appeared really dumb. I was flabbergasted and frightened at this revelation. I told myself I would never have sex when I grew up. Why would I hurt myself just to have sex and produce babies? What pleasure was Alice blabbering about? And how could a huge bulk of a baby come out of a tiny hole? I had by then looked at myself in a mirror and could not even see the damned hole.

In the first place, I did not even know what getting excited meant. Alice had said, "Guys get excited." Did girls also get excited? I asked myself. I know I had this warm feeling come over me when I was watching a love scene in the movies. Maybe that was it, but I dared not ask. I was scared that the other girls would think I was even dumber than I looked.

For days, I could not stop thinking about what Alice had said, and I found it unbelievable and rather gross. They did not show much sexual action in the movies in those days. Films were not so explicit regarding sex then. All they showed was kissing and hugging, which was so romantic. I did not see anything romantic in this sex act—a male organ going into a hole in a woman's body. I could not ever envision doing that act with a man when I grew up. In fact, I did not think I would ever grow up, or even have my periods, and thought that I would die before all these unimaginable things would happen to me. My sexual education came from my peers, and they did not know much either. All bits and pieces of hearsay.

Ma had only explained about girls getting their periods. Even that was strange to me. I absolutely did not wish to bleed. She said it was a normal bodily function, but the sight of blood always frightened me.

All this talk about sex, erections, and getting excited puzzled me, and I wanted to know more details. We all asked innumerable questions to Alice.

"I'll ask my cousin for more details next time I see him," she said.

Talking to a boy about such things was unimaginable to me.

A few days later, Alice was trying to draw a man and a woman lying on top of each other to show the sexual position to us during history class. At the time, we did not know that other positions existed until one day she brought the *Kama Sutra* to school. We huddled around her during recreation to look at this book. I thought it was all very disgusting. The paper that Alice had drawn on was subsequently confiscated by the teacher. "Rubbish," said the teacher—she was a spinster—and threw the paper in the waste paper basket, glaring daggers at us.

"Who is teaching you this?" she asked. No one replied. "You are all punished. No recreation today."

We groaned.

The instruction of Arabic at the Armenian school was strong. I was lagging behind in that subject, and I knew it was going to affect my overall score. I did not like that one bit. I had to be first like I was in all the other subjects. I found out the reason, and I was enraged. One of the girls in class told me about a scheme they had adopted, asking me not to divulge the secret. Some of the kids were supposedly taking lessons from the Arabic master. There was no taking lessons per se. He was being paid by them and thus giving them the test results before the exam. I was furious when I found out.

"Ma, I want to take Arabic lessons to be better in that subject," I blurted out once when she was looking at my grades in my monthly report card. All tens except for Arabic.

"We can't afford it, so forget about it. Just study harder."

"Ma, you don't understand. Some pupils are paying for the test answers."

She was astounded. I was sure she was going to tell Grandpa, and subsequently, the Arabic master would be fired.

"Maaa, I can't study any harder. It is quite difficult. I want to get the results also. What are you going to do about this? Are you going to tell Grandpa?" I was apprehensive.

She thought about it for a few minutes, squinting at a distant object in the living room, while I was waiting impatiently for her reply. She then agreed that I take the so-called lessons also because she wanted me to excel and did not want to have the poor slob fired from his job. She told me that she would get the money somehow. And she did.

She took up nylon mending. Nowadays, we throw our nylons away, but in those days, they were precious and expensive. She bought a machine that mended runs in nylons. I learned to do it also, and we made some extra money mending the nylons of neighbors and friends. It was fun for me. It was my first "paid" job. All the money I made was given to Ma.

I approached the master after class one day and told him that I wanted to take Arabic lessons. He thought for a minute or two and then looked at me with his glaucomic, grayish eyes and suggested the following:

"The day before the Arabic exam, I will pass you the test results. On the way to school in the morning, as I am walking past your balcony, you will lower a basket, and I will put the paper in it, and then you can pull it up, and there you go. And you don't have to pay me," he added. I looked at him aghast. I realized later that the reason for this was that he did not wish Grandpa to find out about this side game of his.

The basket procedure was very common in Cairo. When we ordered ice cream from the vendor on the street, we would lower a basket, and he would put the ice cream in it, and then we would give him the money in the basket. It was a dumb waiter kind of thing.

This Arabic lesson procedure suited me fine. Ma was surprised that we did not have to pay and at first objected, saying that it was not fair, but then she agreed and kept her mouth shut. It was our secret. Even Pa did not know about our little arrangement. Not that he knew much of the family goings-on. Ma felt uneasy, though, I could tell. Well, what the hell, *when in Rome* . . .

So, during the whole year, I also excelled in Arabic.

Problem solved.

When I was in third grade, I had jaundice. One day Ma noticed that my skin was yellow all over and also the whites of my eyes had turned yellow. The doctor was called, and he confirmed that I had jaundice. My grandmother then came up with the bright idea that I should drink my own urine, that this was a cure from old times. Ma asked some of the neighbors and they all agreed that this was a known cure.

"I am not drinking urine. Are you crazy? I'd vomit it straight out. Even the odor makes me puke." And I ran away from the room.

No more talk of urine drinking. Ma did not seem eager about it either. This happened during the summer holidays and, therefore, I did not miss any school days. I lost weight and had to take it easy for a few weeks. It was not pleasant to be skinny and scrawny and tired all the time. Ma tried to overfeed me but I had no appetite. After a few weeks, I got better and could attend school in the fall.

A funny anecdote about my freckles. When I was engaged to my ex-husband, my future mother-in-law thought I would look better without them, and she advised me to take them off with a solution of white vinegar and ground mother of pearl buttons. I rolled my eyes when she said this and looked at my future husband to see his reaction.

"Don't you dare try and take off your freckles. They are so cute. I love them," he said.

That was good enough for me. I did not like my mother-in-law anyway. She was too old-fashioned. For her, a creamy white skin was "ne plus ultra." My fiancé and I considered ourselves out of the norm, having modern ideas and liking everything that was American.

It is only now that I am proud of saying I am Armenian, but then I was not. I wanted to belong to a powerful country. Armenia was a Communist country, a satellite of the Soviet Union, and I did not like that one bit.

# CHAPTER VII

## Everyday Life

My fascination with men came to me early in life. It started with actors in American movies. There was no movie rating in Cairo, and children could see all sorts of films. It was the parents' decision. Crime was not so bloody or lovemaking so explicit in the old films. It was more romantic, and I would imagine myself in the place of the heroine. I remember falling in love with Clark Gable as Rhett Butler after I read *Gone with the Wind* at age fourteen. I fell head over heels in love with Rhett and wanted to meet a man just like him when I grew up. He was so manly with his dimples, his eyes, and his masculine sexuality. I could almost smell his maleness when reading the book. I was so angry with Scarlett for letting him get away. How stupid could she be to prefer the spineless, ashen Ashley? I saw the movie when I was fifteen, and it reinforced my attraction for Rhett. Tyrone Power was another actor I was enamored with. I met Tyrone in his dressing room in Montreal after a performance. It was such an exciting encounter. More about this later. I would daydream about those movie stars and imagine being whisked away to some romantic hideaway.

I was a hopeless dreamer with a fertile imagination.

A curious event comes to my mind when I think of Hassan, the doorman. He had only one son, who was about ten years old. One day (when I was about the same age as him) I noticed that he was walking holding his *galabeya* in front of him with two fingers, away from his body.

"Ma, why is he walking holding his *galabeya* away from his body?" I asked.

"Because he just got circumcised, and he is trying to hold the fabric away to avoid it chafing against his penis."

I looked at Ma, dumbfounded.

"What do you mean circumcised?"

Ma then explained to me what circumcision was, and it shocked me. Why would people want to be mutilated like that? I wondered. Later on, I was told that it was for hygienic purposes because boys did not always draw back their foreskin to clean their organs thoroughly. I also learned that circumcised men take longer to have orgasms than uncircumcised ones.

"Your uncle, the doctor (we always called him the doctor and never Uncle Kevork, which was his name) performs circumcisions on newborn infants in his clinic." Ma then went on to say, "if you want, I suppose you can watch it done one day."

Watch a circumcision? How gory would that be? But I did watch one year later and almost fainted. Part of this poor baby's organ being chopped off and he screaming his head off.

I ran out of the room as fast as I could.

"I will never do that to my children," I told Ma, who then went on to explain that this was a practice among Muslims and Jews and also some Christians, in order to avoid infection if boys failed to clean their organs properly by pulling back the skin.

"If God made boys that way, why cut a part of them off?" I argued.

Now that Pa had lost the building, the rent was collected by the new owner, a mousy, thin, nerdy fellow with black horn-rimmed eyeglasses. He always stumbled on the stairs. His lenses were not strong enough, I guess. We called him the mosquito. He would come around every month to collect the rent. When Ma did not have the rent money available, we would not answer the doorbell. We had a vintage window in one corner of our apartment from where we could see who was at the door. Ma was always late paying the rent, and there would be arguments with Pa. When Pa was the owner, he never went around collecting the rent himself. He sent his assistant. Those were the affluent days.

It was extremely humiliating for Ma but not for Pa. He couldn't care less. He was a "bon vivant" and thought one day he would be rich again. He was a big dreamer. Everybody adored my pa. He had a great sense of humor and was entertaining—the life of the party. I am also a dreamer and have inherited that trait form him. I try to focus intensely on my dreams and pray that they come true. Most of them have fortunately come true.

Ma was quite an authoritative woman. You had to be if you were living in Cairo as you had to deal with all kinds of vendors and especially, food vendors. One had to bargain for everything. A meek woman would never be able to manage any bargaining. There was no set price on the fruits and vegetables. Ma was an excellent cook but got extremely anxious and nervous while preparing food because she wanted everything to be perfect. Her reputation in the neighborhood was at stake.

One unfortunate day, Pa broke our refrigerator by poking at the ice with an icepick. In those days, we were the only ones owning a refrigerator in the neighborhood. It was a remnant from our wealthy days. The brand was "Frigidaire," and we always referred to it by this name. Pa was an extremely impatient person and always did things in a hurry, a fact lamented by Ma. As we no longer had oodles of money to buy another one, we made do with a small old-fashioned icebox.

Our rich days were really over.

The icebox had a faucet for drinking water. It dripped into a bowl on the floor from where Sandy, the cat, and Roxy, the dog, had their drinking water. Ma had put four bowls filled with water under the four legs of the icebox to keep out ants and cockroaches. The pets sometimes used the water from these four bowls. Obviously, they did not know the difference between water dripping from a water faucet and water full of ants and a cockroach or two.

Whenever Ma got angry, we kept quiet and out of sight. She was easily excitable. I think I have inherited that trait from her. One day her rage was unleashed in a big way. She was giving a dinner party for some ten guests, to be held in the formal dining room, where we had all the Art Deco furniture and all the vestiges of our wealthy days. Pa had painted a mural on one whole wall. It was an autumn landscape with red-leaved trees and shaded lanes. He had done it from memory of some place he had visited while in Europe. Under the table, there was a buzzer to call the maid to bring the necessary food and utensils or what have you.

"How can I plan an extravagant meal and keep it fresh in this mouse-size icebox?" Ma kept lamenting all day long. We kept out of her way because she would certainly scold us without reason for something or other. To keep the food unspoiled for the party, Ma needed a good-sized block of ice to put on the coils in the icebox. Ice was delivered daily by the ice man, whose shop was also around the corner from our apartment building. Everything seemed to be on the same block, which was extremely convenient for shopping—the baker, the shoemaker, the ironer, the butcher, the fruit vendor, the iceman, the ice cream man, the bicycle shop, and the clothes mender. The latter had a tiny shop with one table and one chair, and he sat outside his shop all day long mending clothes. He was an expert. I thought he was a genius. If you accidentally tore a dress or a suit, he would mend it so well that you would absolutely not see the spot of the damage, even with a magnifying glass.

On this particular day, Ma was frantic. The iceman had not yet delivered the ice.

"What's keeping him?" she fumed, pacing up and down, talking to herself about the unreliability of the help. The maid cowered in the corner to escape her wrath. My sister and I made ourselves as invisible as possible. The pets were also out of sight, sensing the highly charged atmosphere.

Finally, the doorbell rang. It was one of the younger sons of the iceman, delivering a block of ice wrapped in burlap flung over his puny shoulder. This was the way ice was delivered to the homes. Ma had one look at the block of ice and scowled. She screamed at the boy, gesticulating wildly. We came out of our hiding place to find out what the ruckus was about.

"What does your father take me for? A fool? He wants me to pay for this miserable-looking piece of ice? I don't accept it, and this is what I am going to do with it."

With one sweep of her arm, she grabbed it from the shoulder of the poor kid and threw it down the stone steps. The ice did not break. We gasped and stood petrified watching it. Ma was so angry that we thought she would explode any minute. The maid ran away to the kitchen. The cat, who had come out from his hiding place, hissed and hunched his back. The dog was running around in circles, barking. The poor kid did not flinch; obviously, he was used to this kind of behavior from women clients. He just scurried down the stairs, picked up the ice, and went back to the store to tell his father what the "crazy" woman had done. The father was used to complaints from his customers. I imagine it happened quite often. He sent his son over with a much bigger piece and told him to apologize for this "unintentional" mistake.

When Ma saw the new bigger piece of ice, she smiled and accepted it.

"This is certainly better," she said. "Tell your father not to play any more tricks on me." She gave the kid a pat on his back and a piaster (equivalent to twenty-five cents) as a tip. This was good money in those days. We all relaxed. The maid took the ice and put it on top of the coils in the icebox. The cat raised his tail and meowed for food. The dog walked away and lay down in his usual spot.

Everything was normal again.

Ma carefully and meticulously arranged the food in the icebox, but it so happened that all the food did not fit in it as the icebox was still too small. She cursed under her breath. We were not supposed to hear it, but we did. She then sent the maid to ask the iceman to deliver another piece of ice, and this time "it better be the right size." The maid went unwillingly. Ma reassured her not to be afraid of the guy. She would deal with him if he gave her any trouble. The maid returned with the iceman's son carrying another block of ice, which was then put in the huge kitchen sink. The rest of the food was placed on top of the ice and covered with a dishcloth to keep the flies away. Saran Wrap did not yet exist.

Now we were finally ready for the dinner party. Four couples arrived with their children. The crystal chandeliers were on, and the dining room table was set for ten people with Limoges china and Baccarat Crystal wineglasses—which we used for beer or whiskey and soda, Pa's favorite drink. We did not drink wine in those days. We had no money, but we still had our expensive Limoges china and Baccarat Crystal from our wealthy days, so it felt like we were still rich. The children's table was set up in the adjoining sitting room. We preferred this because we were away from the constant supervision of the parents looking to see if we were behaving or eating all the food placed in our plates. Sometimes we threw unwanted food at one another for fun, and we would then call the cat and the dog, out of parents' earshot, to eat what fell on the floor.

There was music, and everyone was having fun listening to Pa telling his usual jokes, some of which he invented. He was an inventive storyteller with a great sense of humor. The guests were enjoying themselves, and the maid kept bringing up the food, and Ma was beaming.

This was life in Cairo in the 1940s. It was the good old days.

One day Ma decided to teach us how to shop for food.

"Come with me to the market and watch to learn how I shop."

"But we're only kids. We don't need to do this now. We'll never go and buy food on our own, so why learn? It's ridiculous."

"It is not. It is very useful, and you should learn. I insist."

We could do nothing but unwillingly obey.

"The first thing you have to learn is be careful that people don't gyp you. Vendors will always try and take advantage of you if you are naive. You have to act confident for people to respect you."

This was the motto in the Middle East. It was *verbotten* (German for forbidden) to be meek and weak.

We set out for our shopping adventure.

Ma also dragged the maid along to carry the provisions back home. There was no wheeled cart in those days. First, we stopped by the *Kulle Shei* store (meaning the everything store in Arabic) to buy some soap and toilet paper. Toilet paper was not packed up but sold individually. When the shop owner got a roll of toilet paper from the shelf up above, one of these brown ugly cockroaches flew out of the cylinder. I screamed my head off.

"For God's sake, shut up," Ma said, pulling me behind her. "It's only a cockroach, not a mouse." Cockroach or mouse, I don't like seeing flying insects coming out of ordinary objects. From that day on, I always inspected toilet paper before using it.

It was time to buy the chicken. Up to this day, I'll never forget how this was done. The chicken vendor had placed himself on the sidewalk of the market street with his chickens running around in a couple of large cages. A few of them were huddled together, and Ma looked at them, scrutinizing to see which one appeared healthy. The vendor chose one and gave it to Ma, who inspected the belly meticulously.

"You have filled it up with too much corn. Choose another one, and don't cheat me," she told the guy in an authoritative manner. The vendor then got hold of some other poor, frightened chicken—I bet it knew its fate—and gave a presumably acceptable one to Ma. She agreed on his choice. Its head was then cut off right in front of our eyes, and the chicken went around and around without a head, blood spewing out of its neck.

I was speechless and almost vomited my breakfast.

On the way back, we stopped by the fruit vendor. Ma wanted to buy watermelon. The vendor kept tapping the belly of several, trying to see which one made a good noise like "boom, boom" before he was satisfied that he was selling the "European lady" an acceptable one.

"If, after cutting it, it is no good, just bring it back," he said.

The last stop was the butcher, whose shop was right next to our building.

The butcher shop was all white with blood splattered on the walls and on the counter. It was cold—not with air-conditioning. There were huge fans and ice all over the place. The meat had been freshly delivered from the slaughterhouse that day, the butcher informed Ma. He was a tall, burly and flashy, bellicose guy with a bushy black mustache that went from ear to ear. He seemed to be quite proud of it because he kept touching it incessantly and trying to elongate it with his bloody fingers. His apron was bloody also. The whole shop smelled of fresh blood. There was also a young urchin shooing the flies away from the meat with a fly whisker, making a swishing sound.

The carcasses of beef and lamb hung from gigantic hooks from the ceiling. I pitied the poor animals.

He said with a wide smile, baring prominent yellow teeth, "How can I help you today, *ya madame*? (That was how vendors addressed European women shoppers.)

Ma chose some lamb chops off the carcass, craning her neck to see better. These were then cut right off the body of the poor slaughtered lamb and put on the scale.

"No cheating with the scale," Ma said.

"I swear on my mother's tomb I would never cheat you," the butcher said and wrapped up the lamb chops in newspaper, and Ma gave the package to the maid. Newspaper was used in lieu of wrapping paper.

This was the way people shopped in Egypt.

"If you don't show authority, the vendors will fool you and laugh behind your back," Ma said.

I did not want any part of this life.

"I can never shop like this," I told Ma. "It is impossible for me to choose a chicken. I would not be able to tell if the belly is full of corn or not."

"You'll get used to it, or if you will be wealthy enough, you could afford a good cook who will also do your shopping if you can trust her."

After that food shopping experience with Ma, I decided that I was not made out for life in Egypt. I was very influenced by American films and magazines and was absolutely sure that things were different there. I never saw the parents of Debbie Reynolds or June Haver going shopping in this uncivilized manner, killing chicken in the street, seeing cockroaches flying out of toilet paper, bargaining about everything because vendors were prone to cheating.

"How else are you going to be able to run a household if you refuse to do mundane work?" Ma always said.

"I'll have a maid."

"What if you can't afford it?"

"I will try and marry money, or else I will make money. I will not live poor. That's for sure." I was adamant.

Actually, I never learned any household duties or cooking in Cairo. I hated any type of housework. Later, when I was in Montreal with my first husband, I was obliged to do quite a bit of housework. Hubby helped, of course. As I did not know how to cook, I wrote to Ma for recipes of my favorite foods. It never dawned on me to buy a recipe book. I wanted to eat the food I was used to and craved.

I had decided to go to the United States by hook or by crook. In fact, one day I had the bright idea that I should get adopted by a distant uncle who had escaped the Turkish massacres of the Armenians in the 1890s and had moved to Detroit. Pa used to correspond with him once a year, usually at Christmastime. Postcards with short notes. When I was about twelve years old, I wrote him a letter, unbeknownst to my parents, asking him to adopt me. I still have a copy of that stupid letter—so childish. Of course, he wrote back to Pa, asking what was happening "to this child." I got reprimanded and was told that I was "a very foolish girl, full of crazy ideas and to stop bothering an uncle whom I did not even know or met."

"Life is good here," Ma said. "Do you think middle-class people in the United States have maids? You'll have to do everything yourself, and I don't see you doing that. You are a spoiled brat. Everything is done here for you."

I scoffed but I agreed. Life was certainly good, with lots of laughter and music and entertainment. We had a big house with expensive furniture, nice clothes and good friends. And, most of all, despite our lack of money, we enjoyed ourselves. What else did we need?

There was quite a lot of folklore in our daily lives.

The vendor walking along in the street selling lemonade would announce his presence in a singsong manner. This always happened when I was trying to take my afternoon nap so I was not too happy hearing him. All the *fellahs* in the street drank with the same cup. They were not afraid of germs. Their immune system seemed to be strong.

The garbageman pushing his cart led by a donkey would also singsong, making us aware that he was in our neighborhood. Garbage was collected every day from the apartments for free. The garbage guy would come up to each door in the building every day, collect the pails of garbage—plastic bags did not exist then—go down the stairs, dump them in his cart, whereupon his son would stomp on it with his bare feet to make more space. No such thing as keeping garbage overnight. It would create haven for cockroaches.

The Copts—the Egyptian Christians who were descendants of the pharaohs, so they claim, and who are the largest Christian minority in Egypt—were mostly of the middle and upper classes, but surprisingly, some were also the *zabbaleen* (garbage people) as they were called derogatively. They lived in apartments in garbage dumps on the Mokattam Hills, which was known as Garbage City, on the outskirts of Cairo. Images of the Virgin Mary and Jesus could be seen on the walls of their dilapidated buildings. They were staunch Christians. The recycling of all Cairo garbage was done in that city by the Copts, and some of them became very wealthy with this recycling business. Actually, they are known to be the best recyclers in the world. We had affluent Coptic friends who did not like the idea that their people were doing this filthy work. Filthy or not, there was a lot of money to be made.

There has always been antagonism against the Copts in Egypt by some of the Muslim population. The Government does not tolerate it but cannot control it. The Muslims are not against the Christians in general, but they seem to be against the Copts who are Christians. I don't quite know how all this started, all this antagonism. Is it because the Copts considered themselves superior, being the direct descendants of the Pharaohs?

Most workers sang while working. I would watch the laborers going up wooden planks, carrying bricks on their backs, for a building being constructed across the street from our apartment building. They would always chant monotonous tunes, all simultaneously. They had no conductor but they chanted in unison. I guess it helped make their job less boring. It was fun watching them, not dropping one brick off their shoulders. It was hypnotic.

Ma insisted on teaching us how things were done, in case we would not be in the money in future.

We never had our sheets ironed, although we had a maid. Two people, sometimes us kids, would stand apart, pulling the sheet this way and that, straightening it out, folding it, and then putting them all under a settee on which we sat on day in and day out. The sheets were thus "ironed." Only our clothes were sent out to be pressed by the expert ironer down the street.

As for cleaning the house, it was done on hands and knees, barefoot, soaping and washing the tiles. The whole house was tiled. No cleaning products were used, just soap, water, vinegar, and *Eau de Javel*, for the bathrooms. Our apartment was so large we couldn't expect the maid to do all the cleaning. She was a teenager and was my mother's helper in the kitchen and our playmate in the afternoons. I had taught her to play board games, and we used to play together.

A man was hired once a month to do the big job of cleaning the whole house. His name was Ali, and he was an expert. He was fast and furious and never uttered a word. The silent one, we called him, though he did hum some unintelligible tune under his breath. There was no vacuum cleaner, of course, and the Persian carpets were flung over the railing of the south-side balcony and were beaten by a special contraption that looked like a tennis racket. This was done always on that balcony, which overlooked the garden of the tenant on the ground floor. It could not possibly be done on the north side. Too many people walking by.

The maid slept on a mattress in the hallway. At her home, she just slept on a mat on the dirt floor, so this was luxury for her. The mattress was then rolled up and put away in the small bathroom for the day. My parents took very good care of her, and she was treated like a real employee with decent work hours. She was not treated like a slave like some selfish employers did, who kept their maids awake at all hours of the night when guests were present. Some servants preferred to work for Europeans who were more compassionate of their plight.

I vividly remember our last maid who was in her late teens. She spoke fluent Italian because she had been working for an Italian family. She changed jobs for more pay, a pittance. In no time, she spoke Armenian as we spoke that language at home. She had never gone to school but had the knack for languages. We took her to Alexandria on vacation in the summer. I had sewn her a bathing suit from a remnant fabric because I wanted her to go in the water with us. I was already an "expert" dressmaker by age twelve. I loved sewing, and I learned from Ma how to use the old-style Pfaff sewing machine with a pedal. It had belonged to my grandma. In school, we had sewing classes once a week, where we sewed everything by hand. We also had an embroidery class.

Up to this day, I still use my expertly embroidered tablecloths and napkins. I look at them with nostalgia.

This maid came to visit us a few years later, and she could now speak fluent French, having been with a French-speaking family for a couple of years.

After many years of living abroad, we went back to Egypt at one time in the 1980s and made it a point to visit our apartment. Nothing had changed in the street except for all the neighbors. They had all been mostly Armenians at the time as it was an Armenian neighborhood. A great many of them had left Egypt to go to the United States, Canada, and Australia. Insecurity had set in for non-Muslims after Gamal Abdel Nasser came into power. They did not feel they had any future in Egypt anymore. The very rich had not left, though, even though their companies were nationalized. They still had enough money to lead a very comfortable life, and they did not want to start afresh in another country.

The new Egyptian tenants were so kind. They kept saying, "This is your house. You are welcome. Please come in." And we did. It was not the same as I remembered. Somehow it looked smaller than I had imagined. My father's mural on the dining room wall was still there. I was happy seeing it and told them it was Pa who had painted it. The shiny black and chrome bar Pa had built in Art Deco style was still in the great hall. The tenants offered us something to drink. We thanked them but refused. I went from room to room reminiscing, and a wave of nostalgia passed through me like a welcome breeze. I suddenly could not control my tears. We thanked the tenants and went down the old, worn-out stone stairs one at a time—in another life, I used to jump three at a time—out into the street. I almost had a panic attack. I yearned to be a child again and have my life back in that apartment, just for one day.

The butcher, the ice cream parlor, the ironer, and the fruit vendor were still there in the same shops in the street, and they were all so glad to see us and welcomed us, asking whether we came back to stay.

"I would like to offer you a leg of lamb," said the butcher to Ma, but she thankfully declined. Where would she cook it? We were staying in a hotel. The ice cream guy offered us ice cream; we accepted that. The fruit vendor gave us navel oranges, and the ironer asked us if he could iron something for us.

"I am at your service," he said.

Such pleasant people. Having visited a few North African and Middle Eastern countries, I find the Egyptians are the most hospitable people in the Middle East.

# CHAPTER VIII

## The Neighbors

When Pa was working for the American army in Suez during WWII, he would bring home American goodies. He brought Tootsie Rolls, Fig Newtons, Coca-Cola and American comic books. The comic magazine *Little Lulu*, who had a chubby boyfriend called Tubby, was our favorite, and also *Dick Tracy*. We adored these comic books and devoured them. How I wish I had kept them. Worth a fortune today.

When my own children were little, I bought them a lot of comic books in English, French, and Italian. They are keeping them for their own kids, if they have any, at the rate things are going.

As the neighbors were envious of us, Ma would distribute some of the goodies to them so that they would "take their evil eyes off of us," she would say. Ma believed in the evil eye, and so do I, for that matter. I have been the victim of the evil eye numerous times in my life. That is why, up to this day, I never talk about a project to anyone until it has been completed, not even to my husband.

Ma had a ritual to ward off the evil eye from us. She used to make a list of people, liable of casting evil eyes, on a piece of paper. It had to be an uneven number—don't ask me why. I asked Ma the reason, but she did not know it either. She had learned the ritual from her own mother, who had been brought up in Greece. She would choose an uneven number of fat cloves (the number according to the list of names on the paper) and burn one at a time on the point of a needle and mutter something like "Have so-and-so's (a name from the list) evil eye go away from my daughter," while turning the burning clove around my face. She also said a little prayer. If the clove made a hissing sound, then that person had surely cast an evil eye on me, and I kept away from her. Usually, it was a *she*. If the clove did not make a sound, then that person was okay, and I could continue associating with her. She would then put the burning clove in a glass of water to extinguish the flame. After the ritual of burning them was over, I would take a sip from the water. She did it separately for my sister and me.

Ma had warned us to be especially wary of blue eyes, not that there were that many in Cairo. We also used to wear a blue eye stone around our necks or pin it on our pillow to ward off the evil eye. Although I do believe in the evil eye, I don't do Ma's ritual. Maybe I should, as I am quite superstitious.

Our building was populated only with Armenians to start with, when the building was owned by Pa. Actually, the whole street was Armenian with a sprinkling of Christian Arabs (Lebanese and Syrians) and a few Muslims. Everybody knew everybody else's business. Whatever happened in a home was rarely private. All the neighbors would eventually learn about it. Gossiping was a favorite pastime. People spoke in loud voices, and sometimes they shouted at one another if they were at a distance.

A lot of shouting in the building was also done reprimanding the children. Parents were very strict, and there was a lot of sanctioning going around. We often heard snippets of conversations from the neighbors.

"What will the neighbors think about your behavior?"

"You can't go and play outside. No, you're punished."

"You have to do your homework first."

"Help the maid set the table. She is not your servant."

On the ground floor lived a family of three—husband and wife and their grown-up son. The rumor was that the mother and son shared the same bed. Nobody had seen this, however, so I don't know how this rumor started or whether it was true. This was never mentioned when "the children were present," but I had my ways of eavesdropping.

We always knew when the ground-floor woman, whose name was Alice, was home because she screeched in a high-pitch voice when she spoke. One day she was peeling potatoes in her backyard. Our Maine coon cat, Timmy, was being pursued by the Siamese, and he blundered over our third-floor balcony railing, where sheets were spread out to dry. He obviously thought the sheets were some kind of flooring. He fell off, taking a sheet or two with him, and landed right smack in Alice's bowl of potatoes—the peeled ones. Luckily, his fall was somewhat impeded by the clotheslines hanging on the second-floor balcony. Alice gave one shrieking yell as though her house was on fire. I am sure the whole building heard her.

"Araxie," (Ma's name) she screeched, "your damn cat has landed on my potatoes!"

Ma, Judy, and I rushed downstairs and saw Timmy crouched in a corner with his back hunched, hissing at Alice. He hated people who yelled. We retrieved the cat and cooed over him. "Poor Timmy, don't be scared. It is all right," we said. Such a silly name for such a huge cat. We should have called him Pasha, but we were kids when we got him and thought Timmy sounded cute and American.

We were America crazy then.

Ma calmed Alice as best as she could. Her husband was not at home. He was a quiet man, a carpenter by trade, and he was scared to death of the shrew.

One time, Alice called Ma over to dress her husband's gashing wound. I went along with her. He had had a motorcycle accident, and the gash on his shin was bone deep. Alice could not stand the sight of blood. My brave Ma, she could have been the nurse of the building—the number of times she was called to take care of this and that child who happened to be sick—cleaned up the wound and put on a new bandage while Alice was trying to pray on the side. Oh yes, she was religious when it suited her.

Another day, Alice was visiting us to show Ma some dress models. She was a dressmaker, but Ma never gave her anything to cut without strict supervision because Alice was impetuous and worked in a hurry, and sometimes she cut it wrong. The first time she had cut a dress for Ma, she had taken the wrong measurements. Ma had had to buy new fabric. From then on, Alice was used only in patternmaking but never for actually cutting the fabric.

One day, Mickey, our Siamese cat, was lying down on the sofa next to her, and Alice started playing with him. Mickey did not appreciate anyone playing with him or teasing him. He was not castrated. People did not castrate their cats in Egypt. Not many people owned cats anyway. Some had dogs. People in Egypt were not known to be animal lovers. Mickey always looked very serious, and I could tell he was in a foul mood when Alice was trying to play with him. Ma tried to tell her once or twice to keep away from him, but Alice did not heed her advice. Mickey only tolerated being touched by our family and a cute little boy who lived upstairs, who could pull his tail and do all sorts of things to him, but he never objected. I guess he knew it was only a kid, and that kids like to play and tease.

Stupid Alice tried tickling Mickey's testicles. Now what sane person would do that? She had a husband with bigger ones, for God's sake. Mickey jumped and bit her arm and would not let go. Mickey was a biter, not a scratcher cat. Alice gave out one of her notorious screams and tried to pry the cat away from her arm, but Mickey would not release it. He would have bitten off a chunk of her arm had Ma not intervened and pried open Mickey's jaw and released Alice's arm. Mickey scurried away and hid in some corner, looking daggers at Alice and ready to pounce had she tried to resume her unorthodox behavior.

As Mickey was not vaccinated against rabies, he had to be put in quarantine for a week, and Ma went every day to feed him and console him for being locked up. She had to take two smelly buses to reach the destination, which was in a vile part of Cairo. She was very conscientious and was determined that Mickey have a good time and not get depressed. She also took food with her to feed him some home-made stuff.

From then on, Alice stayed away from Mickey, who would hunch his back and hiss every time he saw her.

Below our floor lived a family of four. The man was Pa's uncle, a very dour, nondescript, stooped-over individual who rarely spoke. He worked at the largest tobacco company in Cairo, which had been started by wealthy Armenian tobacco merchants from Turkey. It was later sold to the British. One of my secretarial jobs in Cairo was with that company. It was called Eastern Tobacco Company after the Matossian Brothers sold it.

This neighbor's wife did all the talking and had a controlling nature. She was a shrewd, envious, wiry woman with bulging green eyes. "Envious snake eyes," Ma said. "She may also suffer from thyroid disease, which would account for her protruding eyes," she added.

Well, there were now two people in the building with snakelike attributes. The other person was me. My ex-husband commented that I looked like a snake when I licked my upper lip with my tongue.

This woman was a good seamstress but could not finish anything she started. She had sewer's block. She wanted it to be perfect, but she never did achieve the perfection she sought. She sometimes asked Ma for her opinion in an offhand manner because she did not wish Ma to think that there was anyone better than her. She criticized everyone and thought everyone was inferior to her in everything, whether cooking, sewing, or what have you. She was jealous of Ma having married a wealthy man, although Pa had greatly depleted his wealth big time. Nevertheless, we had expensive furniture and carpets and had an American boarder who got us stuff. She resented the fact that she was married to a blue-collar worker. They had two children, a girl my age and a younger boy. She influenced her children not to befriend us. The daughter was too young to know any better. The boy was innocent and often blabbered too much about what his mom said about us. We had a young double agent in the making.

Fifty years later, Sara, the daughter, confided in me that her mother was envious of everyone. Sara had somehow changed her attitude toward us after she got married. But the marriage ended badly.

Next to this family was a childless nondescript couple. We did not have much rapport with them. They were just colorless, ordinary people, minding their own business.

Above us lived a family of four. They had two girls, about our age. The younger daughter developed a kind of autism and would clench her fists and not move from her sitting position and refused to speak for hours on end. Ma often asked us to go and try to cheer her up and get her out of her mood. There were no doctors treating this kind of illness at the time. Later on, she immigrated to Canada and was the girlfriend of a guy I dated in the United States a decade later. We were two very different types. I don't know how this guy dated me after having been with her in Egypt. She was such a quiet, mousy girl who did not have much to say but was rather pretty.

And I had a lot to say.

On the same floor in the next apartment lived a family of three—Arabic-speaking Armenians. They were Protestants. The Armenian Protestants were mostly Arabic-speaking. Their family had converted to become Protestants by American missionaries in Turkey during WWI. Eventually, they moved out, and a Christian Arab family moved in—an older couple with a son. We had no rapport with them at all. They kept to themselves.

A few weeks after they moved in, we were awakened by a howling. We jumped out of bed and looked at one another, wondering what it was. The howling sounded like that of a wolf, not that I had heard any, but I had seen them in movies. We listened closely and determined it was coming from their apartment. Ma wanted to immediately go and investigate, but Pa told her to wait until morning. It was around two o'clock, and he did not think it appropriate to go knocking at people's doors at that hour. We knew they had a dog. It was a small scrawny dog. He could not possibly howl that way. We had never even heard him bark. Did they also have a wolf by any chance? Were they hiding it inside their apartment? Eventually, the howling stopped, and we resumed our sleep.

The next morning, Ma went upstairs and rang their doorbell. I left our apartment door open to listen to what was being said. Ma spoke in Arabic and was very polite, inquiring about the howling.

"Good morning, *Madame* Souria. I hope you are well. We heard howling coming from your apartment last night. Is everything all right?"

"So sorry, *madame*, I don't know how to tell you this, but our son howls when there is the full moon. We can't do anything about it. There is no remedy for it. We are really sorry if it woke you up. He is quite normal otherwise. He has a full-time job, but the full moon disturbs him, and when he wakes up he does not even remember having howled."

Ma came downstairs and reported the conversation.

The son howled when it was full moon? What was that all about? There was nothing we could do about it, of course. We all felt very sympathetic toward that family from then on.

So, every time there was the full moon, their twenty-eight-year-old son—who happened to be an accountant and who looked quite distinguished, by the way, always well-groomed and dressed in a suit and tie for work—would howl. My god, was he a werewolf? I guess he was. So next time there was howling with the full moon, we just tried to go back to sleep and got used to it after a while.

Although there was a lot of envy and conflict among neighbors, we were quite neighborly, meaning we helped one another in time of need.

One night, for example, the son of "snake eyes" was running a fever, and she woke us up around two o'clock, asking us to call our doctor. Our family doctor was Greek and lived two blocks away. They did not seem to have a family doctor. That was bizarre. In those days, doctors in Egypt were either Greek, Italian, or Armenian. As we were the only ones in the building who had a telephone, Ma obliged and called our doctor, waking him up. He was unmarried (the rumor being that he was looking for a rich Greek wife.) No

Greek doctor in Egypt would ever marry out of love. Money and a dowry were important factors. He was quite handsome, which was a plus, of course. He hurried over, and the son was diagnosed with meningitis. He was taken to the Italian hospital and eventually recovered. Nobody in his right mind would go to the local Egyptian hospital if they wanted to stay alive.

After a couple of years, the howling man's family left, and an Armenian family moved in—a couple with the cutest little boy. He was six years old and the most adorable child. He always smelled of soap. His mother was extremely finicky about cleanliness. She had obsessive-compulsive disorder. We did not know the name of this affliction at the time. She told us one day that when she made the bed, she had to measure the sides of the coverlet hanging over by a tape measure. Wow, what a weirdo, but she was a fun woman to talk to.

I never liked children when I was a teenager, but this boy, I did. And I hoped to have a son just like him when the time came in my life to have children. He would tease the Siamese cat, although I told him umpteen times not to play with him because he was unpredictable. Surprisingly, though, Mickey never bit him. He just let him do whatever he wanted, pull his tail, tickle his ears, and so on. He was an intelligent cat and could tell the difference between a child and a stupid grown-up woman like Alice.

We now had a man who howled like a wolf, a woman who looked like a snake, a crazy woman who screamed like a banjee, an autistic teenager, and an adorable small boy who looked like Tintin (the French comic book character). Life was never dull in the building, and our life in Cairo was also eventful—the war, neighbors, school, movies, and later on, boys, of course.

Ma was the disciplinarian in our family, and Pa left all the sanctioning to her. Actually, Ma sort of controlled my life until I was seventeen. I couldn't go anywhere without her approval. I couldn't wear lipstick, for instance. I wore my first bra and stockings at age seventeen.

Ma believed in me and relied on me quite a bit when I was older. She became my pillar of strength. She also encouraged me in whatever I undertook. She wanted me to look after Judy and guide her. "She is not as *bejerikli* (Turkish word for wily) as you are," she often said.

Pa was an optimist by nature. I liked that about him. Never giving up hope.

Whenever I got discouraged about something, he would urge me to go on and would say, "You can do it, I know you can, so just do it."

I miss them so much. I would have liked to have them around me now, giving me unconditional love and supporting me in my endeavors.

At this point in time, Pa was working as an independent contractor, but he did not earn enough to sustain a family of four, the reason being that he was not really a businessman but an artist. He could never give a correct estimate for a job to be done. It was always too low. He thought he would not get the job if the estimate was too high. There were no contracts in Egypt. Everything was verbal. And some people did not pay on time, or they did not pay at all. There was always a last-minute bargaining. Ma was so frustrated at this state of affairs that whenever Pa came home from yet another disappointing day, they would bicker. We, kids, hated to hear them quarreling and would go to the other side of the house to be away from the squabble. Ma was not a bitch, but she had a family to feed.

I vowed never to quarrel with my husband when I got married. In fact, I never did instigate a shouting match with my husband, or husbands—only two—later on in life. I just shut up, pretending he was right, and went away from the room. I hate getting into a pissing match. Let him think he is right. So, what? I know how I feel. He won't make me change my mind. You can take everything away from a person, but you can't take away his thoughts.

# CHAPTER IX

---

## The End of the War

The war was finally over. The British, American, and French troops left Egypt but not the civilians. There was a big French community in Suez because of the canal.

Pa came home one day imparting important news. This was sometime at the end of 1945. He told us that Stalin had decreed and encouraged all Armenians in the Diaspora to repatriate to Armenia, even the ones born abroad. This caused a great commotion in the Armenian community in Egypt. Some were for and others against it. There were all sorts of rumors about Communism—restrictions of movement, lack of food, learning Russian, and accounts of people being sent to Siberia if they were considered enemies of the Communist regime. We heard many conflicting stories.

I was very enthusiastic about this repatriation idea. It seemed like a great adventure for me. In fact, the whole family was looking forward to this venture, and we decided to take the necessary steps to repatriate. We thought Pa would have better job opportunities there. We put our names down on a list somewhere. I don't remember where.

Ma's cousin, Kohar, who was a well-known soprano singer in Egypt, had met an Armenian guy who had come to Egypt from Iran, and had decided to repatriate. He asked her hand in marriage, and she agreed on the condition that, if she went to Armenia, she would continue to have a career in singing. He eagerly agreed. She would make good money, and they would not have to live with shortages.

Her story is amazing. She took on her husband's name, Gasparyan, and became a famous singer in the Soviet Union music circles, won the Stalin medal, and traveled all over the world, giving concerts and acting in operas. She monopolized the Yerevan Opera (Yerevan is the capital of Armenia) for over thirty years. Whenever I speak to a Russian or Armenian person, whether in Europe or in the United States, they know of her. I think she should have kept her maiden name, Kachatourian, the same as the great Armenian composer. People would have thought she was a relative of his, and perhaps she would have had an illustrious career sooner. She had not heard of marketing in those days.

As she was gaining more and more fame, her husband became envious of her notoriety and tried to strangle her one day. The police were called. The government then intervened, and she was declared Russian property to be protected by the state, if she would divorce her husband. She did divorce and eventually married an opera singer much younger than her—a good-looking man. She was rather short and chubby, not particularly beautiful, but she did attract men because of her personality and fame and the money, of course. She had charisma.

I met Kohar once when she was in New York on an opera tour, and she invited the whole family to visit her in Armenia, all local expenses paid by her. She said she was making loads of money and did not know where to spend it. She never thought of defecting from the Soviet Union while on her trips. She was happy there. She had everything she needed—a family, fortune, and fame. It seems artists were taken very good care of in the Soviet Union and were treated with respect. This encouraged us somehow to go there, but we gave up on the idea after hearing some horror stories.

After Kohar's departure to Armenia, her parents asked us if they could move in with us until their name was called for repatriation. They could not afford their rent now that their daughter had left and, as we were in need of money and had this huge apartment, Ma accepted.

Pa's work, after leaving the U.S. Army, was precarious and had its ups and downs.

In those days, we did not mind having a lot of company in the apartment. The more the merrier. Now everyone wants to have his or her own room.

They brought a truckload of their belongings—furniture, kitchenware, and clothes. They planned to take everything to Armenia. They also brought Kohar's gray tabby cat. The poor cat refused to eat, and one day he jumped out of the window of our sitting room into the rooftop next door. We tried to coax him back up to the window by putting an ironing board, joining the rooftop to our window. We would try to feed him by putting a plate on the ironing board. He refused to get back in the house and hardly ate. Eventually, he died, from heartbreak, we thought, since Kohar had gone away.

Tante Arous, Kohar's mother, asked Ma to have her own dining area and her own space in the kitchen, where she would cook her own food. She wanted to economize. She was very frugal and did not want to share the expenses of the whole household. Ma agreed, of course. Her husband, Dayday Michel (Dayday is Turkish for uncle—that's the word we used for uncle) was given one of our rooms for his study. This room was, in fact, our library with bookcases and brown leather armchairs and an imposing mahogany desk that we never used. He was an accountant and spoke perfect Arabic. I emphasize this a few times in my narrative because foreigners, even though born in Egypt, spoke with an accent, and the local Egyptians called them *Khawageya. Khawaga* means mister in Arabic and is applied to Westerners only. Dayday Michel was extremely shortsighted. Some days I would sneak into his study to get a book from our library, and he would not even notice me. To speak with you, he had to be right on your face with his thick horn-rimmed glasses.

The first boat of repatriation sailed in 1946. Our names had not been called. In hindsight, it was lucky for us. Imagine me getting stuck in Soviet Armenia, away from Hollywood.

Family and friends of the departed ones had agreed on a code in their correspondence to give information on how things really were in Armenia. Well, after a few months, news was coming that things were not that good, in fact, not good at all. The only thing that seemed to be fine was education and employment. Everyone was educated and employed. The lower class of Armenian population from Egypt who could not afford secondary education would have ended up being shop girls and apprentices in factories in Egypt. In Armenia, they thrived and became doctors, architects, musicians. I learned about this subsequently when we started receiving "good news" letters.

Nevertheless, we decided not to repatriate and took our name off the "famous" list. Whatever news was trickling from Armenia was not that terrific. So, life went on as usual. Our life in Egypt was quite comfortable. I liked school, I had a lot of friends, and we were always playing in the yard or playing board games at home, lots and lots of board games.

Our favorite pastime, however, was the movies.

As far as I can remember, we were movie crazy. We went to the cinema three times a week even during the bombing of Cairo. There were three good movie theaters in Heliopolis, and they often showed double features. They were open-air cinemas, not drive-ins. They had regular armchairs, made of rattan, set up in an enclosed space. People from neighboring apartment buildings could also watch the screen from their balconies. Some theaters had lodges that seated five people. It was more expensive, but we sometimes cheated and sat seven in a lodge. After all, my sister and I were only children, and my parents thought they should not be considered as persons. We sat on their laps.

"One day you are going to die in the movies," said the doctor, Anoush's father. We called him the doctor and never by his first name, Kevork.

When we walked to the movies, which we often did as they were within a couple of miles away from our home, Judy and I would take turns sitting on top of Pa's shoulders, singing our hearts out. I felt like a princess being carried down the street in a chariot, looking at my kingdom from my perched position.

"Ma, I want to be a movie actress when I grow up," I burst out one day walking home from the movies. This was when I was nine years old. The reason I wanted to be an actress was to have all these handsome actors like Clark Gable, Gary Cooper, Tyrone Power sweep me off my feet.

Besides dancing the tango with Pa during intermission at the Roxy movie theater, the only theater with a stage, I danced the swing with my sister at home. My auntie, Shamiram, who was only nine years older than me, taught me the boogie-woogie. It was the rage during the war, and we danced to the music of the Andrew Sisters. I imitated whoever I saw on the screen and gave dance performances to the family in our huge hall at home.

There is one thing I detest, and that is any kind of insect, especially cockroaches. I can't even look at a cockroach in a movie. Alexandria was full of them. We used to rent a summer apartment in Aboukir (a town near Alexandria), which we nicknamed *Abou Sarasir* (meaning father of cockroaches in Arabic). Arabic names often go with the word *"Abou"* at the beginning, meaning "father of."

This was just after WWII. We could not afford a swanky place, so we rented an apartment with no electricity. We had to light gas lamps. I remember when we arrived at the door of the apartment in darkness, after climbing two flights of stairs, we could see the cockroaches, these big brown ugly insects, scurrying around in the dark. We used to jump from one foot to the other to make them go away so as they would not climb on our feet. Finally, we would get in the apartment, light the lamps, and they would disappear. Mickey, our Siamese cat, would take over and would squash them with his paw if one would venture out of his hiding hole. Mickey did not eat the cockroaches. He just killed them and left them on their backs to be swept up by us. He was sophisticated in his dietary choice. He had the best food Ma prepared for him.

I remember once, one cockroach flew and perched on top of my head when I was combing my hair. I screamed my head off, and Ma came running, thinking I had had an accident.

There are also a lot of cockroaches in Florida. In fact, when we moved in our condo and took the filthy wall-to-wall carpet off, some were still moving underneath, and others were dead.

Flies were rampant in Egypt. Before restaurants opened up for the noon lunch, the help would tightly close them up and spray them with DDT. Then after half an hour, we would be allowed in the restaurant. The odor of the chemical was overwhelming, but there were no flies. They were all dead on the floor and would immediately be swept away.

Ma taught us to be wary of flies and often repeated, "Don't eat any food if you see flies on it. They carry all sorts of germs as they cluster around *kaka*." Three things I hate most since childhood: flies, cockroaches, and dog poop, the last one rampant in the streets of Geneva also. We had so many fights with dog owners in the park of the apartment building where we lived in Geneva. The dog owners never scooped up the poop. The ones who had no children would allow their dogs to poop in the sandpits designated for the little ones. There was no dog poop law in Switzerland at the time.

When the war was over, some Americans, British, and French remained in Egypt. The Americans still kept a base. To make ends meet, Ma rented rooms to American GIs. One person stayed with us for a couple of years. His name was Jimmy. We called him Uncle Jimmy. He was a navy guy, about thirty-five years old, bald, with a big beer belly. I would tease him a lot.

"How do you float with that huge belly of yours?" I asked one day, pointing at his stomach that bulged over his pants.

"I float better. Look at how boats float. Their bellies keep them afloat," he said.

We loved him a lot and had great fun with him. We adopted him as an uncle, and he adopted us. He became part of our family. He told us stories about the States, and I listened attentively and asked him a lot of questions. I was curious and wanted to know everything because that was where I intended to go. American movies made a great impression on me, not the European ones, which did not show jovial teenagers prancing around. European movies were rather somber. He also told us that he was engaged to a Greek woman from his hometown in Greece and that he would marry her when he got out of the navy. He was a Greek American but born in the United States.

The funny thing is that in Egypt, he was a big shot, an American naval officer, but when we visited him twenty years later in Greece, where he had retired, he seemed like a small, ordinary man living in a dingy apartment with his childhood sweetheart, now his wife. They did not have children. By the time they had gotten married, she had been too old. I was so disappointed in seeing him diminished. He used to be my hero, my American "uncle," the powerful naval officer, my contact to the great country where I vowed to go one day.

Some years later, Ma told us that the gossip in the building at the time was that, "surely Araxie was sleeping with this guy to get all those goodies from the U.S." These were not gifts, however. We paid for them. But gossip is gossip, and the women were envious of Ma, also because she was pretty, and they were rather ordinary-looking and did not have a "handsome husband and beautiful clothes." When he was in the money, Pa had bought enough clothes for Ma to last many years. Ma altered them during the years to follow the existing fashion, so it looked like she was always dressed up in new clothes.

One day Uncle Jimmy got us the Montgomery Ward catalog, and we ordered a few items. I ordered a beautiful doll. I was passed the age of playing with dolls, but as I had broken most of them, I wanted one to keep this time. Judy also ordered one. Ma wanted to order some clothes, but she was disappointed at the dresses in the catalog—they were rather dowdy. They were made for American housewives, and Ma was certainly not a housewife. Yes, she cooked and sewed, but my parents often went out, and Ma was accustomed to wearing stylish clothes. She copied everything from French magazines and chose beautiful fabrics imported from France and Italy. She also made our clothes.

We ordered very few things from the catalog.

A few months after Uncle Jimmy left, in September 1947, there was the cholera epidemic in Egypt. There had been a few epidemics over the years before that date. This epidemic started in a village and quickly spread to other villages. We immediately got vaccinated against it. Ma used to boil our drinking water from the tap, and we added lemon to it for a whole year, even though the epidemic abated around December. Just being cautious. She also washed the vegetables in permanganate solution diluted with water. Luckily, the Heliopolis water came from a well, and it was considered safe. The *fellahs* in the villages were accustomed to drink the Nile water full of germs. I suppose that was how they got their immunity. The news was that about thirty-six thousand people died within a few months and that Cairo had only thirty-two deaths, the least of the other cities. We were relieved to hear that.

# CHAPTER X

## The Arab–Israeli War

And now another war started—the first Arab–Israeli War concerning Palestine. It seems when Israel declared independence, some Arab countries were not too happy about the loss of Palestinian lands, and a war ensued. This started in May 1948, around the end of the school year, when I was graduating from the Armenian elementary school. There was again turmoil in the streets, and riots erupted here and there. But, we were relatively safe in Heliopolis.

There were bomb scares all over again. The sirens would blast, scaring us to death. However, we still went to the movies, and our handbags were checked at the entrance of the theater for hidden bombs. We avoided, which we never did before, some Jewish-owned cinemas and department stores because, obviously, these would be targeted.

Again, we covered our windows with purple paint and dimmed the lights. It was so boring not being able to do anything in the dark. I wanted to read and sew and was utterly frustrated that I could not. I could hardly do my homework with the light of a candle. The only thing I was able to do in the dark was to knit and thus became an expert knitter. This latter activity, which I pursued for many years to come, together with typing on a manual typewriter, caused me to have carpal tunnel syndrome. I was operated on both wrists later on in Geneva, when I was about thirty-three years old.

This war lasted for about a year. The rumor was that the Arabs were not well organized, their arms were faulty, and therefore, they lost the war. We did not see much in the news at the cinema, not like WWII, when the news was abundant. The Egyptians did not want to show and admit their defeat. Thank God things started getting back to normal, and we resumed our life as though nothing had happened. The sad news is that this conflict is still going on after seventy years.

Around this time, a great calamity happened to the doctor.

The doctor's family lived on one floor of an apartment building in Cairo, divided into two sections: one was their residence, and the other was his clinic. He was a gynecologist. He also happened to be the doctor of the wives of diplomats in the Russian and Iraqi embassies. He was on friendly basis with both.

One day, a diplomat from the Iraqi embassy called him up.

"I just picked up my wife from the airport, but before going to the hotel, I would like to dump a couple of suitcases at your clinic, if you don't mind."

"Sure, you can," said the doctor. "My door is always open."

In fact, it was.

A few hours later, two Egyptian detectives came over and interrogated the doctor and picked up the suitcases. They found illegal drugs in them. Lots of drugs. Probably the Iraqi guy was being followed. The doctor feigned ignorance, but nevertheless, he was arrested as a collaborator. His lawyer told him to deny he knew anything about the suitcases being dropped off, but the doctor insisted on telling the truth—that he was told about them beforehand but was unaware of their content. He got two years in jail for being honest. The lawyer could have gotten him off on ignorance of the fact.

Lesson learned. It does not pay to be truthful all the time.

Poor Tante Nevart went to the prison almost every day to bring him edible food.

When the doctor came out of prison, his hair had turned all white, and he had lost a considerable amount of weight. He resumed his work in his clinic. During his absence, Tante Nevart had rented part of the clinic to a couple of other doctors.

The downside of his going to jail, of course, was that now Anoush was branded with the reputation of having had her father in jail, which reduced her potentiality of catching a good husband.

# CHAPTER XI

## St. Clare's College

I had definite ideas which secondary school I wanted to attend after graduating from elementary school. I chose St. Clare's College, a few blocks away from our house, run by Irish Franciscan nuns. It was convenient as it was within walking distance. I still pursued my dream of going to the States, and that was why I chose an English language school. I wanted to be damn good in English.

The college was attended by Christians, Muslims, and Jews. There was no tension amid the students regarding religious differences.

I started school at the fifth grade, but after a couple of months into the term, the class sister thought I was too strong and suggested that I skip a grade and go on to the sixth, which I did. I was not particularly keen to do this as everyone else had already started their year, and I thought I would lag behind. I hated the possibility of that. I always wanted to be first. My English was not that good yet. All I had had were two classes a week of English in Armenian school. By skipping a grade and going to a higher grade, I would be confronted with Shakespeare and the like. I had already started reading novels in English, but Shakespeare?

"I want to go back to the fifth grade," I told my parents after one week. "I want to get a better command of English before I can confront Shakespeare. How can I understand that guy with my limited English? Thou, dost, thee, cometh, and so forth! It's crazy."

Whereupon Ma went to the school and talked to the sixth-grade sister, who was confident I could tackle it with a little extra work.

"But, Sister, I cannot understand Shakespeare even if I tried harder," I told her and refused vehemently to stay in the upper class. They were obliged to transfer me back to the fifth grade, where I excelled in everything, which was what I wanted.

I liked the atmosphere of this school. It was serene, and the nuns' attire was impeccable, a dark brown robe with a crisp, starched white collar and a white rope at the waist. Some of the nuns were pretty, with blue eyes. Almost everyone had brown or black eyes in Egypt except those who were of Albanian origin, like King Farouk. Therefore, I was fascinated by blue eyes. I was also fascinated by the nuns' demeanor of silently gliding on the floor without making any noise.

During my first year at St. Clare's, I had visions of becoming a nun. I did the Way of the Cross every day, although I was not a Catholic. The sister of my class liked that. Perhaps she thought I could be converted to Catholicism. I soon gave up on the idea of nun-hood when I became more and more interested in boys. They were constantly on my mind. I was fourteen then. Boys were much more exciting than being a nun and celibate. I had started reading romance novels and American magazines. I was crazy about *Seventeen*, *Photoplay*, and *Modern Screen* magazines. I would devour and cherish them. Never threw them out.

In seventh grade, the nun (one nun was assigned for each grade) took a dislike to me because I had managed to do an algebra problem, which she had not been able to solve after several attempts, on the blackboard. During her trials, some of the students blurted out, "Peggy did it, Sister." That pissed her off, and her cool, composed face became red as a tomato. She threw down the chalk on her desk and continued the algebra instruction as though nothing had happened.

After class, she took me aside and gave me a lecture.

"You are too clever for your own good. I think I might not promote you at the end of the year if you keep on boasting."

"But I am not boasting, Sister."

"Don't stand there as cool as a cucumber and contradict me," she said and walked away. You could never win an argument with the sisters. You had to say "Yes, Sister," to whatever they said.

Then during the summer, the sister called for me through a friend of mine and informed me that I was going to skip the eighth grade and go to the ninth when school reopened. I was surprised. One day she threatened me that she would not promote me and the next day, that I would skip one grade. The nuns were unpredictable. I think they were frustrated about their predicament (being without a man) and took it out on the students. You had to always try and be in their good graces; otherwise, they would make your life hell.

The idea of jumping grades at this time enchanted me a great deal. As I had improved my English considerably, I was now ready to tackle Shakespeare as well as Chaucer.

The nuns were not that much in favor of gymnastics for girls, and I missed the rigorous gym sessions of the Armenian school. The gym master in Armenian school had been trained in Germany, and he led us like we were soldiers in the army. He was always in a white short-sleeved shirt summer or winter.

We wore a black cotton gym uniform in Armenian school. It consisted of a one-piece outfit (shorts with a top). We also wore gym shoes. This outfit as well as our school uniforms were sewn by the mothers or seamstresses. Most women in those days knew how to sew. It was part of being a woman. You cooked, looked after the house, sewed, mended, knitted, and looked after children and husband. A full-time boring job. If you were lucky to have a maid, you did not have to do the washing up, washing clothes by hand, or cleaning the house. But otherwise, you were stuck. And I was adamant not to get stuck with housework. My young, undeveloped mind was occupied with different scenarios. Become wealthy, marry a passionate guy, and have a fabulous career as a fashion designer in the States and eventually have a couple of intelligent children.

We were cold in winter with this short-sleeved outfit but were not allowed to wear a jacket on top. We were scared to show how cold we were because the gym master had a sadistic mania of making us stand still and shiver even more, if we complained. So, we pretended that everything was fine. We were eager for the sessions to start so that we would move, jump, run, or whatever. He would also hit our hands with a clapper if we did not take the right positions. It hurt like hell.

In St. Clare's College, however, we did some semblance of gym in our school uniforms. How can one do gym with a serge skirt and white blouse and pompoms and just ordinary shoes? The gym teacher was a man, and maybe the nuns considered shorts were too sexy and that he would get lascivious ideas looking at our young legs.

At that time, I did not realize that exercise was so important, and I did not mind our stupid gym class. At least we were outside in the yard and not stuck in the classroom.

There was an American girl in my class who had experience with boys.

"Why do you stay in Cairo and not go back to the States?" I asked her one day. She was from California, the land of Hollywood, where I wanted to go.

"In California, I am like everyone else—blonde, blue-eyed—whereas here in Cairo, I stand out, and boys pay attention to me."

That made sense.

She invited me to party once, and after a few dances, it was decided to play spin the bottle. I had never played this game but had heard about it. *What the hell am I doing with this group? I do not belong here. I have not even danced closely with a guy yet, and I am supposed to kiss him?* When my turn came to go to the designated room for a kiss, I hesitated but was obliged to go to the room where the kissing was supposed to take place; otherwise, I would be considered a dumbass, which I was. I was extremely shy. I didn't know what to do, how to act. The guy came towards me and held me close. I stammered and said "no". He looked at me like I was from another planet, shook his head, and walked out of the room dumbfounded. I followed him out of the room, looking down at my shoes, trying to hide my blush. I didn't look up for fear that he would snicker and tell the group what had happened. I was so ashamed, and I hated myself for being such a prude. Luckily, he did not utter a word. Otherwise, I would certainly have been branded an idiot. I just wanted to run away from the party, but I stayed, pretending I was enjoying all this.

I wanted so much to grow up and be part of an older, more sophisticated group, but I was so timid. I think the reason I was shy was that I was not physically developed like my peers.

One day during the Bible class, the sister came out and said that only Catholics would go to heaven. All other Christians would go to purgatory. She did not mention the Jews or the Muslims. Whereupon I put my hand up.

"What is purgatory, Sister?"

She explained that it was a place where your fate would be decided, whether you were going to heaven or hell. It scared me to death and, when I got home, I related to Ma what the sister had said. Ma got upset, although she was not that religious. She went to school and confronted the Mother Superior and asked her "to please ask Sister to refrain from filling her child's mind with Catholic stuff, that this was a school attended by all religions and that the sisters should respect that."

After Ma's visit, we never heard any more nonsense during Bible class. Bible class was not obligatory to non-Catholics, but I liked to attend. I liked the stories.

Overall, the sisters liked me because I got good grades and helped them out by tutoring the other students. They thought I could explain the assignments better in a language that the students would understand. Their Irish drawl was sometimes incomprehensible. In seventh grade, I was asked to coach the girls in algebra and explain geometry to some who had not grasped it. They also asked me to correct their tests. Unpaid, of course. I was only fifteen, but I managed to do what was asked of me. It made me feel important, and it built up my confidence.

We had nine years of schooling all in all. The tenth grade was for the advanced class of the Oxford/Cambridge levels. I did not do that level in Cairo. I wanted to work and make money to help the family. I did that final year by correspondence when I was in Geneva because I had the intention of going to Geneva University at that late stage. But the thought evaporated. I was intent on continuing to work and make money and also advance my artistic career.

Later on, after I had left Egypt, I heard from the new generation of students that my test papers were kept and shown as examples of well-written papers. I wished so much that I could go back and look at them myself, but the opportunity never arose. The school was eventually closed, and it became an Egyptian Catholic school run by local nuns.

# CHAPTER XII

## Teenage Years

Ma had the habit of always saying no at first to whatever I suggested. One day I found out that there was going to be a Girl Guides group in Heliopolis—Armenian Girl Guides. I wanted to be part of it. It sounded like fun, and I have always been a fun-seeker, even now at age eighty-four. We were approached by the two leaders of this new group, who came to our doorstep one day. Not everyone had a telephone, so people just dropped by. If no one was at home, they would leave a note and would try the next day.

We were always prepared to receive visitors, day and night, so we were presentable-looking. No walking around all day with dressing gowns. Some of our neighbors did that. These two young women gave a pitch to Ma. They were persuasive, and Ma finally accepted. After they left, she called Tante Nevart and told her that her daughters were to become Girl Guides. Tante Nevart warned Ma that the chief leader was an extremely wealthy Armenian woman who was married to so-and-so and that she was also the mistress of so-and-so. Ma relayed this message to us and told us she regretted giving her permission.

"Who cares about the morals of the chief?" I blurted out. I certainly did not. I admired that woman, not because of her morals but because of the way she dressed, always very chic and *à la mode*. I was already quite fashion conscious and I wanted to be like her when I got older.

The Girl Guides episode was a fun time in my life. We were given a hut on the grounds of the Armenian school and were divided in three groups, each with a leader, and given a corner of the hut to meet with our group. I became the leader of one and decorated our corner. The other leaders did not have any ideas of how to decorate, so I gladly helped them. My early decorating skills were emerging. Like father, like daughter.

We had weekly meetings where we learned a few things, one of which was how to tie the six most important knots. I still have not forgotten them and use them whenever the occasion arises. The rest of the time was consecrated to play, play, and more play. A charmed life, being young. We went camping one day in some deserted park, and we were given a tent for three girls each. It was a great adventure for us to be away from home for three days. We never slept at nights though. We played board games with a flashlight, and we had to go out to do our business in the bushes. We always went in twos because we were scared of the dark and crawly insects and spiders.

The fights that my parents had, all about money, infuriated me and I could do nothing about it. How I hated those arguments. Pa just did not make a decent living. We scraped by. He was a very generous man, mind you. Whenever he cashed any money, he would buy us gifts, like the latest issue of *Photoplay* or *Modern Screen*. He knew we wanted to learn about our favorite actors and their shenanigans. I loved both my parents equally, and I wanted them to get along and not argue. Pa was fun, and Ma was so loving. She was the disciplinarian. Pa never scolded us. If he did not agree with something we were doing, he would tell Ma. She, in return, would reprimand us.

At a very early age, I decided that when I grew up, I would work and provide for myself, not to be at the mercy of a husband. Some of Ma's friends were unhappily married, but they did not dare leave their husbands because they could not get jobs. Some of the others just accepted their fate that a woman's place was in the home. There was no work for married women with children anyway. Who would take care of the children? I did not agree with this and told Ma that I would not follow in her footsteps and be a stay-at-home mom. I would strive to have an exciting career.

"How can you do that in this society?" she asked. "You get married and look after the house, husband, and children."

"I'll think of something," was my reply.

I had not yet figured out what I would do nor how I would achieve what I wanted to do. How could I achieve my dreams? I was constantly thinking of different scenarios. Should I go to university? Should I continue with painting lessons? The answers were not obvious. Staying in Egypt was a deterrent to a career for me. By this time, I had set my mind to be a dress designer. But where would I do that? Egypt was out of the question. So was Europe. My only hope was the United States, but how to get there? It was an impossible dream, and it required money.

In the meantime, I wanted to have as much fun as possible in a restrictive society. The nephew of Ma's ex-fiancé, Aram, who was our friend, would sometimes take us to the Italian Social Club. I was fifteen at the time, and he was an older boy—about eighteen—and I thought I was in love with him. I think that was my first real crush. Actually, no, my first crush was when I was six or seven and met Pa's army buddy, Johnny Pendergast.

Aram was now in my horizon, and I wanted him to take notice of me. I was smitten by him. He did not dance with me during these outings but danced with my cousin, Anoush, who was a couple of years older than me and had some curves on her body. I was only fourteen, with no curves whatsoever, and he considered me a kid, I guess. I was extremely jealous. I was a better dancer, but he didn't know that until a couple of years later.

I was quite excited when Aram asked me to go over to their house one Sunday so that he would carve my portrait in *bas-relief*.

He thought I had an interesting profile. Another one to be added to the list of the admirers of my goddamn profile. Who cared about my profile? I wanted to put on some weight and not be a scrawny teenager with no boobs or ass. I did two sittings with him on two different Sundays. He was a serious guy, did not laugh much, and did not crack jokes either. I soon lost interest in him when other boys came into my vision.

# CHAPTER XIII

## The Armenian Social Club

One day in 1949, Pa came home and gave us some great news. A certain Armenian millionaire, who had a metalworks factory in Cairo, had just donated a considerable amount of money to open an Armenian cultural/social club a couple of blocks away from our house. We were thrilled, of course. The principal object of the club was to have cultural activities and have social get-togethers for the Armenian community.

An anecdote about the millionaire. He asked for Shamiram's hand in marriage. She was an attractive young woman, tall and blond (from the bottle). She refused categorically. "I won't marry a midget," she said. "I am taller than he is. He'll have to step on a stool to kiss me."

Her family tried to talk her into it. "He is cultured, and he has money," they argued.

"I don't give a damn," was her reply.

She was an independent young woman, and she made a substantial living by giving private piano lessons. She was also the piano player of the Armenian kindergarten, where she earned peanuts, and the organist at the Armenian church.

Actually, the true story of her refusal was that she had a lover—a married man with four kids—who lived a couple of houses away from her home. Pa tried to talk sense into her, but to no avail. She preferred her lover to the millionaire. She ended the relationship with the lover because he had threatened her with a gun one day out of jealousy. He had seen her speaking to a man in the street. She ended up marrying a man who earned much less than she did—a salesman of fabric material at one of the renowned fabric shops in Cairo, a good man.

The family was relieved.

The club was going to have a theater, a couple of ping-pong tables, and a dance podium, outside in the yard, for Saturday night dances. And also, lots of board games. It had a kitchen, where the members would cook for the social events. There were plenty of volunteers. There was no membership. Any Armenian could go anytime and hang out. It was financed by fees paid for the activities. As most young people did not have a telephone, that was where they met, formed a group, and decided what to do or where to go for the evening or on the weekend. It was a convenient place, especially to meet young people. Lots of activities were planned at the club. In fact, after school, around 4:00 p.m., the Heliopolis teenagers and the young singles of Heliopolis met there to socialize. Judy and I went there often. Homework came much later in the evening.

Parents usually went to the club for special events or for weekend shish kebab dinner and dance parties.

"You are making yourselves too visible. The boys will take you for granted," Ma kept telling us.

"So, what? All my friends go there, and I want to be with them," I retorted.

"Well-brought-up girls should refrain from socializing with boys so frequently," she said. "Be less accessible. You will be more appreciated, and the guys will not take you for granted."

In fact, this was true because when I did not go to the club for a few days, the boys asked what had happened to me. They said they had missed me. I was flattered and just shrugged, beaming internally.

I loved Saturday nights when there was dancing. For big events, there was an orchestra, for smaller ones, just records with loud speakers, playing American, Italian, and French dance rhythms.

Families with their children, young and old, would sit at tables in the garden, have shish kebab prepared by volunteers—Pa being one of them—and the girls, all dressed up in their Sunday best waiting eagerly for a boy to come and ask them to dance.

I was fifteen at the time and went with my parents to these events. Although I was a good dancer and was dying to show off my talent, no young man would come to our table and ask me to dance. The music was calling me. But the guys did not. I was skinny, no boobs, no ass, nor any makeup. The young men considered me a kid. Then at one dance event at the club, a friend of my father asked me to dance. After taking permission from Pa, I got up, my heart thumping like a drum, and did a real sultry rhumba. Bam, that did it. Everyone from then on noticed me, and I was asked to dance at every function.

It was sheer bliss.

Amid all this turmoil of Pa's inadequate employment and Ma's frustration, Pa came home one day and announced that he was going to work for a bookie. He said this triumphantly as though by doing this job, all our financial troubles would be solved. Ma looked at him speechless. She froze. She was suddenly transformed into a stalagmite compared to Pa's jovial stance. Judy and I were nearby and hid behind a wall to listen.

The stalagmite then melted, and Ma managed to say "What on earth are you talking about?"

I later learned, by pestering Ma for an explanation, what a bookie was.

Being a bookie was strictly against the law in Egypt, and offenders were imprisoned. Pa adored horses and had owned a few back in the old days when he was wealthy. He used to have them compete at the racetrack in Heliopolis. He gambled on his own horses. I remember going to a couple of races when I was a child.

"Yup," he said, "I am going to be this bookie's assistant. I met him at so and so's. I will procure clients and phone in their bets. And I'll get a percentage of their earnings. I will lose nothing. All there is to do is use our telephone."

"Are you crazy?" Ma raised her voice. No more stalagmite. Now it was fire and brimstone.

"Of course, you're crazy. I have never doubted that since the day I married you." This was supposed to be a love marriage, by the way. "Have you thought about being caught by the police and being whisked off to jail? And a stinking jail at that? And I will have to come over every day and bring you homemade food as though I have nothing better to do? And the shame you will bring on the family and on top of all that, we would be totally broke."

All this in one breath. Ma always projected the worst that could happen in any circumstance. She was right, of course.

"There is nothing to it," Pa kept on repeating, trying to appease her. "Nobody will know. We just won't open the door on the Sundays when I am using the phone for this job."

He was as excited as a kid. He was finally going to make some money.

"The Egyptian police are not dopey, you know," said Ma. "Look at what happened to the doctor. He was jailed, and he was not even guilty."

This is how Pa's bookie business took place.

On Sundays, all the windows of the south side of the apartment were closed. Pa would commandeer the informal sitting room. Everyone had to be quiet, pretending nobody was at home. No one could use the phone except Pa, who placed his bets in a low voice. If anyone rang the doorbell, we looked through a secret window on the south side of the apartment—nobody knew this window was part of our apartment—to see who it was. We feared informers and police. We could not allow anyone in the apartment even if it was a friend visiting, because Pa's bookie business was supposed to be top secret. We were warned not to tell anything to a soul.

This business went on for a few months until Pa found gainful employment. Actually, he got employed by the company that was owned by the "midget" millionaire suitor of Shamiram. He turned out to be a miserly employer, stingy and demanding. Pa finally left that job to become manager of a hotel in Helwan, a spa resort.

Yup, Pa could almost do everything except make money. He was an artist through and through.

# CHAPTER XIV

## My First Boyfriend

The summer of 1951 was the best year of my life up to now—I, finally, had interaction with boys. I mostly loved the Saturday night dances at the club. That was when I blossomed.

One of the guys at the club, Dick, a good basketball player, a few years older than me, took a liking to me, and I would dance with him sometimes during the social evenings. He was tall and handsome and had a nice smile. Quite a few Armenian guys in Cairo were basketball players, some were soccer players, and others played both. There was an Armenian sports arena in Heliopolis and another in Cairo called HMEM (the Pan-Armenian Sporting Organization, in English). We would often go to the two clubs to watch the guys play matches with other ethnic groups. These were exciting times because there was always dancing and dinner after the matches.

Dick started following me, coming to the movies with our group, passing in front of my balcony four times a day, glancing up, and waving at me. I looked forward to his daily walks. I was positive he was in love with me, and it made my heart flutter. At parties, we danced cheek to cheek but not at dances at the club. Boys and girls never touched each other physically except while dancing. It was taboo. Simply not done. It would create a scandal, and people would talk. The cheek to cheek was a very mild one, nothing hot and steamy. I did not even let Dick put his arm around me at the movies. I was prudish and shy, extremely prudish and shy. I thought he would think badly of me, all because of what Ma had instilled in me—to be a good girl and not an easy one. I was so tired of hearing the words "good girl", "easy girl."

I was very much interested in Dick, but nobody was aware of it, not even him. Actually, I thought I was in love with him, the first time ever that I really thought I was in love aside from my fawning on actors. I was reserved, though, and did not at all show my feelings toward him. "A girl has to play hard to get," Ma always said over and over. We never dated; that was not permitted. But we did go out in groups to nightclubs, parties, movies, picnics, cycling, the zoo, the Pyramids, and so on.

An activity Ma expressed her disapproval was my wish to join the Armenian junior girls' basketball team at the Armenian sports arena.

"Everything I want to do, you say no. I wish I did not need your permission for my activities," I told her. I was so fed up of having to take permission for everything I wanted to take part in.

"You are still a teenager. You have a long way to go."

"I am sure it is not like this in the United States. Teenagers seem to have a lot of fun," I said. American movies and magazines pictured another kind of life. I always thought about the United States and my impossible dream to live there. I thought everything was so rosy over there. Reality struck me much later.

"Nice girls do not play basketball and exhibit themselves. I am sure only lower-class girls are on the team," she argued. There was a consciousness of class among the Armenians and, in fact, among all the ethnic groups in Cairo. Lower class also meant being poor, and people looked down on you if you were poor. Money was of great importance. That was why Ma always kept us well dressed and groomed and pretended we still had some money. After all, we were still living in our huge apartment with fancy furniture, and we had a maid and a monthly cleaner and a telephone. That was important. People did not know that Pa was not earning a good income. Ma was adamant about keeping up appearances.

After my insistence and the insistence of some other "good family girls" who were members, she agreed, and I joined the basketball team. I hated to play while the boys were watching though because I looked so skinny in shorts, flat as an ironing board, legs like matchsticks, and thighs that did not meet. The other girls were fleshy and lumpy, female attributes much sought after in the Middle East, even now.

I forced myself to eat more food to put on a few pounds. I sewed my own clothes, pretty clothes, and did my hair Veronica Lake style. No makeup, though. Ma did not allow me to put on lipstick until I was seventeen, and even then, I was allowed a very pale hue.

Basketball turned out to be one of my most enjoyable pastimes as I was finally in contact with boys, the basketball players. We also formed a ping-pong group at the social club, and I enjoyed that game also.

I was fascinated by the play of two older guys who were the ping-pong champions of Cairo. They would almost always beat all other ethnic groups during interclub matches.

It is uncanny how life catches up with you sometimes. Years later, in 1963, when I was separated from my first husband, one of these guys became my boyfriend in New York. His name was Arty. He wanted to get married to me after my divorce, but I decided to go to Switzerland instead and have European experiences. I was not that much into him. He was a nice guy, but he was fresh out of Egypt and had not yet started to earn a living in the United States. He had plans though, plans to open up a handmade ceramic tile business in L.A. We kept our friendship through the years, and subsequently, he got married to someone else, and he has passed away since.

The other one, Jack, is in a nursing home in LA. Poor thing. He had been Anoush's secret boyfriend when she was fifteen. Her mom never knew a thing about it. The last time I met him accidentally was in Venice about forty years ago, when my sister and I were visiting that city and met him there in the street. He took us to a Dalida concert—Dalida again—then we drove him back to Geneva in our VW Beetle. He made us laugh the whole time with his anecdotes and jokes in Arabic. He was such an unusual fellow, had an outrageous humor, was good company, and a spendthrift. He sometimes calls me from L.A., but I don't understand a thing he says. His diction is incomprehensible. He is about ninety years old now. All his flamboyance is gone. It is too bad old people lose all their verve. I hope I never do. But then I get tired being energetic all the time.

I must admit we had quite an active social life, even though Ma persisted in not allowing us to go to every social event at the club or to go to every party in friends' homes. And there were plenty of invitations. Her first answer was always no. Ma insisted that Judy always go with me. Judy felt out of place most of the time because guys did not often invite her to dance. She was only thirteen but looked older as she was taller than me. Ma insisted, however, and Judy hated it. She felt like a wallflower.

As most of the guys did not have telephones, they would come to our apartment in twos or threes to ask permission from Ma. They did this ritual with every girl's family.

Pa was a very active member of the club but was rarely home. He would have allowed us to go more often. Ma's permission depended on her mood or on what Tante Nevart would advise her.

"Are you crazy allowing your daughters to go to parties? They'll never find a husband later on," she always told Ma. A mother's principal worry was that her daughter or daughters would not find suitable, well-to-do husbands if they acted in a certain unacceptable manner—meaning having contact with guys.

Tante Nevart and Ma were the best of friends. They told each other everything, or, rather, Ma told her everything but not vice versa. Tante Nevart was very secretive, especially about money. She did not want their financial situation to be known. Anyway, both mothers warned us girls not to be all over the *piazza* as they called it. We often used foreign words in our vocabulary; they were more apropos, in making a point.

Tante Nevart being stricter, Anoush did a lot of things in secret. A few times, when her mom found out what she had been up to, she was grounded for a few days, but Anoush never flinched. She continued defying her mother.

Ma once got annoyed at my insisting to go to a particular party, and she came out with "You are not studying. Your head is in dancing. Where will that lead you? All you think about is parties and boys, boys, boys."

"What's wrong with that?" I retorted. "My grades are not suffering, are they?"

After that argument, I did not receive any more comments about my dancing mania. I would still have to plead with her to let me go to the parties I was invited to, but to no avail. I would then lie to her and tell her I was going to a movie with a group of friends—she insisted on knowing their names—but I would go to the party instead. I loved dancing parties. I lived for dancing parties. I dreamed of dancing parties. The music was European and American.

Guys took notice of me through my dancing and not because of my "voluptuous" figure. I was far from having one. I was considered to be the best dancer at the club (all dance steps copied from American movies) and was much sought after. I was flattered and became quite popular, although still very slim with no curves whatsoever but dressed in the latest fashion, copied from magazines. The way I danced was uncommon in Armenian circles. Up to now, when I talk to my old, old, very old friends—even those I have not seen since they were thirteen—they remember my dancing. I just talked to one of them in Sweden the other day, and he said he has a photo of me dancing at the club and e-mailed it to me. Another guy I met in a school reunion introduced himself, saying that I would not remember him as he was younger than me in the 1950s, but he remembered my dancing.

A major reason I wanted to go to all the parties was that I did not want Dick to dance with other girls if I was not there. And this would surely happen. I could not imagine him standing at the bar, just twiddling his thumbs, looking at the dancers. Although I sometimes vacillated in my feelings toward Dick and became interested in a couple of other guys, I still wanted him to be interested only in me.

One day I was walking home from the movies with three guys—the other girls had already been dropped off—and Ma saw me from the balcony. She scolded me when I stepped through our doorway.

"What will people think and say?" she asked. "Are you out of your mind?"

She was very concerned lest the neighbors thought I was an easy girl.

"Better than walking with one guy," I replied. "Then they would really talk."

About kissing, if a boy tried to kiss a girl, it was either because she was an easy girl or that he was really interested in her and planned to marry her in some distant future. No girl that I knew allowed herself to be kissed willingly. Girls played hard to get. It was a game. I am not saying the words "easy lay" here because that would never have applied in those days. There was no such thing. The guys would go to prostitutes for that activity. One wealthy guy, a friend of ours, had a *garçonnière*, and that was where he and his friends would take the street prostitutes to indulge in their dirty business. We also heard that some "easy" girls were taken there. We girls were curious to know which guys frequented that apartment.

Men having a *garçonnière* was a common practice in Mediterranean countries, where young women were not allowed to have relationships with guys until wedding bells chimed. If a guy was wealthy, he could afford to rent one by himself. Otherwise, two or three guys got together and rented an apartment for the purpose of taking prostitutes or loose women there. Some were even married women, not sexually satisfied by their husbands. It was all very hush-hush. These guys usually lived with their parents for all the conveniences of having their needs taken care of by their mothers. They went to work and were never home in the evenings. Mothers in the Middle

East favored boys and took good care of them. Girls were supposed to help their mothers.

Even though we had school, we spent most afternoons at the club. One of the games we played was "truth or dare?" I always lied when it came to questions about what guy I liked. I did learn though that Dick considered me to be his girlfriend. He came out with it in the game. People in our group started whispering to each other and gossiping. I denied it, of course.

Dancing was the only time close contact was permitted, so to speak. We never held hands in public either. Never went out openly in couples, a real no-no. All outings were done in groups. Some older girls sneaked and went out alone with guys. We would go to the Pyramids, the zoo, movies, nightclubs, and parties. Lots of parties. Ma would allow us to go out with the group after finding out who was going to be there and gave us a curfew time.

"All men want is to touch you, and then you become an easy girl, and nobody will marry you," she often said. This was true to some extent. Men did not consider such girls as possible wives-to-be. Even if a girl wanted to say yes, she would say no. It was all a game the girls played. This is also true to all societies in the Middle East.

During that summer of 1951, Judy and I went on a two-week vacation at the YWCA camp in Alexandria. It was an all-girls club and quite an adventure for us, sleeping in straw huts with no flooring—the cots were directly on the sand. We had to beware of insects crawling on our cots. We carefully examined them before going to sleep lest a bug or two would be nestling under the sheets. There were small frogs in the toilets and showers. Their croaking sometimes kept us awake, but we dared not harm them. They were so cute to look at. I would have liked to catch one and keep it as a pet.

It was sheer pleasure to spend two weeks going to the beach every day and taking part in all sorts of activities. We also put up amateur theater shows in the evenings. I was one of the actors in these plays, and I loved it. I wanted to take part in everything. We were not allowed to leave the club on our own on any pretense unless a parent's permission was granted. Well, Ma was in Cairo, no way would she give us permission to leave the club, even if we asked her. Dick was also in Alexandria, and Jack, and Arty. They were all eager to take us out to tea dancing—that was the rage in those days—dancing to records in a club in the afternoons. They were kind of discotheques—which became the rage in Europe in the 1960s.

What to do? How to maneuver an outing with the boys? I had to revert to underhanded means. Judy was scared lest we get caught. She was always the reticent one. She needed to *obey the law*. And I was the mischievous one, trying to go around the law.

I took a decent piece of paper, scribbled a note, and signed it as though it were my mother's signature, and gave it to the club manager. She was a fat-bellied woman, middle-aged, with a no-nonsense, stern demeanor. She looked at the note twice, and then she looked at me with eyes that distrusted me. I felt panicky and was trembling inside, but I kept my cool and did not lower my gaze. I looked straight at her. After all, nobody knew what Ma's signature looked like—she had never signed anything at the club—so why should I be scared? A telephone call to Cairo was too expensive, so there was no fear of that either. I did not know what would happen if she caught me out in the forgery and the lie. I would certainly be banished from the club, and my summer would go to hell, and my parents would never trust me again. All these scenarios were going in my head as I looked at the warden—as we called her—without batting an eyelid. I got away with it.

The note read, "Please allow my daughters to go out with their cousin Jack when he comes around to pick them up."

From then on, we managed to have some clandestine outings. What joy. The cousin Jack was actually the guy who is now in a retirement home in L.A. I am a good forger, by the way. I have even done a few changes in a friend's Egyptian passport in Montreal—changed the dates of its validity. I also forged my sister's signature at her bank in Montreal—with her permission, of course. She worked too far away from the bank, and I used to deposit and withdraw her money. I think I have missed my calling. Well, maybe in my next life. I have so many ideas for a next life that I think I need several next lives.

That same summer, many Armenian families in Heliopolis had rented houses and were vacationing in Alexandria. We also rented a place in September—a rather modest one. Our wealthy cousins, who lived in Dokki (a fashionable suburb of Cairo), had rented a cabana at the poshest beach in Alexandria, called Sidi Bishr No. 2. There were No. 1 and No. 3, but they were not attended by the hoi polloi. The No. 2 was the one to be seen in. Even King Farouk's extended family and entourage sometimes visited this beach. Beautiful young women, dressed in the most fashionable bathing suits, walked up and down the promenade in front of the cabins. We spent the whole day at the beach, swimming, playing games, and dancing on the sand in the evenings. Dick was also there, and he taught me how to swim. We often went to the movies and to tea dancing. That was a big thing in Alex (short for Alexandria).

During all that summer and fall, my thoughts were on Dick, on what he whispered in my ear, how he held me while dancing, whether he would dare kiss me on the cheek, and so on. And when he left to go back to Heliopolis before we did, life stood still for me. I was suddenly bored and wanted to return sooner. There were other boys around, but they did not fill up the vacant space that Dick had left behind.

Dick never knew how much I liked him. I never showed any affection toward him. I firmly believed he would then take me for granted. I wanted him to be always the pursuer. "Look but do not touch"—that was my motto. And it worked; it made him pursue me relentlessly.

I guess things do not work like that anymore, but I do prefer the old ways. There was more flirting, drama, and conniving. It created intrigue.

One thing I learned later in life, when I was single and between marriages, is that men always pursue the girl who plays hard to get. They want to conquer her. Well, things don't go that way anymore—there are so many women on match sites pursuing men that the latter take them for granted.

Dick wrote me a couple of love letters, which I have still kept. I am a hoarder and have kept every single letter I have received from family, friends, and boyfriends. Ma had read one of Dick's letters, which I had foolishly left on my night table.

"What is this?" she asked one day, brandishing one of the letters. "Why is he sending you kisses?" Dick had put "xxxx" at the end of the letter. She was a curious woman and wanted to know what her daughter was up to.

"It's nothing," I said. "He's just being friendly." After that incident, I hid the letters in a safe place, away from her prying eyes. However, as I was still scared she would discover my hiding place, I wrote Dick asking him not to write to me anymore.

One day, after we were back in Heliopolis, I saw Dick talking to another girl, and I was extremely jealous and pretended not to notice him at the club and refrained from talking to him. I ignored him for a whole week. He finally realized something was wrong. Guys can be dumb sometimes. He sensed my aloofness and, after a few days had gone by, he came to sit next to me at the club, trying to be friendly, but I still ignored him. I finally gave in after his several attempts at friendliness, and we were the same again.

At one point, I thought I really loved Dick. I was so eager to be in love. I wanted to experience the emotion. How silly of me. Love. What did I know of love? I wanted him to love me in return, of course. I wanted him just for me. He often complimented me on my hair, my clothes, my dancing, and my acting.

Yes, I also acted in plays at the club. We had some good playwrights in the community. One play was about an American-Armenian girl coming back to Egypt to meet her relatives. I had to speak Armenian with an American accent. I adored that role, and the press was very kind to me.

"Ma, I want to be an actress when I grow up."

"Ma, I want to be a dancer when I grow up."

"Ma, I want to be a fashion designer when I grow up."

This latest wish did come true when I went to Boston and Manhattan, later on in the early 1960s.

I firmly believe that if you focus steadily and intensely on a wish, it does come true. You have to believe in yourself and be relentless in your pursuits and never stop dreaming. Reaching for the stars was my hobby. In fact, I daydreamed all the time.

One unfortunate day, I made the idiotic mistake of bringing three Syrian Christian girls, who were in class with me, to the club. This was supposed to be an Armenian club and not really open to foreigners. It was a kind of loose arrangement, however. Some people who had foreign friends would sometimes bring them along to a few functions. Stupid girl that I was, I brought along these girls. One of them made a beeline for Dick. She was not pretty, but she had boobs. I did not even wear a bra, never mind having boobs. She often tried to make him play ping-pong with her. I used to watch him like a hawk. He would always decline, sensing my displeasure—at least he was capable of being sensitive to my moods this time—and would come and sit next to me. He had learned his lesson, ha ha.

One thing I should explain about this Dick relationship. It was all about doing things in a group and not me alone with him. There was no hugging, kissing, or anything of that nature. The only time girls and guys had any physical contact was through dancing. Sometimes the guys would hold you too close, and you could feel the bulge in their pants, but you just ignored it and pretended you did not feel it. You often saw girls keeping their lower bodies away from contact while dancing. We, girls, referred to the bulge as the "package".

Almost all the guys knew how to dance the contemporary dances, some better than others. I hated it when a guy, who was not such a good dancer, would ask me to dance. I could not refuse and then get up and dance with a better dancer who came along. So, I would accept to do one dance only and then sit down, hoping a better dancer would make an appearance. Dancing was a big deal in Cairo in those days. All the ethnic minority clubs had their own venues and events.

And I was dance crazy. And, I still am.

I acted very prudish with Dick. I should have at least allowed him to put his arm around me at the movies. But I was apprehensive of people in the back (other Armenians) seeing me, and then there would be gossip. Wherever we went, we met Armenians. They were all over the place, just like ants, and they loved gossiping. When Dick would put his arm around my seat, I would lean forward so that his arm would not touch me. Ma had instilled in me the idea that if I would allow a guy to touch me, he would consider me to be "an easy girl." I was so tired of hearing these words. Of course, I would have liked to be touched by Dick, but I was shy and did not want to do anything to mar my pristine reputation. I did not wish to be considered "tainted."

And then I got mad one evening at the club because Dick danced with the Syrian bitch, my classmate. I had quarreled with him earlier for some triviality and had ignored him the rest of the day.

After that incident, I never invited them to the club, but they were cheeky and kept coming uninvited. The Armenian guys were interested in them because they let them be touchy, touchy. The Armenian girls, on the other hand, were more reserved and were furious at this turn of events. They complained to the club committee that foreigners were invading our club.

The club committee, Pa being one of its members, came to the decision not to allow non-Armenians to frequent our club. I loved that rule. So now Dick was all mine. No more hanky-panky with other girls, at least not during my presence. I was sure things were going on in the *garçonnière*, though, but that was beyond my control.

# CHAPTER XV

## Political Upheaval

Although 1951 was the best year of my life socially, it was also a turbulent one politically.

The British had controlled Egypt for many years, and even after WWII, it was felt there was some resentment from the local population but not from the ethnic minorities in general. I was only a teenager, and I was not really aware of all that was going on, nor was I particularly interested in politics. All I wanted to do was continue having fun. On certain days, there were massive demonstrations in the streets, but nothing major had yet happened. Schools and businesses would close for a day or two, and life would go back to normal the next day. We were aware of some danger but were not too apprehensive. We just avoided going to Cairo on those days when there were demonstrations. We considered our neighborhood safe. Demonstrations never happened in Heliopolis.

Political trouble started in Egypt around September/October of that year. The Egyptian outrage toward the British occupation of the Suez Canal had become quite vociferous in the towns around the Suez Canal.

In January 1952, the British troops, which were stationed in Ismailia (a town on the canal), had a confrontation with the Egyptian police in their barracks. In the skirmish that ensued, the British killed more than fifty auxiliary Egyptian policemen. News quickly spread to Cairo and, the next day, massive riots broke out in Cairo and in Alexandria. Gangs of hoodlums and peasants (the consensus being that they were instigated by the Muslim Brotherhood) put fire on all buildings owned by foreigners, and there was extensive looting. Cinemas, department stores, clubs, and almost all foreign-owned businesses were scorched. News did not get to Heliopolis until much later in the afternoon; therefore, we were not aware of the riots in Cairo. The radio station was not working that day, and of course, there was no TV yet. And not many people had telephones.

The way we found out was when the doctor (Anoush's father) rang our doorbell that same afternoon. Ma opened the door and came face-to-face with him, dressed in a wrinkled *galabeya*, breathless and disheveled—very unlike his usual well-groomed self—and told us that Cairo was burning, that their building was set on fire, and that he did not know where his wife and daughter were. We were speechless. We had had no news of these riots. Ma and Pa ushered him inside and tried to calm him down. Luckily, Pa was not working on that day.

This is what had happened.

The rioters, some on foot, others in cars and trucks full of gasoline containers, were burning many buildings in Cairo. We later found out that about 750 buildings were scorched. Their apartment was above the Ouzo factory in downtown Cairo, and they started scorching that too. The doctor had his apartment on one side of the floor and his clinic on the other. He told us that his male nurse, Ali, who had never gone to nursing school but who assisted him in operations and taking care of the patients, had lent him one of his *galabeyas*, ushered him out of the clinic as though he was a patient, past the violent mob that was trying to get into the building, and put him in a taxi. The only place he thought of going to was our home. An hour later, my auntie and cousin arrived. They were also in bad shape, frightened to death, and had a hard time explaining what had happened. They were in shock, and so were we. Their nurse had also saved them from being dragged by the mob before it got to the second floor of the apartment building to cause more havoc. After sending the doctor in a taxi, the nurse had found my aunt and my cousin huddled in the bedroom. He hurriedly threw a couple of black *milayas* (the Egyptian peasant woman garb) over their shoulders and got them down the stairs, asking the mobsters, who were climbing the stairs, shouting anti-European slogans, to "let the patients of the clinic go out, please." He then put them in another taxi, and they also came to us, their only relative who had a big house.

So now there were three households in one apartment—Tante Arous and Dayday Michel, the doctor, Tante Nevart, Anoush, and the four of us, plus the live-in maid. We the children (Anoush, Judy, and myself) were thrilled and planned all the fun we would have. Here they were with only the clothes on their backs and the jewelry and money in their pockets and we, the teenagers, were already planning on going to the club to play ping-pong and other games. That's how children are. Elusive childhood. Gone without a backward glance.

The day after the riots, when all was quiet again, we went to the doctor's building to see what had happened and whether there was anything to salvage from there. Great disappointment—everything had burned; not even a photo was left.

On the way back home, I noticed a young fellow in the street wearing one of Tante Nevart's jackets. I had the eyes of a hawk, I had often been told.

"Auntie, Auntie," I said, "that guy is wearing your jacket. Let's go and take it away from him."

Tante Nevart refused and said she would not wear anything that had been on that dirty urchin's back. We let it go. What was one jacket among all that had been looted?

When school reopened after a week, we were asked to keep one minute of silence for those killed in Ismailia.

Six months passed after the riots, and we received astonishing news. King Farouk was overthrown by the Free Officers of the Egyptian Army (as they called themselves) and asked to abdicate. This happened on July 23, 1952. (It seems the number 23 figures many times in my history—date of my birth, date of my present husband's birth, the Battle of El Alamein). It was a bloodless coup perpetrated by them, headed by Maj. Gen. Mohammed Naguib. We later found out, however, that an army officer by the name of Gamal Abdel Nasser was the real head of the revolutionary group. The revolutionaries had trapped the king in Abdeen Palace, and he was asked to abdicate in favor of his infant son by his second marriage. He sailed away in his white military uniform on the royal yacht to Italy. Egyptians had class, not like the barbarian Iraqis who dragged their king through the streets of Baghdad, tied to a truck, thus killing him.

We later learned that the revolutionary council had political ambitions of abolishing the monarchy in Egypt and the Sudan, establish a republic, and end the British occupation.

There was again a lot of chanting anti-British and anti-French slogans in the streets. We were careful in our outings and were apprehensive of what else would ensue. We were especially careful when we spoke in public or on the phone because we were told our phones were being tapped. We trusted no one. Not even the neighbors.

The new leaders of the coup started nationalizing and liquidating foreign and even Egyptian-owned properties. They were against the aristocracy and targeted wealthy landowners—Egyptian Muslims and foreign nationals alike. The ethnic minorities feared the outcome of such measures and some people with foreign passports started leaving the country. They opted for Europe, Canada, and Australia, whichever would accept them. We were going nowhere. We had nowhere to go, and we had no money abroad like some of the wealthy people who made plans to leave. We did not even have passports, and getting one was a hurdle. And if we had, they would be Egyptian ones, and with those, we would have a hard time obtaining a visa to any country. Only Ma had a British passport.

Following the coup, schools and offices were closed for a few days. Later, we heard that the new government leaders reassured the ethnic minorities that they were safe and had nothing to worry about. And surprisingly, they asked all those, whose belongings were burned on Black Saturday (that is what they called the day of the burning of Cairo), to make a list of what they had lost so that they would be compensated. This was very surprising news indeed and quite unbelievable. The Free Officers wanted to make a good impression.

Up to this day, it is not quite clear who instigated the riots.

The plan was that the men of the family—Pa, the doctor, and Dayday Michel, who was extremely fluent in Arabic—would sit down and make a list. They sat in the small sitting room, and we were not allowed to interrupt them. This was serious stuff.

Two separate lists were made: one for the clinic and the other for the apartment. They toiled day and night preparing these lengthy detailed lists. The doctor would dictate the item to Pa, who wrote it out in French, and Dayday Michel would translate it into Arabic. Of course, some fictitious items were added, and the lists were padded as the doctor did not believe that he would be fully compensated. Who could trust the revolutionaries?

There was the problem of getting a wardrobe for the destitute family and fast. Pa could not lend any clothes to the doctor because he was a portly man, and Pa was slim. Ma's clothes did not fit Tante Nevart. My clothes fit Anoush, so she was able to borrow some of mine, the little I had.

The women, including us teenagers, started to frantically knit sweaters and sew clothes for Auntie and Iris. We had lots of dress materials at home and also knitting wool stored in a trunk. We finished one sweater in two days. We were like working bees. This did not prevent us girls from going to the social club to socialize. Iris did not seem to be emotionally affected. She was a fun-loving, optimistic girl and a daredevil. She left the worrying to her parents.

The way the three families lived was as follows:

We, the teenagers, shared one king bed in the master bedroom. We were thrilled about it. My parents had another bedroom, and

Tante Nevart and the doctor were given Dayday Michel's office. A bed was found for them. Tante Nevart hated sharing the same bedroom as her husband because the doctor snored like roaring thunder. Tante Arous and Dayday Michel kept their own bedroom and their own eating area in the hall. Dayday Michel had to work in one of the halls.

The three women shared the kitchen. What a bleak place that was and rather small for four people (the maid included). When the women were at work in there, we would not dare interrupt them with silly questions. Tante Arous kept to her habit of cooking for herself and her husband, but Tante Nevart joined hands with Ma to cook for us all. We used the formal dining room as it had a large table and could easily accommodate all of us.

On the other hand, we only had two bathrooms, so that was tough. Apartments were not built with several bathrooms in those days. People shared. There was also the maid who shared the small bathroom.

After a few days of knitting and sewing, we had the bright idea to go to the largest department store called Orozdiback to buy some clothes. We had more than ten luxurious department stores in Cairo and Alexandria. They were geared toward the large European population and the wealthy. They carried French and Italian merchandise. Most all other department stores had been ravaged by the fires and were not yet refurbished, but this one had been spared because it was owned by Omar Effendi, an Egyptian Muslim, although originally, the name of the store was that of two Austrian Jews who had built it around the 1890s. People still used the name Orozdiback when referring to that store.

We bought some clothes for auntie and Anoush, and we also stole some. Yes, we stole some. Tante Nevart and Anoush were so angry about their predicament of having lost everything except the clothes on their backs that they did not think it was wrong to steal.

We did this a couple of times until Anoush got caught. We became quite good at it. This was how we operated. Three of us—Anoush, my sister, and myself—would go in front of the scarves counter and ask to be shown a scarf. Whereupon the salesgirl would unfold a scarf on the counter to show us the pattern. One of us would sneak a hand underneath and take a scarf out of a pile and quickly put it in a tote bag. We would never buy the scarf. Scarves were big in Cairo in those days.

For clothes, the modus operandi was different. We would choose some clothes—there was no control on the number of items going into a dressing room—and six of us (my sister, Anoush, my two aunties, Ma, and myself) would go in the dressing room, which was huge, and try them on. Tante Nevart and Ma would start trying on some dresses and then wear one on top of the other and come out and buy only one or two items. One day Tante Arous noticed what was happening in the dressing room. She had been unaware before. She was a very honest and straitlaced person. The two sisters had different characters, Tante Nevart being shrewd and the other naive. When Tante Nevart started wearing one dress on top of the other, Tante Arous glared at her.

"What are you doing?" she asked.

"Never you mind. I am pinching some clothes," was the reply.

"You mean you're stealing them?"

"Well, yes, if you had all your clothes looted by savages, I think you would do the same," she said, and without blinking an eyelid, she continued doing so.

Anoush and I then got brazen and did the same thing. My sister abstained. She did not like doing illegal things. We continued on our stealing rampage at this store for a couple of weeks.

During one of our stealing sprees, Anoush got caught. I was looking for her in the store and could not find her. Then I passed in front of an office—the door was open—and I saw her sitting down, being interrogated by two women. She made a discreet gesture to me to walk on and not come in. Otherwise, had I gone in the office, I would also have been apprehended and questioned. I was watching from the corner of the corridor. She was crying and gave a sob story of how her house was burned down during the riots and that she did not have any clothes and to please let her go because her mom would punish her and so on. She was a good actress. Luckily, they took pity on her and let her go. She was only a teenager, but she was wily.

From then on, we stopped stealing. By then, the family had enough clothes. Our frenetic knitting and sewing compensated for some of the lost apparel.

The men in the family did not have any inkling of what the women were up to. Tante Arous kept her mouth shut after being sworn to secrecy by her sister. The doctor would have raised hell.

We, the teenagers, were thrilled to have so many people in our apartment. Card games and backgammon every night. Anoush forgot the hardship of losing all her possessions. We still went to school, went to the club for social events, and went to the movies and, most importantly, socialized with boys.

A few days after the riots, all English street signs and street names were covered up, and Arabic signs went up. Before 1952, all street signs were written in English. Obviously, the Egyptian government did not want to have anything to do with the British. They were claiming their independence. Foreign goods were boycotted now and again. This was somewhat unsettling news. The situation in Egypt was unstable, and the foreign population was apprehensive.

A month later, one of our neighbors, downstairs—a childless couple who had a two-bedroom apartment—moved in with a relative and rented out their apartment to Anoush's family. Tante Nevart bought a piano and had Anoush practice. Anoush hated it, but Auntie thought it would make her more marriageable now that they had lost all their belongings and, presumably, had no money. A cultured bride was the next best thing to a moneyed bride.

Anoush used to practice the piano every day. All I could hear was "Für Elise," the same tune over and over. I could hear it from our south-side balcony. It bored me to death, but hearing it now reminds me of the good old days.

As for me, my free time at home was spent reading or sketching. Pa encouraged me in the latter. I sketched all the time and also did caricatures of people. My textbooks were covered with my doodling, and Judy got irritated when she inherited them.

# CHAPTER XVI

## The New Boyfriend

Around September 1952, I half-heartedly accepted Dick in my life again but was rather aloof toward him. At about the same time, Kourken, the son of a wealthy family from Heliopolis, came into my life. He was one year older than me and looked like Peter Lawford, one of my favorite actors. We had gone to the same elementary school, he being one class higher. I heard he was attending Victoria College in Alexandria, a posh boarding school for boys, where the sons of anybody, who was somebody, went there. Omar Sherif was a schoolmate as were some princes, the sons of Pashas and of wealthy Europeans.

Kourken's father owned two photography shops—one in Heliopolis and the other in Cairo. At that time, everyone loved to have their picture taken. However, the father's upbringing was not a rich one. He was an orphan of the Armenian Genocide and was eleven years old when he went on the death march with his family toward Iran. Everyone else perished during the march, but Kourken's father managed to survive and was taken to an Armenian orphanage in Iran, where he learned photography. He eventually came to Egypt, opened his first store, and amassed a small fortune.

Today I wish I knew more of his story but, in those times, I was not interested in history. I was only concerned about my own life. It was me, me, me . . . and then Kourken and me. I did not even know my own grandfather's story of the genocide or any general facts because the subject wasn't covered in the Armenian elementary school. We studied Armenian ancient history, how the Armenians were persecuted by the Persians and how brave Vartan Mamigonian—an Armenian hero whose name has been given to countless Armenian boys, one of them being my younger son—led the Armenian army to victory by sacrificing himself to keep our Christian faith. I later learned that the Armenians were the first nation that embraced Christianity.

My relationship with K—I'll call him K from now on as I did in my diary—started one day when the gang met at the club and decided to go to a basketball game at the sports club in Cairo. One of our friends had borrowed a small jeep, and the rear seating was two benches opposite each other. Dick was already seated at the far end of one bench, and as I was climbing in, he called me, patting the seat next to him. Despite him making overtures toward me to get things back to being civil between us, I was still mad at him. I was rather proud and did not want to give in. I therefore ignored Dick and sat at the opposite end of the other bench. K then climbed in and took the empty seat next to me. We hardly spoke because I was very shy. Dick was looking daggers at me for ignoring him. I smiled inwardly as I stared at the passing scenery.

After the game, there was dancing at the sporting club, and K asked me to dance. He was the best dancer I had ever come across, and after all these years and many partners, he has never been bettered. As he held me tight, causing butterflies in my stomach, he complimented me on my hair, told me I was cute, and said I was a very good dancer. From then on, we became firm friends, and he always asked me to dance at parties and at the club. Dick got jealous and wanted to monopolize me at these functions, but I ignored him and preferred K.

My infatuation with Dick was over.

K had come into my life, and from then on, I concentrated on him.

I remember one day at a party, when Dick asked me to dance the *paso doble*—a dance I adore—I refused and then got up to dance with K. I was being spiteful to Dick, and I felt good about it. I had not forgotten or forgiven him for dancing with the Syrian girl at our club.

He eventually got the message when he saw his attempts at getting me back were futile.

K was allowed to drive both family cars, but his elder brother had first choice. They had a Cadillac and a Fiat "Topolino" convertible, which is more commonly known today as the small Fiat 500. K having a car at his disposal was a plus for our group, and all the guys wanted to be his friend. No one else had the regular use of a car. We would pile in, eight of us sometimes in the Cadillac, or six in the Fiat when the top was down, some of us sitting precariously on the back edge. We never got in trouble with the police in Cairo for overcrowding the car.

I remember one time in Geneva, we were seated three people in a two-seater, and the police stopped us in the middle of a busy square and asked one of us get out of the car. Very sticky with rules, the Swiss are. This was in the middle of the 1960s.

I was truly smitten by K, and I wanted him to be smitten by me. I still had a body image problem. I knew that young guys liked curvaceous girls, and I weighed only about one hundred pounds.

When I started interacting with guys, I kept a diary. I found out, by Ma's offhand remarks, that she was reading it. I could have hidden it somewhere in our large apartment, but instead, I invented a code. I would write a number of words, mostly gibberish, to make up a sentence. Then I would take the third letter of each word and make up the actual word. After a while, I realized this was taking too much time and effort, and I invented a second code, undecipherable according to me—symbols representing the letters of the alphabet. I became an expert at reading the second code because I read my diaries sporadically through the years. It is like reading a novel, even better, because there is so much intrigue I had completely forgotten. I sometimes could not even remember who I was talking about. Writing dialogue in the diaries made them more interesting and alive. I am still surprised at some of the conversations we had as teenagers. Those diaries have become extremely useful in reconstructing my memoir.

I was deliriously happy to have K in my life, and Ma noticed a change in me.

"People are gossiping that you have a boyfriend, this Kourken fellow," she said one morning while we were having breakfast.

"No, Ma, he is not a boyfriend. He is just a friend in our group," I lied, not looking at her.

When K started coming to the house to pick me up to go to parties or to the movies—always in a group—Ma got to like him.

"He seems to be a decent chap," she said one evening as I headed to the front door, "well mannered, but you are not to go out alone with him. You either take your sister along or you go out in a group. You are not even seventeen. Remember that. We are in Egypt, not in America."

Judy hated coming along with us. She wanted her own boyfriend, but she did not have any—not yet—she was two years younger than me.

Some of my schoolmates were getting engaged at seventeen, and I was envious. I wanted to become a fiancée too, and I had set my eyes on K. In my eyes, he was the only candidate because he was so different from the other guys. He was not a mama's boy and certainly not "Armenian-minded." Armenian-minded meaning being under the influence of the Armenian society as a whole and following his parents' old-fashioned beliefs.

We met often at the social club for events.

When nightclubs reopened after the riots, the atmosphere was almost the same as when King Farouk was in power. We started going to the Mena House Hotel nightclub, where an Italian band was playing, and at the Semiramis Hotel Rooftop with Bob Azzam as the band leader. We adored these two bands. On the whole, we did not give a damn about things like politics as long as they did not affect our lives directly.

Yup, we could go to nightclubs as teenagers. We only ordered one drink. I did not even drink as I hated alcoholic beverages. I would have one coke which lasted me through the whole evening and the guys had one glass of whiskey and soda. And, we would dance all night until the nightclub closed around 4 a.m. Ma did not seem to mind our coming home that late in the evening or rather that early in the morning as long as we were in a group. I would then sleep till 12 noon.

On the political front, the news was that General Naguib was head of the revolutionary council, and he seemed to be a decent guy. My parents and their friends alike thought well of him as far as the interests of the ethnic communities were concerned. Nobody knew at the time that the real boss hidden behind the scene was Gamal Abdel Nasser, the man who would come to global fame for his political victory in the Suez Canal crisis.

One evening, before his abdication, we saw King Farouk and his new bride, Narriman, seated in a corner of the Mena House nightclub. There were no visible bodyguards. He was still handsome then, but Narriman could not be compared with Queen Farida, who was slim, elegant, and a classical beauty. Narriman was of middle-class stock, fleshy and vulgar, and ordinary-looking.

"It is a good thing you are slim," K remarked as we discussed the king's choice. "Otherwise he would snatch you away from me." The king was known to take any women he fancied, even if they were married. So, my thinness saved me.

On my seventeenth birthday, K gave me an 18 karat gold bracelet with "Peggy" engraved on one side and my birthdate on the other. When Ma saw the bracelet, she thought it was inappropriate and asked me to give it back. I refused to do so. It was precious to me. It meant that K was serious about me. It wasn't a ring, but it was a step in the right direction.

"Why is he giving you a gold bracelet? What does he want in return?" asked Ma.

"Nothing. Why should he want anything in return?"

"Don't act dumb. You know what I mean. Don't you ever give him favors." I guess she meant sexual favors, but that was not even in my mind.

"In any case, this Armenian jeweler will tell the whole community, and people will gossip. You wait and see," Ma added. Most jewelers in those days were Armenian.

"Don't be ridiculous, Ma. It's only a birthday gift."

"An expensive birthday gift from an eighteen-year-old!" she retorted.

I still wear this bracelet and have never taken it off. It is a gift from the first man who really loved me. I was also in love with him—my first real love.

K and I now became an item in the Armenian circle, and people did gossip. He only danced with me at club events, and that was the only thing they saw, but it was enough to set tongues wagging. Usually everybody danced with everybody. But he did not want to dance with other girls. He was enamored by me big time and wanted to spend all his spare time with me. I was also obsessed by him—the first guy I was in love with. I realized that Dick did not really count. I had not really been in love with him. It had been an infatuation.

Did I prefer K because he was a good dancer? Dancing played a very important part in my life—it was my first obsession. I was really into K but did not show him the extent of my puppy love. I was often aloof, which made him chase me even more. We still had school to attend, and yet we saw each other almost every day at the club, movies, parties, and nightclubs. I preferred nightclubs because I could unleash myself dancing there as it was seldom that we met any Armenians in nightclubs. We would dance cheek to cheek, and he would sometimes kiss me on the cheek. That was still considered hot dancing in those days. However, we were more cautious at the club.

After a while, Ma allowed him to come to the house to visit me and play games—usually cards or backgammon—but then complained he stayed too long and was preventing me from studying and going to bed early. Even if we had exams the next day, we still saw each other every day. Nothing deterred us from spending time together. He would bring me home and then stay a long time at the door, saying goodbye. Pa once complained to Ma that K and I spent too much time at the door. I guess he suspected that we were doing more than just talking, and in fact, we were. Our embraces got hotter as time went by.

When K phoned me, we had one-hour-long conversations. I really don't remember what we talked about, silly teenage talk, I guess. And a lot of arguing. Perhaps he was seeking to be the dominant male. K often got mad at something I said or did, and he wanted me to apologize. I did not think I had done anything wrong, and I often refused to do so, but then I would give in just to keep the peace. I hated arguments.

Our friends started teasing us, saying I was K's girl, and no other guy dared approach me. I denied it, of course, but K did not. He wanted everyone in our group to know I was his, and he became extremely possessive and jealous.

"What were you talking about with Samy?" He would ask me when he saw me talking to him—one of our friends.

"Why did you accept to dance with Bello?" He was a guy I had met in Alexandria during the summer.

Our constant bickering went on in person or on the phone. It got to be quite annoying, and I certainly did not like that possessive trait in his character. But then Anoush would tell me, "It is because he loves you, silly."

At the time K was doing his freshman year at the American University in Cairo, he told me his parents had decided to send him to the United States to study architecture. So, my so-called boyfriend would vanish into thin air. I didn't cherish that news at all. I made sure I did not appear affectionate toward him because what was the point of falling for a guy who had plans to go away? Inwardly, I wished my parents could have afforded to send me to college in the

United States as well. I was quite envious of K's future and had quite a few sleepless nights.

One unfortunate day, K was taken to the hospital and was diagnosed with paratyphoid. Ma forbade that I go and visit him, telling me that it was very contagious. We wrote letters that were transmitted by a good friend of his. No such thing as writing to him at the hospital, and in no way would we use his mother as the courier. His hospitalization lasted a month, and I missed him terribly. When he came out of the hospital, he had lost a lot of weight, and his mom did her best to fatten him up.

The first time we saw each after his discharge, he told me that he had decided not to go to the States after all since I had become the romantic fixture in his life. I felt more secure with our relationship then. His sacrifice proved the extent of his love toward me. I felt a little guilty that I had robbed him of this so sought-after opportunity, but I was overjoyed at his decision.

Bahi, the Egyptian lawyer,
me and a friend at the beach

Arty in L.A.

Painting auto-portrait
in Montreal 1959

First painting done in Montreal

Nubarian Elementary School, 5th grade

Dining table on USS Independence in 1962     First Solo exhibition in Montreal

Judy and me                              Engagement party

Judy, Emile, me and K                    K and me, dancing boogie

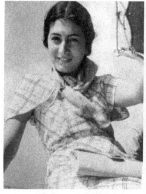

Ma on sailboat  Mickey sitting at the bar

Dick and me  Modeling in Montreal

My parents' wedding photo

Pa posing
for photographer

Paternal
grandparents

A play I am acting in

The bachelors at the Social Club

Family with cats in Heliopolis

Maternal grandparents

Timmy, hissing at Alice

Uncle Jimmy, Judy and me

Wedding photo

American G.I.s at home

# CHAPTER XVII

## Life with Kourken

At this time, I started to take art classes at the Leonardo Da Vinci Art Academy in Cairo. It was an Italian-run school. I did not particularly like the classes. They were not avant-garde. The professor was Italian and hell-bent on teaching us how to draw from real life. We had an Egyptian nude model, a fleshy, lumpy female. I always drew from my imagination and did not adhere to the rules. I changed the painting to my liking. He would then come and draw a cross across my paintings. I hated the professor. I still attended the class, however, because this gave me an opportunity to see K on my return. Either he would pick me up by car or we would take the metro together.

At one point, although our outings alone were clandestine, his parents got wind of our relationship. They were aghast, and they forbade him to see me. His father told him he would throw him out of the house and would not give him the Heliopolis photography shop to manage. He would thus be out of a job with no prospects in Cairo if he intended to stay put. The elder brother was managing the Cairo photo shop. We continued seeing each other in secret, and things got to be extremely complicated.

One time, I was in the metro, and the plan was that he would get up at the next station after getting a signal from me at the stop.

There were always a lot of Armenians around—in the streets, in the theaters, in the metro. This idea being to show people who may be watching—and there were a lot of those—that we met each other by accident. I was seated at the window, and he came down the aisle and took a vacant seat opposite me. He was jabbering away as usual, oblivious of people around him. After a couple of stations, I had the shock of my life. I saw his father coming down the aisle and take the vacant seat next to K. The space not being wide enough, he had to squeeze himself in between K and the other fellow. K did not notice his father and kept talking to me. I froze. I wanted to give him a signal to stop, but I could not. His father had his eyes on me the whole time. I looked out the window, not paying attention to what K was telling me.

"Why are you not listening to me?" he asked.

I turned and looked at him and said nothing and kept looking out of the window. My heart was beating frantically. When we arrived at the first station in Cairo, the father got up and bade us farewell in Armenian. K's jaw dropped.

"For God's sake, how come you didn't realize your father was seated next to you?"

"Because I only have eyes for you," he said and sang the first verse of the song. That made me feel much desired, but our relationship had been unmasked by his father and confirmed. We were apprehensive as to what the father would do and decided to be much more careful from then on.

We also had to be careful of the new Egyptian morality code. The military government had enacted strict laws concerning public behavior between the sexes.

We could no longer hold hands in the movies or have K's arm around me. We could not be seated close in public places. This rule pertained also to married couples. There were plainclothes policemen and power-hungry, uneducated soldiers, with rifles slung over their shoulders, trying to enforce the new law. In the movies, out of nowhere, a guy would pop up and go up and down the aisle, brandishing his flashlight on our bodies. Any inappropriate sitting position would mean a march to the *Karakol* (police station in Turkish and Arabic). I remember one time, K had his arm around my chair, not even touching my shoulder, when one of the ushers came up to him, brandished his flashlight on his face, and told him to sit in an appropriate manner.

No discussion there; K took his arm away.

Another time, K and I were seated on a bench in the park in front of Baron Empain's palace. We were careful to be seated quite apart from each other. A uniformed guard with a rifle was going up and down the path. He was a mosquito-size man, but his rifle gave him power. He looked at us several times. He had nothing else to do. There was no one around. We were only talking. Then he came toward us.

"Follow me to the *Karakol*," he said.

"Why is that? We were only talking," said K, who spoke fluent Arabic.

"You can explain it to the *rayis*" (chief in Arabic), the diminutive idiot said.

His attitude was uncalled for, but of course, K could not reason with a rifle-brandishing idiot.

Off we marched to the police station. I felt weak in the knees and had visualizations of ending up in a stinky Egyptian jail, full of prostitutes, getting lice and bedbugs and God knows what else.

K saw the state I was in.

"Don't worry, I know how to fix this," he said in a hushed tone.

He could fix things? How could he?

We went to the police station, and the proud nincompoop ushered us into an office and informed the chief that "this couple was holding hands in a public park."

K asked to use the telephone very politely. Luckily, the chief obliged.

K then called a friend of his, who happened to be a lieutenant in the army and also one of his customers. This guy rushed to the police station and brandished his badge to the chief and asked K what had transpired.

"Release this couple immediately," he ordered the chief in a commanding, no-nonsense tone of voice, "and ask your power-hungry, stupid underling here to refrain from harassing innocent people."

Egypt had a military government, and people with high ranks in the army had extensive authority over other branches of the government and did not hesitate to exercise their power over people below their rank.

The chief apologized profusely, told the idiot off, criticized his unwarranted zeal, and out we marched from the *Karakol* with a sigh of relief.

There was one good thing about this morality law.

Harassment of girls and women in the streets was rampant. It was usually a harmless type of harassment, and a girl could walk alone in the streets of Cairo safely. Sometimes I would be harassed by a young passerby while walking in front of a café, where locals with *galabeyas* were seated with their *shishas*. They would all get up in unison and shoo him off, calling him a *mugrim* (criminal in Arabic).

Yes, we were safe in Cairo. There was no grabbing of flesh like in Italy. It was all verbal but not really dangerous. The *fellah* kids did not dare touch a girl.

The morality code in Egypt was strictly enforced. No man was allowed to touch a woman in public, even married ones. We were very careful how we greeted each other in public or how we walked. No hand in hand or arm in arm.

One day, while we were at the movies, a guard with a flashlight walked by and directed the flash toward K's lap. There was nothing going on in K's lap. He did not have his "weapon" out or anything. I would never have tolerated it, in any case. Another day, while coming home by cab, K had put his arm around my shoulder. The cab driver, the idiot, asked him to take his arm away. The same thing happened one day while we were riding a horse cart in town. In the center of Cairo, we often took horse carts for short distances. The horse cart driver turned around, why, I don't know, and told him to sit properly. The funny thing is that they never addressed the female; their disapproval was always addressed to the male.

From that moment on, everything started getting on my nerves in Cairo. No freedom either at home or outside. I was hell-bent on leaving the country. My desire to go to the States was reinforced. How I wished my parents had enough money to send me there.

The government had also decreed that any girl could complain at a police station if she was being harassed. So, one day when I was walking along in the street, a bunch of guys in a car started teasing me, opening the door of the car, and inviting me in. They were harmless. They would never dare drag you in by force. Egyptians are known to be nonviolent by nature, and it was safe for girls to walk alone in the streets, even in early evening. Not so now, I gather from the news I get from Egypt.

However, this time, encouraged by the new morality law, I took the license plate number of the car, and the next day, I went to the police station to file a complaint. A few days later, two policemen came to our apartment, bringing over the driver of the car, and asked me if this was the guy. I said, "Yes, he is." The poor fellow looked frightened. He happened to be the owner of a store that sold fabrics. When the police were busy talking among themselves, he took me aside and asked me to please not file a complaint and that he would offer me any fabric I wanted from his store. I did not agree with the offer of the gift, but I did pity the guy. He seemed genuinely remorseful. He was fined and let go. He did not go to jail.

Another time, I went to buy a bathing suit, tagging K's younger sister along. I tried a couple but did not find any that fitted me properly. It was a small store staffed by a middle-aged Syrian store owner. When I brought back the bathing suits to the counter, he picked one and put it to his nose, smelling it. I ignored him and went out of the store. When I related this incident to K, he got stark raving mad. He was of a choleric nature. The next day, he took along his lieutenant friend and went to the store. The friend frightened the guy out of his wits by threatening to put him in jail.

"A hundred apologies. I did not do that on purpose. Please forgive me, sir," he said. I was outside the store, watching what was going on.

They reprimanded him severely and eventually let him off.

It was very useful to have influential friends in Egypt, especially high-ranking officers in the army.

There was one particular thing we were very scared of though.

"Don't ever criticize the government in public," my parents warned us. "You never know who is listening, and you may be denounced and end up in jail."

We were indeed vigilant. We were also careful about talking over the phone.

"Be very careful about what you say on the telephone. No complaints about the government, not even to neighbors. Our phones might be tapped," we were warned by our parents over and over.

We became paranoid, so paranoid that I remember one instance, when I was in the United States, long after all this, a friend from Cairo, who had just arrived to New York, called us on the phone.

"How are things in Cairo?" I asked.

"Shh, don't ask such questions over the phone," he said.

"We are not in Egypt anymore, you know," was my reply.

No matter, he did not divulge any information until he saw us personally. He had gotten out of Egypt via Lebanon because the American Embassy was not giving any visas to Egyptian-born people. Some people with money went to Lebanon and even worked there. From Lebanon, a benevolent Armenian organization called ANCHA, helped obtaining visas for them to the States. That was what most Armenians did.

Amid all this partying and nightclubbing, I was still going to school, and my grades were excellent.

I don't know how I managed to study and have a nightlife at the same time. Although I slept late at nights, I did get up early in the morning to attend school. Ma was always telling me off that by not sleeping enough, my health would eventually suffer. But I did sleep enough. After coming home from school at two o'clock, I would have a late lunch and would take a one to two-hour nap. I was then as fresh as a spring flower for the evening activities. That was what I lived for, getting prettied up and going to parties and nightclubs. You may think I was frivolous. Yes, I was, and I loved it.

Another thing I did a lot was sewing, knitting, and drawing. I had to have new clothes for all the events I attended. I could not show myself with the same dress at the same place. People were very conscious of clothes in Cairo and in the whole of the Middle East, in general. And jewelry and shoes and handbags, they had to match. Egypt had good shoemaking and handbag factories. The leather was impeccable. We also had excellent cotton fabrics. Silk was generally imported from France or Italy. It was a show-off society, and we enjoyed being seen and talked about.

"Ma, did you see what so-and-so was wearing?" I absolutely had to sew something similar or better.

Every week we would go downtown to buy fabrics, shoes, or dressmaking stuff and also wool, to knit sweaters. When we visited each other, almost everyone took her knitting along. Even in the women's compartment in the metro, the Armenian women were knitting when going to and coming from work. (Eleanor Roosevelt did the same thing at meetings as I remember.)

At home, we would cut the patterns of dresses and sewed them on an old-style Pfaff sewing machine, with a peddle, inherited from my grandma. Ma had taught me how to knit and sew at a very early age. Actually, I was an avid learner, and I wanted to know how to do everything in order not to depend on anyone. I also scoured foreign magazines and looked at fashion, hairstyles, and hints about makeup and hair.

Our lifestyle was so different from life now in the twenty-first century. We socialized almost every day. Either we went to friends or they visited us and we played cards or other games. Our apartment was like Grand Central Station, people coming and going all the time. We were never alone, even for one evening. We went to the movies, to the club, to parties, or for rides to the Pyramids, the zoo, the lemon garden, the Barrage.

There were so many interesting places to hang out: The Italian ice cream parlor, Groppi's (a large fashionable space with a long counter and numerous tables and chairs), was a favorite rendezvous spot. It still exists, and the name is now written in Arabic. There were Ciro's, a dancing bar; A l'Americaine, another bar/restaurant with outside seating; Homemade Cakes, a coffee bar with a shaded garden; and of course, a newly opened pizza parlor, where even Egyptian movie actors hung out. It was a tiny shop with one table and four chairs outside on the pavement next to a cinema, and it was very popular. I met the heartthrob of Egyptian movies there one day, Rushdy Abaza, with Barbara Bianchi, his American wife (who was a classmate of mine at St. Clare's). This was the girl who said she preferred living in Egypt rather than in the United States because in Cairo, she was somebody. Well, she was indeed. She got married to the best-looking and most highly regarded actor, who also happened to be wealthy.

While watching an Egyptian film the other night on Netflix, I kept drowning in nostalgia. They had enacted life in Cairo in the late 1950s—my time. They showed Groppi's and people dancing at parties in trendy clothes. As I said before, dancing was a great part of our lives. We were part of the glitterati, and I am glad I had my youth in the 1950s and 1960s. But as always, people think the grass is greener. After arriving to the desired location (as I did from Egypt to Canada and then the United States), I discovered that, in fact, the grass is a dirty brown.

We had such a sumptuous, interesting lifestyle in Cairo, and we were not even aware of it.

# CHAPTER XVIII

## Back to School

It was decided that I would not go further in my studies in St. Clare's College to get the Oxford and Cambridge Board of certification. I would just get the school certificate, which is equivalent to the American high school degree, thus leaving school one year earlier. The biggest reason was that we had no money for the tuition. Although it was a miserly amount, to us every pound (Egyptian pound) mattered. I wanted to get in the work force as soon as possible to earn my own living and be independent. First, I had to study shorthand and typing as secretarial jobs were the highest paid in Egypt. Pursuing my art classes was also very important to me, although they were not satisfactory. I could not do all that and also do my homework and go to parties if I was going to continue my schooling.

"You have to start work as soon as possible," Ma told me apologetically. "You see how your father's job is—so precarious. We can hardly make ends meet."

Therefore, after taking my diploma and when the school year started, I did not attend school. Mother Superior called for me. It was already November.

I spoke to her about my predicament of not having the funds necessary to attend school, and I had a great surprise. She told me that she would accept me in school for free, if money was the problem (but not to tell anyone). She lectured me on the advantages of education and told me it would be a pity for a smart girl like me not to go any further. She made me feel guilty. She said that she would instruct the sister of the highest grade to let me sit at the back of the classroom, where I could do my homework as well as listen to class. In this way, I would be free in the evenings to pursue my art school and my shorthand and typing course. Mother Superior had great faith in me and knew that I could do two things simultaneously. I never expected this coming.

"You can do two things at the same time. I know you can do it," she assured me. She boosted my confidence.

Realization has dawned upon me that most women can, in fact, do two things or three things simultaneously. Men, not, however. I know this for a fact, having three men in my family now—a husband and two sons.

Mother Superior also advised me not to go into the arts as a profession.

"No career in that and certainly no money," she said. "Look what has happened to great painters. They have ended up as paupers."

Yes, I knew that, but art was my passion. It was in my blood. I could not do without it. I used to sketch and do watercolor drawings in my spare time. Pa, being an artist, had introduced me to art. The advice of Mother Superior was that I learn shorthand and typing and seek a secretarial career because that profession was in demand in any country in the world. This was the 1950s. There were big ads in the *Egyptian Gazette* (an English language newspaper) about secretarial jobs in the oil companies, foreign banks, and multinational corporations.

"You can find a job anywhere in the world," she told me, "and you can be an artist on the side." And she was absolutely right. When I landed in Montreal in 1956 as an "illegal alien" (this word makes me laugh. It sounds like being from outer space), I found a job on the third day. And my life in the "greener" grass started.

Actually, I did like the idea of going back to school, and I went with enthusiasm. I was able to catch up the two months I had missed. The sister made an announcement to the whole class.

"Peggy has joined us, and we will restart the trigonometry lessons from scratch just for her and also because none of you have grasped it yet. She may even be able to coach you, if you ask her nicely. She is smarter than all of you."

The sisters had no hesitation of criticizing the students harshly or even insulting them, sometimes telling them that they had the brains of a bird. The meek students cowered with fear. No one dared complain to their parents. Parents were not involved in the school life of their children like they are now in the United States.

Later on, after I had left Egypt, I heard from the new generation of students at St. Clare's College that my test papers had been kept in the archives and shown as examples. I wished so much that I could go back and look at them myself, but the opportunity did not arise. The school was eventually closed, and it became an Egyptian Catholic school.

St. Clare's College was obviously a girls' school, and we did not have much contact with boys. Boys from the English school, a couple of blocks away, would come and hang around our iron fence and gawk at us, trying to get our attention. We snickered and cast them furtive and flirtatious glances. The sisters did not like that one bit.

"Girls, girls, behave. Get away from the fence. Your behavior is not ladylike," they would say. We did not care about being ladylike. We just liked the attention we were getting from the boys.

Funnily enough, much later, fifty years later, when I was in a condo in Fort Lauderdale, I met a guy, another condo owner, who told me, when he heard I was from St. Clare's, that he was one of the boys who came to the railing. We reminisced. What a small world. In fact, my upstairs neighbor now in our condo was in my class at St. Clare's. She recognized me, but I did not recognize her. Poor thing she had aged badly because of circumstances in her life.

# CHAPTER XIX

## Parties and Fun

It was always the same story. Getting permission from Ma to go to parties continued to be an uphill battle. One instance that I will never forget was when Maryse, a blond blue-eyed girl from our group, who was the leader of the pack and who had become Dick's girlfriend after I was out of the picture, invited us to a party. Her mom was a divorced woman. Divorced women were few in the Armenian circle, and they were not well thought of. We only knew of two. They were seamstresses and were ostracized by the Armenian community, mostly by the women, who thought they were out to grab their husbands.

When Anoush and I asked permission from our mothers to go to the party, they refused. Tante Nevart came out with an asinine statement.

"Maryse's mother is using you girls to entice guys to her house. You are going to be considered *orosbi* (meaning whore in Turkish) like her. The same goes for Anna's mother. You should not associate with these girls because you will be considered as being in the same class as them, daughters of *sharameet* (meaning whores in Arabic). Tante Nevart was always very vociferous in her outbursts. These two words were often used in our language because they were more emphatic. I don't know the Armenian word for whore.

Anoush and I were stupefied at this statement. I looked at Ma. She did not seem to agree with Tante Nevart. I waited for Ma to say something—that these women were not whores, that it was okay to go to the party at Maryse's.

"Nevart, don't exaggerate" was all she said.

We cajoled them, but permission was not granted. When the day of the party came, we lied and said we were going to the movies but instead went to the party.

From then on, lying became a habit with us.

"Ma, I am going to so-and-so's house to study." But in fact, I went out with K to the movies.

"Ma, I am going to my drawing lesson." But in fact, I went out with K to Groppi's and so forth.

Lying became second nature, but we were careful that Armenians not see us. They were everywhere—in the streets, in the movies, and at all the places mentioned above.

I remember one day Tante Nevart caught Anoush in a lie, and she slapped her and pulled her hair. They were living on the floor below us at the time, and I could hear her crying. Then Tante Nevart informed my mother about the lie, who did not pull my hair, but she reprimanded me and forbade me to go out for three days. Well, three days was nothing. Iris was punished by having to exercise her piano lessons day and night.

We resumed lying but were extra careful to have solid alibis with friends.

K was my constant companion. We saw each other almost every day. I considered this too much, but he was adamant to see me every day; otherwise, he would get angry. Actually, he was angry all the time. We would talk for hours on the phone, arguing who had done something wrong. It was so childish when I come to think of it. I got fed up of this constant bickering, but I still loved him. The problem was, young guys never stayed home in the evenings. Nothing for them to do there except see their parents' faces. Either they were with their friends around town or, in K's case, as he had a girlfriend, he wanted to be with me.

On my birthday, he gave me a cute ring—an 18 karat gold ring with two turquoise stones dangling from the side. I still wear it; it is such an unusual ring.

"Another gift in gold?" Ma remarked.

"Yeah, isn't it nice?"

"Yes, it is, but where is this thing going? Is he planning on marrying you? He is so young. You can't be serious considering him as a husband. You need a mature man with a solid job. Just because he dances well doesn't mean he is the right choice for you."

During the summer of 1953, K kissed me the French way, putting his tongue in my mouth. I didn't like it one bit. I felt like vomiting, and I pulled away. I hated tasting his saliva. I spit it out in a handkerchief when he was not looking. He also asked me to trust him implicitly because he wanted to do heavy petting. I always felt his "thing" while dancing. He was always excited. Whenever I tried to stop his wandering hands, he assured me not to worry, that we would get married by hook or by crook. But I was not that convinced because of his parents' disapproval, and I rejected his advances to go further. His parents were a major obstacle, and I did not know how far they were prepared to go to prevent our union.

K wanted to ask the spirits whether we would eventually get married. He did and was satisfied with the information he got. I don't remember how he got this "ironclad" information. I thought he was being childish.

I found out that K had a pen friend from the States. I was envious and wanted one also. I found a Swiss one. I don't know where I found him. His name was Fernand. We exchanged photos. Funny thing, after thirty years, when I was living in Geneva, I found out he was an art dealer in Zurich. I contacted him and told him I was an artist. As he was dealing with million-dollar paintings, he was of no use to me.

My life with K had so many obstacles, and I was extremely annoyed that we could not plan our future together. I could see three possibilities:

1. His parents would eventually accept our union (very unlikely).

2. He would get a job in the Sudan (not likely I would join him).

3. His pop would leave this world (sinful wishing on my part; God would punish me for such thoughts).

We found ourselves in a hopeless situation.

K wanted to be with me every minute of the day. I was in love with him, but I felt he was suffocating me. I had no freedom whatsoever. Whenever he came by to the house, I was busy sewing or sketching, and he would complain that I was not paying him enough attention. He craved my attention. I was flattered, of course, but sometimes it was just too much. I just wanted to flap my wings and do my own things.

One thing Pa objected to was our lengthy goodbye sessions at the door of our apartment. When K brought me home from a function, he would linger on. We would smooch and smooch, and he wanted me to do other things as well, which I refused vehemently. He would then get angry when I told him that it was time to leave, that it was already past midnight, and that I had to go to bed early. I had school the next day, and I wanted to get enough sleep, my beauty sleep. But he refused to budge. His persistence annoyed me. If there was going to be so much petting now, why on earth get married? And marriage plans were so far beyond my horizon, like in another century. He was sex-starved and could not let go of me, not that we did any sex at the door or elsewhere for that matter.

I had strong beliefs that a "good girl" had to protect her virginity until the wedding night.

Ma would pass by the door sometimes, and we would stop smooching, pretending we were only talking. Pa would also pass by and ignore us. Pa would never admonish me directly but would tell

Ma to cut our goodbyes short at the door. I guess he, being a man, suspected that some real hanky-panky was going on.

"These kids are exaggerating. Tell them to cut it out," he told her one day.

Ma relayed Pa's remark, and I, in turn, told K. K somehow improved his behavior but not to the extent that I wished. One day K got mad that Ma was harassing me about seeing him too often. He told her off. Ma then got so upset that she forbade him to come to visit me at the house. This lasted a few weeks. I was somehow relieved that I now had some time to myself, doing my sewing or drawing without any interruptions from a possessive boyfriend.

As mentioned before, K was of a choleric nature and always looked for fights. He was not a big fellow, but he was wiry and knew how to fight. I think he loved it. The slightest thing would enrage him. I don't really know if his attitude stemmed from sexual frustration. I hoped that was all it was because I could not envisage being married to a man who would criticize me every day and pick an argument.

I still remember an incident that scared me. The metro between Heliopolis and Cairo was built by the French around the 1980s, and it was above ground. It was the fastest mode of transport between these two cities. We were coming home from a movie one day—K, one of his friends, Emile, my sister, and myself. A couple of guys sitting a few seats away started snickering and were casting flirtatious glances toward us girls. K noticed this, and it bugged him that other men were sort of making fun of him. He asked Emile if he was ready for a fight. Emile was Judy's date, and he was a reserved kind of guy but did not dare act cowardly and tell K that fighting was not in his nature. They both got up, got hold of the two Egyptian guys, and started pounding on them on the floor of the metro. When the metro stopped at another station, a friend of ours, waiting at the stop, saw what was going on and jumped aboard to help. K gave him a punch, mistaking him for another opponent.

Yes, life was indeed quite eventful in Cairo. It was mostly full of fun except for the biggest problem—how and when were we going to get married.

I was scared that no one would marry me after being with a guy for four years, which was common knowledge. If something went wrong, God forbid, and K and I parted, it would be very difficult for me to find someone I liked to marry me. This was my greatest preoccupation. And who would marry me anyway, after being branded as K's girlfriend? I would be considered tainted.

Actually, that was a wrong statement. This same friend who got punched in the metro witnessed a fight between us at the club one day, and K had left in a huff. This guy, whose name was Kevork, volunteered to accompany me home and, when we arrived at my door, he said, "If you ever decide to leave K, I am here." Wow, so there was at least one guy who would marry me. But he was short and ordinary-looking and, most of all, did not dance well. Ma thought my criteria were screwy, but those were the things that were important to me in my youth. Poor guy, I did not want to hurt his feelings and came out with "Thanks. I'll be okay." I met him thirty years later in Los Angeles. He had become a wealthy banker, but he was still short and ordinary-looking.

Ma was concerned at what people would say when they saw me with K so often. She was worried about my reputation. She forgave K for being rude to her as he apologized a few days later, but she still thought he was too young for me.

"So what, Ma? Who cares what people think? This is my life. Am I dependent on them for my livelihood? Do I owe them anything? No, nothing, so please leave me alone."

I did not tell her about the fight in the metro. She would have gone ballistic.

Against her desire, Judy had to be with us whenever we went out to the movies or nightclubs. She hated being a chaperone until the time when K found an acceptable guy from our group to go with us, and we formed a foursome. His name was Emile.

Ma then relaxed her objections, and she became comfortable with the idea of my being with K since Judy and Emile were also in the picture. After a while, Emile's parents got wind of the situation and forbade their son to see Judy. They did not want him to be trapped by a penniless young girl and create a duplication of yet another young couple going their way without parents' approval. Emile was a gentle soul and could not contradict his parents. He defied them once or twice, on K's insistence, but a "couple" was never formed between Judy and him, although they were romantically involved. It was Judy's first romantic interlude. Judy later went out with other guys and, years later, when Judy had joined me in the United States, Emile got married and immigrated to Canada. They never saw each other again. It was a short-lived romance.

We, the young crowd, were still quite oblivious of the political situation in Cairo. Riots or no riots, we still went out in the evenings. We did not pay much attention to politics in those days. All I knew was that Egypt did not become completely independent until after the overthrow of King Farouk in 1952. We had it good while the king was in power. He was considered a puppet king though, which was okay with the ethnic minorities.

Cairo was a cosmopolitan metropolis with ethnic diversity. It was like Europe on the Nile. When the king was overthrown and General Naguib came in power, followed by Gamal Abdel Nasser, things started to decline for the Europeans, the wealthy Muslims, and the Jews. Landowners were targeted. There was a great deal of uncertainty that reigned, and people started to make plans to leave the country. But go where? Exit visas were not granted that easily, and no country was accepting Egyptian-born immigrants. Lebanon was an exception and a favorite destination. But one needed money to live there. And we certainly did not have any.

# CHAPTER XX

────────

## Alexandria

I graduated from St. Clare's College with honors in June 1953. Finally, school days were over, and real life was around the corner. How stupid of me to think "real life" would be better. I think school years are the most careless years in a person's life. I did not know it then and wanted to grow up fast and be independent. I did not think of all the responsibilities of an independent life, away from my parents' support.

During the summer of 1953, we went to Alexandria again for vacation. We rented an apartment that turned out not too clean. The first day, Ma took all the bedding out on the terrace and gave it a good cleaning. Then she washed down the headboards to get rid of ticks. Mickey, our Siamese cat, was the cockroach warden again. He was serious at his task. He killed them but never ate them. He was a sophisticated cat.

An Armenian lady who lived across the street helped us move in. She took one look at me and told Ma that she knew of a prospective wealthy husband for me. In fact, she knew of two guys who were looking for wives. I was seventeen and a half years old. When Ma told me that this woman had arranged for a young man to come and visit me—they call it *akhchig-des* (girl-looking in Armenian)—I objected and refused to come out of my room to meet him.

"My daughter is very headstrong and wants to choose her own husband and, in any case, she is too young to get married," Ma told the neighbor.

You bet your life I wanted to choose my own husband. I was planning on marrying K, and Ma was aware of my intentions. I disliked this Middle Eastern custom of arranged marriages. However, Ma told me that my behavior was rude and that I should at least come out and pretend to be sociable. I finally did and sat like a mummy and did not utter a word. The guy was casting discreet glances in my direction, but I ignored him. I did not like his looks anyway. I could not envisage myself being embraced or kissed by him, let alone going to bed. I was fixated on K, and I wanted to marry K—no one else.

We were making plans—not very concrete ones, though.

As I mentioned before, most of my classmates were already engaged, and some were even married, and I was envious. My future looked so nebulous. We had to wait till K was twenty-one years old to be able to make his own decision, and even then, if his father threw him out of the shop, where would he work?

The whole month of September went by going to the beach, meeting friends from Heliopolis, going dancing, going to the movies, playing cards or board games, and just hanging around. We also went on lengthy walks on the *corniche* (the promenade along the seafront) in the evenings. There was always a faint breeze from the sea, and I loved eating grilled corn sold at every corner of the corniche.

Alexandria had a special smell—you could smell the sea salt a mile away. Cairo had a desert smell, and Heliopolis smelled of jasmine because of all the jasmine plants in the villas along the streets where we walked.

Most of the people we knew were vacationing in Alexandria at the same time. K could not stay a whole month and had to return to work in his father's shop in Heliopolis. I felt very lonesome and wanted to return to be with him, but that was not feasible.

There was an Egyptian lawyer named Bahi who was part of our group. He was tall, good-looking, extremely polite, and respectful. He was a Muslim and a friend of K. When K went away, he would ask me to dance at the beach parties in the evenings. There was one almost every day. I found out that he actually lived across the street from us in Heliopolis. All the Armenian girls were envious of me because he only danced with me. He had a big car, and we would pile up in it to go dancing, usually to tea dances. This was very much in vogue in Alexandria at the time.

"Is Kourken your boyfriend?" he asked me one day out of the blue while we were dancing on the beach.

"Why are you asking me that?" I was taken aback.

"Because if he is, I will not pursue you."

So, Bahi was interested in me. If I did not have K, I would probably have accepted being pursued by Bahi. However, that thought soon evaporated from my mind because Ma would flip if she found out I had a Muslim boyfriend. She did not even totally approve of my having an Armenian one—because of his young age—never mind a Muslim.

I answered in the affirmative, but that did not prevent him from dancing with me.

The fact is I liked being pursued by other men. I was flattered, especially that Bahi preferred me to the other girls who were fleshier and more curvaceous than me. What curves? I had none. Men in the Middle East like girls who are amply endowed. I was an exception and hated my figure.

# CHAPTER XXI

## Same Everyday Life

In the autumn, I started taking a shorthand and typing course at a private school run by a Maltese teacher, a one-man school. The course was quite expensive. But it was worth it because he was an excellent instructor. After a couple of months, I started teaching my sister and my cousin as it would have been a waste of money for them to pay for their courses since I was able to fulfill this function. We rented a typewriter and started pounding away day and night, taking turns. I wanted to finish the course fast, but the other three students at the school—all classmates of mine—were slow. I could not afford to take a private lesson.

At this time, a young Armenian student at St. Clare's College needed tutoring in math and science, and the sister of her class referred her to me. I was elated to be finally earning some pocket money. It would pay my tuition at the art academy.

One day K imparted some disturbing news to me. His father had gotten wind of our relationship being a serious one and had threatened him.

"I will throw you out of the house and out of the shop if you don't stop seeing the Hinaekian girl," his father had told him.

K had a defiant nature, but he did not cherish being homeless and jobless. And what would I be doing with that kind of a guy? I did love him, but I did not want to end up poor.

K was devastated at his father's threats and started pondering the possibility of going to work in the Sudan.

"What do you think about it? There are good job opportunities, and lots of Armenians are working there."

"I hate that idea. What would I do in the Sudan, for God's sake?"

"Well, if we want to get married, that is the only solution. Or else, we can go to Saudi Arabia."

The sky fell upon me when I heard of these two possibilities. There goes my dream life. People would say that if I were really in love with the guy, I should not have minded the locations we were going to live in. But I had a wonderful life in Cairo, I loved my family, I had oodles of friends, I had the prospect of a good job, so why would I displace myself and go to some godforsaken country? It would kill me and my dreams, and it would certainly kill whatever love I felt toward K.

"I don't like either solution," I told him and started sobbing.

He tried to comfort me, but I was not to be consoled. My life was going to turn into hell if we did not find a viable solution soon. I even thought I would much rather be a nun and lead a serene life with no problems than not get married to K. Just gliding on the floor in my long robe and praying, away from the real world, appealed to me at one of my out-of-this-world moments. The thought of that solution lasted one day. There would absolutely be no men in my life if I were to become a nun.

That idea did not appeal to me at all. I got rid of it quite fast.

We were meeting really in secret at this time. Ma and Pa knew about it, though, and we kept away from places where Armenians would frequent. This was difficult to achieve because they were everywhere, just like ants, as I mentioned above. Everybody knew everybody in the Armenian community.

K continued to get angry for one reason or the other every day, either on the phone or when I saw him. My nonchalant behavior irritated him when I did not allow him to be close to me in public, when away from the Armenian crowd. He wanted me to be more affectionate, but I was shy and did not think it was appropriate. I blamed his short temper on his frustration of not having a sex life with me and that, once it happened, things would get better.

In the meantime, he was seeing street prostitutes. I was vehemently against this practice, but all his friends did it, it seemed. They would pile up in a car, two in front and the third in the back, doing the business. How revolting. I asked him to stop doing this, but he said he could not and that he needed release.

"And what about me?" I asked.

"You are joking," he said. "You know very well that there is a difference between men and women."

"Why should you do everything you want and I can't?"

"And what is it you want to do?"

*I would like to hug another man*, I wanted to say but kept my mouth shut.

The discussion went on and on for days and weeks. Stupid guy, he should never have told me. Was he bragging, or what? He would tell me what these prostitutes did—pretend they were having orgasms. He explained to me what an orgasm was. He and his friends would laugh at their phony moaning and groaning. He said these women were as wide as a sink.

One day Ma asked me what was the subject of our constant bickering.

"K goes to prostitutes with his friends, and I don't want him to," I blurted out.

"It's normal. All the young men in Egypt do this. Let him go as long as he takes precautions, and I don't think he is stupid enough not to do so."

Ma's logic surprised me, but little by little, I came to accept it since it seemed to be the norm. After all, he did not love the prostitutes. It was just in and out—that was what he told me—no kissing or petting.

Another bone of contention was my acting in plays put on at the club. I very much liked the characters I was offered to play. I loved acting. My life was overflowing now. K told me that his parents would not approve of it at all.

"They already don't think highly of you, and your acting will make matters worse," he said. What the hell was the matter with these people? Is acting a bad thing? Then why did they come and watch the plays?

"Who cares? They think we are not seeing each other anymore, so what difference does it make?"

He could not argue with me on that, but he still wanted me to give up acting. He did not like my being in the limelight.

I rebelled and refused to abide by his request. Another reason to quarrel.

After King Farouk's forced abdication, the new government in place did not affect our lives that much except for the morality code and the names of streets being changed from English to Arabic. In 1953, the monarchy was abolished. After his expulsion from Egypt, the king's infant son had been declared king, but it was just a ploy. General Naguib became head of the government, but he was, in fact, just another puppet, we later found out.

In the beginning of 1954, Gamal Abdel Nasser started to emerge from behind the scenes. He removed General Naguib from power and put him under house arrest, and he was declared prime minister. Anyway, it did not affect our lives in general. The government nationalized wealthy people's businesses, factories, and lands. We had nothing of the sort, so they could not take anything away from us. Some wealthy people started feeling shaky, and exodus plans were being carried out.

"Are you sure you want to marry this guy?" Ma once asked me. "You are always quarreling. Things will not improve after you get married, you know. Trust me."

"Ma," I replied, "I cannot envision marrying anyone else. I don't even like anyone else. I am sure he will change once we get married." I wanted to believe what I told her.

"Don't bet on it. Men do not change. You are ruining your chances of finding a husband. I heard from a very good source that the Pesnerians' older son has been hinting that he is interested in you."

"He can hint all he wants. I am just not interested. He is too prim and proper, not attractive, and he does not dance well at all. He is as stiff as a board, no rhythm whatever."

"Is that your criteria? Someone who is attractive and dances well?"

"Two of my criteria," was my reply. "And, another thing, he smokes. I don't think I would like kissing a guy who smells of cigarettes. Ugh."

"But you should still give him some consideration. He comes from a good family, and he has a good job," Ma insisted.

"I don't care what family he comes from. I just don't care for his type, too Armenian."

"Well, look around, and maybe you will find someone of your liking," Ma persisted, but I just scoffed.

"What if your prospects with K do not come through?" Ma asked. "Don't forget there is the Aydzemnig ball next month, and hopefully, you will meet some eligible guys there."

Ma's criticism of K almost every day upset me. She pointed out all his faults, and I pointed out his good points to her.

The Aydzemnig ball was the ball of the season, a charity ball that was attended by affluent and some less affluent Armenians. It was a good occasion for families to show off their daughters. I loved going to this ball. It was the second time I would be attending this function. I made myself a pale blue organdy dress just midway below the knees with a frilly neckline. I bought myself killer white shoes, and I mean killer because they hurt like hell. Why did I buy them too small? Women in Egypt were very conscious of their feet. And having big feet was just not considered feminine. The fashion was narrow, pointed shoes that squished the toes. I had to follow the fashion and suffer pain.

K came over the day before the ball.

"You can't go the ball," he said, looking at me sternly.

"Why can't I go to the ball?"

"Because my parents will be there, and we will not be able to dance with each other. Remember, we are supposed to have broken up. So, I'm not going. Therefore, you can't go."

"I really don't care about your parents. They are not going to run my life."

"What's the use of going if we can't dance with each other? And I certainly don't want to see you dancing with any other guy."

K was extremely jealous, so was I for that matter.

After much argument, we decided we would both go, and we would both dance with others intermittently and not hold them close and maybe sneak a couple of dances with each other.

Finally, the day came, and I was excited. I was busy the whole day taking care of myself. I took a bath and lotioned myself up. I put rollers in my hair and then combed it out and brushed it until it fell on my shoulders like silk. I had no makeup on, just a faint blush on my lips and *Je reviens* perfume behind my ears.

The ball was being held in an open-air venue with an excellent band.

I made an entrance with my parents and Judy. We were given a table just for the four of us, quite near the band but not too near. We could converse without getting deaf.

Guys were standing around checking out the girls seated with their parents. An older guy—older by about four years—came up and asked me to dance. I accepted. Actually, I liked this guy. He had the eyes of a fox, literally, and he was quite a good dancer but not as good as K. I was watching K standing at the bar and could tell he was seething. He went and asked a girl to dance. After a few dances with other people, K could not bear it any longer and asked me to dance. He immediately started murmuring love words in my ear and telling me that my perfume was driving him mad. I loved it. I watched his parents. They did not look too happy. They looked emotionless like wax statues, with pursed lips and slit eyes, but they could not create a scandal at the ball, of course.

"You will certainly be thrown out of the house," I told K, "and you will lose your job."

"I don't care. They cannot govern my life."

"Of course, they can. What are you going to do?"

"We'll see."

A few days after the ball, K told me that surprisingly, his father had not yet uttered a word to him about the ball. He did not know what was brewing. He was apprehensive, and so was I. My future was at stake. He was talking of going to Jedda because the shop was not making enough money to support a family in the style we wanted to live. I was going crazy with all his ideas, which did not appeal to me in the least.

Going to Jedda? Going to hell would be better.

Our bickering continued. We loved each other, but he was just too demanding and much too jealous. Sometimes when he got really mad, he would storm out of the house after bringing me home from a function and threaten to leave me.

"Go ahead, leave me!" I shouted at him one time.

It was the first time I had really raised my voice at him. Usually, he did the shouting. The next day, he called and apologized. This happened very often—quarreling, apologizing. I thought that making up was the best time. He became quite romantic, and I liked that. It was almost worth the fight.

To assuage gossip, we stopped dancing together at club events. In fact, we did not go to dancing events there anymore except for the tango contest. That, we could not resist. After all, we were known to be the best dancers, and the tango was our favorite. We would hate to see another couple win if we did not participate. Therefore, we took our courage in both hands and got up and danced. We had practiced beforehand at home. K had the habit of guiding me with the pressure of his hand on my back. We performed flawlessly.

We won first prize. Gossip restarted.

Although I hated our bickering over unimportant things, as far as I was concerned, I loved some of our romantic times, his artistic nature, and his unflinching enthusiasm about our future. And most importantly, he always told me he loved me. Unfortunately, I did not love him like I did in the beginning. But I wanted to get married. I firmly believed that it would take me out of the rut I was in.

One day we were at the Greek club, and a guy came and asked me to dance. I was taken aback and was too shy to refuse, so I accepted. It was not a slow dance, mind you. No closeness. K got mad, however, and broke a glass on the floor. Everyone at our table looked at him, perplexed.

"It was an accident," he said and took me home.

Another day, K told me that the real reason for his parents opposing our marriage was because my two uncles from both my parents' side were loonies, meaning that our children would certainly be crazy too. Actually, one of Pa's half-brothers had autism, and Ma's brother was diagnosed by the British Army doctor as being undisciplined and let go with a handsome pension. These uncles were considered crazies according to K's parents. I was extremely upset by this comment. I hated his parents. I wished they would disappear in thin air.

I was reassured by my parents that my uncles were not loonies, and they gave me details, which I immediately imparted to K.

I really did not know what the future held for me. I could not possibly wait another two years to get married. K would be twenty-one by then, and he would be legally authorized to take a decision unencumbered by his parents' wishes. But still, the future was nebulous. It was too far away. His petting got to be insistent, and I kept pushing his hands away. I had decided not to allow any heavy petting until we got married. I did not want to be considered "used merchandise."

Even though we avoided being together at Armenian social events, the whole Armenian community suspected that we were still together. I hated my life. Everything had to be done sneakily. Some guys took advantage of the situation and started asking me out to the movies with their group or to parties. I refused them, of course. They did not understand the reason. If I had left K, why was I refusing to go with them?

K's going to prostitutes still bothered me. It was eating me up. He said it was normal and not to worry because he would marry me eventually with or without his parents' consent.

"My going to prostitutes does not affect what I feel for you," was his reasoning.

"Well, I still don't like your being in contact with such filth."

"I don't kiss them, for God's sake."

"You're still in contact with their dirty bodies, and then you touch me."

The resistance of K's parents opposing our relationship kept on being a never-ending problem.

One day Pa told us about an interesting but disturbing conversation he had had with K's father, who had confronted him at the club one afternoon. He had broached the subject of my relationship with his son.

"I would like you to rein in your daughter and ask her not to pursue my son," he had said.

"Rein in? Who is pursuing whom? Don't you realize that my daughter has not lifted a finger to snatch your son and that all the pursuing is done by him?"

"After all, your daughter is only a working girl," he had continued, meaning my family had no money.

His elder son was engaged to a Greek girl who worked in a pharmacy. The elder son was much older, so the father could not interfere in his relationship with a woman.

Pa, never for a lack for words, went on to tell him, "At least my daughter works as secretary to the president of Barclays Bank and not as a seller of Vaseline." Vaseline being THE lubricant for the sexual act.

"Actually," Pa had then gone on, "perhaps you should rein in your son. We are not that eager for his relationship with our daughter. He has no proper job and is too young for her."

The old man had nothing further to say and had walked away.

As punishment, K's father did not allow him to use any of the family cars from then on. But K managed to do so in secret with the approval of his elder brother, who was a shady character and was up to his own shenanigans.

K was still working in the photo shop. His father had not thrown him out yet. The threats had not materialized.

"My mother talked him out of it," K said. "She says she is not that opposed to our engagement. She wants me to write to father, asking for his permission. A letter would be better, she advised me."

"Do what you have to do because I am getting impatient. Almost all my friends are engaged or married already. I feel like I am being marinated like a pickle in a jar, waiting to be consumed."

K heard from someone that if he put my handkerchief under his pillow, he would dream of me as his future bride. He did this, and he dreamed of me. We actually believed in such nonsense. I became hopeful that marriage was indeed on the horizon.

# CHAPTER XXII

## My Jobs

Finally, at the beginning of 1954, I was through with my shorthand classes and started looking for a job. There were quite a few advertisements in the English language newspaper, the *Egyptian Gazette*. I applied for secretarial jobs in all the large firms. I went for interviews. I had no experience whatsoever; therefore, I was not considered for any of the prime jobs. Luckily, however, a friend of Ma, whose husband was the manager of the Egyptian branch of the Sun Life Insurance Company of Montreal, suggested that I apply there as they were looking for a secretary. I went and passed a rigorous test and was accepted. I was so relieved. The salary was not much. The hours were fine, from 8:00 a.m. to 2:00 p.m. K would come and take me home by metro or by car if he had the use of one. I would have lunch at 3:00 p.m., take a nap, and then would be ready to go out on the town.

After a few months at Sun Life, I started looking for a better-paying job. The insurance job was tedious, pounding away on a manual typewriter, typing insurance forms in ten copies. If I made one mistake, I had to erase ten copies by hand with an eraser. It was such a bore. Although I liked my boss, the husband of Ma's friend, I was determined to leave. I wanted a more exciting job, where I would meet people. At the insurance company, there was the boss, an assistant, a clerk, and me. No excitement whatever.

The position of confidential secretary to the president of Barclays Bank was advertised one day in the newspaper. I applied. They were interviewing eleven girls. I took an IQ test and a shorthand and typing test. A young British guy, not bad-looking, sitting at a large old-fashioned desk, interviewed me. He asked me questions and made some notes on a notepad. I had a sharp eyesight and was good at reading upside down. I could see what he wrote. "An intelligent, slim girl, very competent in English." The word "slim" pleased me a lot. He did not say "thin" like all Armenians tended to describe me. At one time, I thought I had worms in my intestines and even took worm medicine to get rid of them.

No worms. Much to my dismay, I remained thin.

Another thing that made me feel good was that two actresses, who were not fleshy, made their apparition in Hollywood—Audrey Hepburn and Pier Angeli. People thought I looked like the latter. Same body, same hairstyle. I felt better about my body image from then on.

I got the job at Barclays Bank. The salary was better than that at Sun Life, but the hours were abominable, from 8:00 a.m. to 12:00 p.m. and then from 4:00 to 8:00 p.m. I would take the metro to go back home during the four-hour lunch break. Sometimes K picked me up by car or by metro. One half hour each way, a half hour for eating, and then the rest of the time, I napped to be able to go out in the evenings after work. The management made me work one week in each department to get a thorough knowledge of the business of the bank. It was serious work.

The work was fine, but I could not continue with such ungodly hours, and again, after two months, I was on the lookout out for a better job. I felt guilty about it, especially as they had just bought me a brand-new typewriter. But this was my life, and working hours were important to me. I wanted to have more free time.

My life was not all about money. Two things dominated my life then: my job and my relationship with K.

Right at this time, K's family suffered a horrendous calamity. The best friend of K's brother abducted K's sixteen-year-old sister, Claire, and took her to the Sudan to get married. That was the greatest scandal that overshadowed our own harmless peccadilloes. The parents were frantic. They did not know how to annul the marriage. Egypt and the Sudan had no extradition treaty, and also, they did not know where exactly the guy had taken their daughter.

I later learned the whole story from Claire, when we were both in the States and both divorced from our first husbands. I had remained good friends with her after divorcing his brother. She told me that I was his brother's one true love and that he never got over me. Also, he never remarried and died rather young. I was sorry to hear of his passing away when I was married to my second husband and living in Geneva.

I cried. Part of my youth had evaporated.

In January 1955, my maternal grandma was quite ill, and I spent some quality time with her. She was living with us at the time. She had been to the British hospital (being British), and we were told there was nothing they could do. She had a weak heart. I could not be at the beck and call of K. He did not tolerate anything or anyone keeping me away from him. I admit I was harsh with him sometimes, but he was so stubborn he just did not understand my feelings. I did not like the controlling side of his character one bit. I considered myself a free spirit or rather wanted to be a free spirit. How could I be that, though, in Cairo, in a restrictive society, with a hawkish but caring mother and a controlling, jealous boyfriend?

Grandma died a few evenings later. I was sitting next to her when she passed away. She took one deep breath, and she was gone. I cried and cried, and I wished I had spent more time with her. She had had such an unhappy life, losing three boys, one at birth, another at three years of age from typhoid, and yet another at twenty-two from a motorcycle accident. The fourth, my uncle Aram, had been such a burden on her. He was a genius but unmanageable. Her husband (my grandpa), whom I had never met, had gone to England before the World War II to attend to his textile factory in Lancashire and never returned when the war broke out. Eventually, he died in England before the war ended. It seemed he had not been such a good husband. She was such a gentle soul, and he had taken advantage of her by bullying her.

I resigned from Barclays Bank in January of that year. I had found a better job at Eastern Tobacco Company in Gizeh (a suburb of Cairo), almost an hour away from home. A small company bus would pick me up from home and take me to work starting at 8:00 a.m. Then I came home by 3:00 p.m., had lunch and a long nap, and was fresh for my evening events. Perfect job, perfect salary, perfect life. I was the private secretary of the personnel manager, who was an Egyptian Muslim. What a great boss he was.

Eastern Tobacco had been an Armenian company by the name of Matossian to start with, and then the owners had merged with British American Tobacco around the1920s. The board of directors was all British with its own British confidential secretaries. Most of the other secretarial staff were Armenians. They were envious that I had a private office. They sat in a large hall, all fifteen of them plus the chiefs and clerks. All the secretaries were older than me.

My boss had an assistant, an older guy who annoyed and harassed me. I told him off several times and asked him not to bother me, that I was engaged to be married.

"Where is your ring?" he asked, the dope.

"It is coming," I retorted.

Then another, much younger guy, a Muslim technician, befriended me. His name was Adly. He was a nice guy, polite, respectful, and funny. I always liked guys who made me laugh.

"If you were not engaged, would you accept to be my fiancée?" he asked me one day.

I was taken aback by this question and did not reply.

"Would you?" he persisted.

"Adly, I am engaged, so the question is moot."

I did not want to hurt his feeling and tell him that I would not consider marrying him because he was a Muslim.

As I have mentioned before, in Egypt, an Armenian girl did not accept dates from a guy. If a guy really liked you, and you also liked him, he would ask to be engaged to you, and that was that. You did not go out on dates before being engaged. Some girls did, clandestinely. The rule was not so strict with some other ethnic communities.

At that time in my life, I gave much importance to religion. Later on, as I became less religious, I befriended Muslim and Jewish guys. It did not bother me as long as they were not fanatically religious and did not practice their religion or force it upon me.

At this time, my relationship with K was rather tepid from my side, at least. I did not like kissing him, his breath stank sometimes, and I pushed him away. Not wishing to hurt his feelings, I didn't tell him about his breath. Also, he wanted me to be affectionate at parties, like swooning over him. But I was rather aloof. I did not like the idea of drooling over a guy and was reluctant to show my feelings in public. I wondered if I was having cold feet, or was I having doubts about loving him? I hoped his breath would improve.

Nevertheless, I stayed with K because I was used to him. Some days I loved him, and some days, not. I did enjoy our outings. All I could think about was going dancing. He was such a good dancer, so inventive in his moves.

Upon his mother's suggestion, K had written a letter to his father, explaining his sentiments toward me. His father finally realized that, whatever threats he put out, it did not dissuade K from his desire of marrying me. They agreed on our "engagement" and started visiting us. K respected his father because he had taught him everything about photography, about retouching negatives, and so forth. And he had great affection toward his mother. They also introduced us to their extended family. Boring, old-fashioned people. I did not enjoy their company. K did not particularly like his extended family either exactly for that reason.

However, even with this improvement in our daily lives, K was still picking quarrels with me. He did not approve of what I wore or what I said or did. He overwhelmed me with his attentions and wanted me to do the same. God forbid if I did not greet him with a kiss. We were always fighting for stupid reasons—the way I talked to so-and-so, the way I wore makeup, which was hardly any, but he still expressed disapproval. "It makes you look cheap," he would say. I would therefore only use a discreet line of kohl on my eyelids, a very natural shade of lipstick, and I would pinch my cheeks to get some color on my face. Woe to me if I ever used rouge, he would wipe it off roughly with the palm of his hand. His possessiveness was unbearable at times.

K's jealous moods got on my nerves more and more. During one dancing evening in an open-air dance venue, a good friend of K asked me to dance while K was away in the restroom. When K came out of the restroom, he looked for me and saw me on the dance floor with this guy. He flew into a rage and came over and took me away, reprimanding his friend. "Never, ever will you dance with my girlfriend again," he told him menacingly, ready to punch him. K had a temper, which ignited very easily. The poor guy got scared and walked away with his head down. Nevertheless, they remained good buddies.

"You should not have accepted to dance with him when he asked you," he turned around and scolded me also. He was so possessive as though I already belonged to him. First of all, he did not know that I would never belong to anyone. This is the Middle Eastern way of thinking. Men think they possess women. I had such a rebellious streak in me and K was insecure, I guess. But I obeyed him that time, not to cause embarrassment in public. I was only eighteen then. Later on, I did not take this kind of admonishment meekly.

Right around springtime, I decided to distance myself from K, not see him too often—not twice a day in any case—to rekindle the romance, if it were at all possible.

"We should not see each other every day," I said one day while he was kissing me goodbye at the door and lingering as usual.

"Why not? What's wrong?" he asked.

"Well, it is going to be a long time before we are married, and we will get bored with each other before that ever happens."

"Nonsense," he said.

I did not think it was nonsense. Did he not sense it that I was getting colder toward him and it was all his fault? I guess not. Now I know that young men are extremely selfish and want everything now, now, now. He was always sexed up and often went to prostitutes. I was past caring about that by this time. Was it because I was no longer in love with him? I hoped not.

In love or in lust? What was the difference?

I was upset about the fact that he was touching other women—low-class prostitutes—and I had never even kissed another man. I wanted to experience the thrill of doing so. With whom? That was the big question. Not with Adly at the office, he was a Muslim, and office flirtation never bodes well and not with any Armenian guy, God forbid.

Besides Adly, there was a Greek guy at the office who started paying me attention, but I did not like him at all. He was uncouth and had an aggressive manner. I rebuffed his advances. He did not understand why. Men can be dumb sometimes.

# CHAPTER XXIII

## Our Engagement

Now that K's parents had accepted our relationship, it was time to plan our engagement party. I was excited at the very thought of having a big party just for me and K.

My friend Claudine, who had just gotten married, talked to me about marriage. After her frank talk, I started to get cold feet. All the work and responsibilities of a household overwhelmed me. I realized what Ma was talking about. How would I be able to handle it? Everything was being done for me now at my parents' home. Household work was not for me. All I wanted was to have a good time, dance and paint, just be an artist, and have other people do the tedious work for me. I always daydreamed of some fairy-tale life, stupid fool that I was. By this time, I realized that being in love does not last forever. Love was even going away before getting married, for me at least. Friends of mine, who had not dated their husbands before getting married, were luckier, maybe. Their romance started after getting married, if it ever started, or was it duty? They did not know everything about their partners beforehand. Knowledge came gradually to them, but sex came immediately. I often wondered how they felt about it, but not one of them was talking except Claudine. In my case, my romance came early, and it was already dwindling away before even getting married.

We had a big engagement party. I designed and sewed my own dress. The fabric was a Bordeaux-colored taffeta with gold threading, and it was imported from France. I still have the material and have the intention of making another dress out of it one day. Wishful thinking. The material is in a trunk with other materials to be made into scrumptuous dresses one day when I will again have a highfalutin social life. Laughable. What am I thinking? Will I live forever? I have kept so many things all to be used at a later time. I am a hoarder. They are all going to be gotten rid of by my sons in an estate sale, and I will watch from heaven and sigh or smile.

It was an awesome party. Forty-four people were invited to our house. Friends and neighbors helped Ma to prepare the buffet. It was scrumptious, and Ma was dead tired supervising and doing most of the work. She strived for perfection as always; otherwise, people would gossip. I did nothing to help except get dolled up and enjoy the party. There was dancing, of course. It lasted till 4:00 a.m. for the young people. The older folks drifted away by 2:00 a.m. I had a fabulous time dancing and showing off my dress and being admired—and envied.

K's moods kept on being a huge blemish in our relationship. At one time, we were in Alexandria and driving with friends to go to a nightclub. I made a remark about something, I don't remember what. He got so upset that he took off his engagement ring and threw it out the window of the moving car. His friend Emile was driving. Emile promptly stopped the car and went to fetch it to give it back to him.

"I don't want it. Keep it," K told Emile with a sweeping motion of his hand.

I sat frozen in the back seat next to him and did not utter a word. Then Emile coaxed him, and he relented and asked me to tell him I was sorry for what I had said, which I did just to keep the peace. I did not think I was wrong, but I did not wish to spoil the evening.

Life went on. I had a busy life, drawing frenetically, sewing my dresses, knitting, going to work, and having a social life.

"Don't think that the life you are leading now is real life," Ma told me one day just out of the blue. "You will have responsibilities and children to take care of."

"I don't want children, in any case, not any in the distant future," I told her.

"Eventually, they will come, and you will be very busy with married life. There is no escaping it. K is not so wealthy that you can afford to hire all the help you will need."

I disregarded Ma's warnings. Somehow, I would manage to have the life I dreamed of.

As for children, it was true, I did not like them except for one.

The third-floor neighbors had the cutest little boy, and I adored him and wished that if I ever had a child, it would look just like him. He visited me almost every day, which frustrated K when he was at our house also. It looked like they were in competition with each other. This kid would sit right between us and hold my hand. He was only six years old, but I swear K started getting jealous of him. I saw this cute kid in Montreal forty years later. He was no longer cute. He was just an ordinary middle-aged man, not too tall, married, with a couple of kids.

So many dreams.

It was time for the Aydzemnig charity ball again. Now we were engaged, so we made a triumphant entrance as an engaged couple. I was dressed in a pale blue organza dress, which I had designed and sewed, with a navy-blue sash around my tiny waist—I was known to have the tiniest waist in the whole of Cairo—with a minuscule bouquet of pink flowers in my shoulder-length hair. K was dressed in a pair of navy pants with a white sharkskin jacket, made to measure, of course. People scrutinized us, and they murmured.

We danced the night away and were crowned the prince and princess of the ball. I could feel the envy oozing from the other girls, even my friends. They were looking daggers at me. I had been able to snatch an eligible bachelor.

I now decided that I wanted to get married as quickly as possible and not drag the engagement period ad infinitum and have even more doubts festering in my mind. Ma saw us bickering all the time.

"I have told you time and time again that he has a lousy character, and you better think twice before getting married."

"I'm sure it will be okay," I said.

"Just because he will have sex, he is going to change? Is that what you think?" she asked.

I did not reply.

The atmosphere at home because of Pa's job situation was another reason for my wanting to get married and having my own home. But did I know how to take care of one? I did not have a clear picture of how my married life would be. I did realize that I was harsh with K sometimes and hoped that marriage would solve all our problems, well, at least some of them. I also believed sex would be a big part of the solution.

Right at this time, when things were not going too well between us, I had a naughty thought. I wanted to be kissed by another guy before getting married. I wanted to experience the thrill of a stranger's kiss. But which guy? No one in sight. I was in a dilemma, but I could not see a solution. I was going to marry the only guy I had ever kissed. I do admit that I was very much in love with him at the beginning of our relationship, but the infatuation or love did not last, on my side, that is. He did vow eternal love to me and went to prostitutes on the side.

Adly was still hovering around me at the office, paying me compliments. I don't know what he hoped he would achieve. I was not in any way encouraging him. I had my ring on my finger. And he was not the guy I was thinking about.

There was some imaginary guy at the back of my head.

I don't know the reason why I did not yearn for K anymore. Maybe it was his constant anger. Or maybe it was because "familiarity breeds contempt," as they say. He was also going too far with his criticisms of me. His newest peeves were that I had red nail polish on, or that my lipstick was too bright, or that the sandals I was wearing were not meant for the street. Or yet my skirt was too tight. I hardly had curves. What was the tightness of my skirt revealing? Was he going to teach me about fashion? Our social life was fine. No problem there.

K took part in a Gala des Amateurs at Covent Garden—a chic open-air nightclub in Cairo. He sang an American song. Don't remember which one. He had a good voice and got second prize by only one vote less.

We also had a fight that evening.

Every day was the same old story, quarreling because I did not spend as much time with him as he wished. He was being ridiculous. Things at home needed my attention. Judy fell sick quite often and was having problems finding a good job, and finances were strained in the family, as always.

There was also a problem that occurred after my grandmother's death. Her only living son, my uncle Aram, tried to commit suicide in our storage space above one of the bathrooms. He cut his wrists. Ma discovered him and, as he was a British subject, he was rushed to the British hospital.

What bothered K the most was that he could not be alone with me often enough to smooch and do other stuff. His apartment was out of the question, and our apartment had people going and coming all the time. He sometimes insisted in making out even when my parents were present, in the doorway, of course. But I was uncomfortable, and I did not feel like being romantic in doorways. I just wanted him to say goodbye and leave. He said that he wouldn't get married unless I change my ways. Really? *My* ways? What ways? What about his ways? I did not pay too much attention to what he said or did because the next day, he would apologize, and things would resume.

Because of all these arguments, I sometimes thought of breaking up my engagement. Ma was right. Things were getting out of hand. I was fed up putting up with his volatile moods. A good reason to leave him would be if I could somehow leave Egypt and go to university in the United States. But we had no money, and my savings were far from being adequate.

My mind was in constant turmoil.

I asked Adly to help me find universities that would possibly give me a scholarship. He was surprised and sensed that I was having doubts about getting married, but he did not utter a word.

We researched and found none.

"So, what have you decided? Are you going to finally marry this fellow?" he asked.

"Yes, I suppose I will marry him. I see no other way out of my predicament in this country. I like him enough. Had I found a way to go to university in the United States, I would probably have left him. It is not that he is a bad guy. He is just too choleric and immature."

*Was I mature?* I asked myself.

"What about considering me? I would marry you, if you stayed."

"Adly, let's be serious. My parents would not allow me to do so. We live in a restrictive society. Christians do not marry Muslims. You know that."

He was disappointed and looked crestfallen.

I liked him, but marrying him? No.

I was bored at work, I was bored at home, and lately, I was bored with K. I wanted something new. Something was definitely wrong with my attitude and feelings. No girl who was engaged should think or feel this way. Was I a weirdo? The way things were going, I did not think I would even like the sexual part of marriage. How I wished I were still in love with K and not have these doubts that kept torturing me.

At the office, Adly was not giving up. He came by one day, when I was in a bad mood, and out of the blue said, "Your lipstick is fascinating and tempting." I liked that, and I almost blushed. I did not know what to reply, so I said nothing, just looked down at my keyboard.

One day K was very rude to Ma, and of course, Ma reiterated her opinion of K. She told me, *"Il a un sale caractère"* (he has a bad character). Ma wanted him to apologize, but he did not agree that he had done anything wrong. A big quarrel ensued. He left in a huff. Then he got on the phone with me and started crying.

"I love you so much," he said. "Nobody appreciates me, and you don't treat me as your fiancé, you are cold, you don't invite me over, you don't prepare dinner for me, and your mother is against me also," and on and on he went.

Prepare dinner for him? I did not even prepare dinner for myself.

He even threatened that he would commit suicide if I left him. What could I do now? I did not love him with that early inextinguishable passion that I had at the beginning. I realized that passion dies eventually in a relationship, and a kind of comfort zone sets in. Would the same thing happen with any other guy that I would ever befriend? I didn't know the answer. I had no experience. But I wanted that passion very badly. I wanted my heart to jump in my chest when I saw him.

What a romantic fool I was.

One question in my mind was, "Will I be happier married to K or being single?" Being single in Cairo was out of the question. I wished sometimes that I had not taken up with a guy so early in my life, at sixteen, for God's sake. I should have gone out with several. Only then would I have been able to make a choice. But that was not possible in the Armenian community in Cairo. A girl would be considered a slut.

I started yearning to meet other guys. I told this to my best friend, and she thought I was crazy. Yes, I was crazy. But the truth of the matter was that K had lost all his initial charm for me. I did not like the way he talked, the way he walked, the way he looked even. What was I then doing with this guy? I realized that I did not want to be tied down. I just wanted to have fun and flirt. As this was impossible, I was resigned to my fate. I had to get married and get it over with. Things might hopefully get better. I had to have an optimistic attitude. He was a good guy, I kept telling myself. I did like our romantic evenings and outings after all. I am not saying that all was bad.

Around December 1955, we realized that, if we wanted to go to the United States, we had to go as students. The Egyptian government would grant student visas only after having been accepted by an American university. I was scared to face that future. How could I live so far away from my family? And my cats? When would I ever see them again? All these thoughts kept going around in my already cluttered brain. Well, I thought, if after marrying K, I was dissatisfied with my life with him and if another guy took my fancy, I would either divorce or take a lover on the side. Simple. All those "ifs." I had seen too many movies. My mind wandered all the time. I did not think I could be faithful to any one guy throughout my life. Imagine not having kissed anyone else. That thought still bothered me.

Lately, K had become negligent about his appearance. And I didn't look forward to kissing an unshaven guy. He also smelled of liquor after bringing me home from an evening at a nightclub. That added to my reticence to kissing him. He would then get into a funk, and another quarrel would start. How could I tell him the reason for my reluctance? It is difficult to tell someone who loves you, "Hey, you don't smell good, and I don't like the taste of your lips."

I had a fertile imagination, and I kept falling in love with actors in the movies and would imagine love scenes with them. They fed my fantasy. Actually, I was in no way a mature person and should not even have thought of marriage, with all its obligations.

Around this time, we had another death in the family. Anoush's father died of a heart attack. My aunt blamed it all on his life in prison a few years before. His health had deteriorated. She was devastated. How would they live? What money? Anoush would never find a husband. She had come down a couple of notches in Armenian society because of the death of her father. She was no longer considered a wealthy bride-to-be. My aunt was frantic. She had to find a husband for her, quick. Anoush had clandestine boyfriends unbeknownst to her mother—a couple of Armenian guys, a Greek guy—but they did not propose marriage. It is doubtful she would have married them, if they had.

My job at Eastern Company was fine. The practice in Cairo at workplaces was quite relaxed. In your free time, if you had no work, you were allowed to read or knit. Then one day my boss told me that he had gotten word from the board of directors that they needed another confidential secretary and wanted me to be transferred to their department.

"Why me?" I asked my boss.

"It seems because you are half-British from your mother's side, and they only hire British girls for that job. They have decided to transfer you. I'll be sorry to let you go. I don't trust the British too much. They are shady characters. If anything goes wrong, I am here for you, and you can always have your job back."

I was elated. It meant more pay and a more prestigious job. I was to share an office with two English young girls, serving a team of ten board of directors. I liked working with the English girls and had an exciting time talking about boyfriends and sex. They were so open-minded. A novelty to me because Armenian girls were rather reserved. I told them about my situation with K. They understood. They wanted to invite me to a party and introduce me to their circle of friends, and maybe I could pick up a boyfriend. Although I did want to go to the party, I could not leave K behind. I could not lie to him either and go unbeknownst to him. So, I lost my opportunity of meeting other guys. On the one hand, I was eager to meet other foreign guys, but on the other hand, I was engaged, so what was I thinking?

Gladys and Joan, the English girls, encouraged me to leave K when I told them about the troubles I was having with him. They were English; they did not know the problems of being an Armenian girl in Egypt. I would be branded. Fingers would point at me in social circles. And I was not in foreign circles to find a substitute. I was not a member of the posh sporting clubs, where membership was expensive, and we could never afford it. That was where one would meet the foreign residents of Cairo.

Gladys even wanted to introduce me to one of her ex-boyfriends, a German guy. But the guy did not wish to meet me because he was leaving Egypt within three months and did not want to be attached to a girl if he liked her.

So that project also fell into the water.

After I left Egypt, Judy told me that Glady's father, an employee of the Marcony Company, had been arrested for being a spy for the British and was jailed, together with an accomplice. They were released after about a year. Poor Gladys. I don't know what happened to her.

I soon found out that Joan, the senior secretary, was the mistress of the chief director, a surly, older guy. She spoke openly about it. He was married, of course, but she did not seem to mind. She was getting what she wanted from him, whatever that was.

I was smitten by a young member of the board, and the feeling seemed to be reciprocal. He kept coming to see me at my desk often, giving me stuff to type. This was unusual because the board members never came into our office. We were sent the material through a messenger. The girls even noticed this guy's behavior and kidded me about him. There was no way we could have made further contact though. How could it ever happen? The company van took me back and forth to work. He could not come right out and ask me out. And, in any case, I would not have been able to go out with him in the open.

Although I was eager to go to the United States, some doubts took hold in my mind. If I went, I would be away from parents to whom I was extremely attached. But on the other hand, I could have the career I wanted, that of fashion design. If I left K and stayed in Cairo, I would be single and have no career, and who would I marry? Adly? Kevork? God, no. It would be very difficult for me to find a husband, and I could not see myself going through life as a spinster. What a horrible future that would be.

The decision was made for me one day. We heard sirens again in February. The rumor was that an Israeli attack was imminent. We, therefore, decided that it was time to seriously plan our departure from Egypt. We did not want to get stuck in Cairo because of a goddamn war. We wanted to start new lives. There was some urgency. I felt very panicky, and K tried to assuage my fears, but I was terrified of the future. What if we did not succeed to leave Egypt?

One day at work, a mistake was made by Joan, the head secretary, and the bitch blamed it on me. I don't remember what it was about, but it must have been serious enough because the next day, I was taken out of my job. I went crying to Mr. Orphy, the Egyptian personnel manager, for whom I had worked before. He consoled me and told me that I could get my old job back. He had a temporary secretary, so it was no big deal to get rid of her.

"Did I not tell you not to trust the British ever?" He reminded me.

I was humiliated and wanted to die and cried my eyes out. I went home that day and related the incident to Ma, who advised me to resign rather than be demoted to my old job and suffer humiliation. I was getting married in two months anyway. If we did not succeed in going to the United States, then I would have to seek other employment. I certainly was not going to be a *hausfrau*.

# CHAPTER XXIV

## Wedding Plans

My feelings for K were in a seesaw position. I loved him, and I loved him not. But I had made a final decision. I would marry him. I had loved him before, so maybe I would love him again. I had to have stability in my life. I could not go on flip-flopping forever.

Plans were made, and I designed my own wedding dress. I chose a white satiny brocade fabric and designed a kind of *bonbonnière* type dress, just above the ankles, different from ordinary wedding dresses. I disliked ordinary in everything. I wanted it to stand out. I also put pink flower bouquets around the hem that was gathered up every foot or so for the bouquets.

"Pink?" Ma said. "People will think you are not a virgin if you put colors on your dress."

"Do I really care what people think? You know me better than that."

I never gave a damn of what people thought. I liked being scandalous. I did not take part in the sewing of my dress though. It would bring bad luck, I was told. And I was superstitious. I just gave instructions as to how it should be sewed.

To me, the wedding day was like a huge party, nothing more. On that very same day, when I was getting all dressed up, with Judy, Ma, and a friend hovering around me, I had a most bizarre realization—that I did not really love K. After a four-year courtship, the passion had slipped away quietly but surely. He did not know anything of my real feelings toward him. However, I could not and would not cancel the wedding. I would be the world's most stupid fool. Who was going to marry me if I broke off the engagement on my wedding day? People would classify me as a real loony.

First of all, there was nobody in the whole Armenian community whom I wished to marry. Second of all, I wanted to leave Egypt. I could not bear the thought of staying there forever. And getting married to K was the opportunity as we had decided to go to the United States, where a new life awaited us.

We had applied to George Washington University, had been accepted, and were doing the necessary papers for student visas and exit visas. You had to get an exit visa if you wanted to leave Egypt for any reason.

The prospect of what this marriage would bring me excited me. It was a new beginning, and I thought that perhaps, once we were in the United States, my love for K would be rekindled.

I was being delusional.

I remember the night before my wedding, I lay down with Ma on her bed to be held by her one last time. She was my pillar of strength and my confidante.

"You're sure you want to get married to K?"

"Who else will I marry, Ma? There are no prospects around. I do like him. I don't think I can fall in love with someone else in Cairo. K is the best I can get. All my friends are already married, and I don't want to be left by the wayside. I don't want to continue working in Cairo as a secretary, however prestigious the job. I will not have a meaningful career here. A husband and children would not satisfy my needs. I want to go to the U.S. and become a fashion designer. And most importantly, I don't want another Armenian husband."

"You are pretty and talented. You will find a nice guy eventually."

"No, not eventually. Nothing can be certain. K is okay, basically a good guy, and he loves me. I am used to him, and I can handle him. If it does not work out in the States, there is always divorce, you know."

"Are you crazy, girl, not even married and you are thinking of divorce?"

"Yes, that is always a possibility. I will not continue being married if things do not work out. I want to be independent and make my own life, and in the U.S., I can do that. People will not look down on me if I am divorced."

"You are arguing with him all the time, my dear," said Ma. "It is not going to get better as years go by, you know. It will get worse. Think carefully."

"What am I supposed to do? Cancel my wedding and be the laughingstock of the community and start my life over again here?"

"Why not?" she asked.

"Because my future is in the U.S. That's why," I retorted.

Ma just shook her head. She was done discussing with me.

"I hope you know what you're getting into," she concluded.

We had rented an apartment some months prior, in case the American prospect would not go through. I rather liked the apartment. It was in a quiet residential neighborhood of Heliopolis and had two bedrooms and a large patio. Who was going to keep house though? I had never touched a broom or a casserole in all my life. We were going to have a maid, that's for sure, but cooking? I did not think too seriously about that.

Something would materialize, I thought.

Our wedding was one of the most sumptuous weddings of the Armenian community in the Armenian church of Cairo. The church was a landmark. The architecture was unique as are all Armenian churches around the world. There were about five hundred people. All could not fit in the church, and people were standing outside in the yard. Besides friends and relatives, many people came to see this rebellious couple who had made it to the altar despite the objections of the groom's parents.

I was ecstatic with all this attention. Pa walked me down the aisle, and there I stood at the altar, opposite my husband-to-be, smiling and happy. It was one of the most exciting moments of my life. To me, the wedding was like one big party, and all I cared about was being admired. I was the belle of the ball. What else did I want? I was in a dream world.

The priest uttered some mumbo jumbo, which I did not understand and to which I did not pay much attention, anyway.

At the end of the ceremony, family and friends lined up in the aisle, and they passed in front of us, shaking our hands as they each offered me jewelry. That was the custom among the Armenians. Relatives and close friends would offer jewelry to the bride. I received an exquisite 18 karat bracelet with tassels from my in-laws. They wanted to outdo everyone else and not because they particularly liked me. K's brother offered me matching earrings. (I sold this jewelry fifty years later in Miami to an estate dealer.) They were collectible handmade pieces designed and made by an Armenian jeweler. Armenian jewelers were known to be the best in Egypt.

On our dining table at the home of my parents, all the other gifts were laid out. The question remained. What to do with them since we were going to the United States? We took stuff that could be crammed in trunks, and the rest we left behind.

There was no reception afterward. After all the congratulations were done, we spent the night in a luxurious hotel in town. The next day, we flew to Alexandria for our "real" honeymoon. I was scared to have sex and wondered how the other girls did it. How was I supposed to have pleasure while six inches would go into one of my holes, pierce me, and make me bleed? I thought girls were crazy to go through this. And this was supposed to give a girl an orgasm, with all the pain of the hymen being pierced? After one glass of champagne, I finally managed to overcome the fear of being deflowered. What a stupid word.

Before going to the States, we stayed in my parents' house. I felt very strange to be "legally" sleeping with a guy (my husband nevertheless) in my parents' home. Why would a priest's mumbo jumbo and a piece of paper give us the right to have sex?

I was still in a daze. Yes, I was married. Yes, he was a good guy. Yes, he loved me a lot. But what about me? What did I feel? What did I want? I certainly did not want kids. I wanted a career, and I wanted to feel passion. How could that happen with the same man, the same lips, the same hands, the same body? And sometimes he had bad breath—a real turnoff.

My love for K kept diminishing. I remember at the beginning of our relationship, whenever we smooched, I felt thrills, passion, and excitement. All this was gone even before we got married. Maybe passion drifts slowly away after "being married." Yes, that was it. There was no longer the excitement of clandestine get-togethers, stolen moments of passion, eagerness to see each other. Everything was now legal, everyone knew you were married, and sex was part of it.

I kept thinking how could two people vow to be together for a whole lifetime? Impossible. There surely would be occasions of meeting other men and desiring them. The same would apply for the groom, of course.

# CHAPTER XXV

## Getting Out of Egypt

To be able to get out of Egypt, I needed a passport. I had applied for an Egyptian one since I was born in Egypt, but it was not being processed quickly enough. The bureaucracy in Cairo was unbelievably slow. You needed to bribe people to get things done. Our departure date was set for early September. K had an Iranian passport through his father who had lived in Iran.

Our plan was that after setting foot in the United States, we would not go to college—since neither of us had the funds—but make our way to Montreal and become immigrants there. We had heard that it was very easy to land in Montreal without official papers. We just had to cross the border, and bam, we were there, and we would ask for the necessary papers after arriving. And then, sometime in the future, we would find our way to the United States. But how?

That was the one-million-dollar question.

We had already booked the voyage by ship from Alexandria to Naples, and from there, we would be crossing the Atlantic with an Italian ocean liner to New York. But, I still did not have my passport.

We found a solution to that.

I applied for an Iranian passport as the wife of an Iranian citizen (K was Iranian through his father), and I was given one immediately. These were the days of the Shah and not the Ayatollahs.

We were allowed to take only one hundred Egyptian pounds each with us on leaving Egypt even on a student visa. Since we could not take out more money, we bought stuff. We bought a lot of stuff. We could take with us as much Egyptian made goods as we wanted. We bought Egyptian cotton sheets, towels to last us decades, blankets. I am not kidding. I was still using the same sheets and towels thirty years later after having divorced and remarried. I also had clothes made, every kind of dress, suit, coat that you can imagine. We bought Egyptian artifacts to sell there and make some money—camel saddles, oriental brass dishes, mother of pearl inlaid boxes, leather goods, and small replicas of pharaonic statuettes.

We used the two huge ocean liner trunks that my parents had used on their trips to Europe. We stuffed all the goods in them. I finally got rid of these trunks fifty years later when I moved to the States again with my second husband, but this time from Geneva.

The biggest problem was to get my jewelry out of Egypt. *Verboten.* Not allowed.

My father had the solution to that dilemma. He had an Armenian friend, a facilitator, as he called him. He was a short, wiry, and wily guy; spoke excellent Arabic; and was a wheeler-dealer. He had piercing black eyes—as though to better look into your soul—donned large brown horn-rimmed glasses, and talked a mile a minute. You had to concentrate hard to understand him. He had six children, two of whom my sister and I went to school with, and one of whom later on wanted to hook up with my sister. No go, she did not like him. This facilitator had a lot of connections in the government—in the crooked government. Which government is not crooked? I have not seen one after having lived in six countries since then.

This guy, I shall call him Inkjian—it is not his real name, but I don't want to have any problems with his family—charged a lot of money to muster up deals for people, but he did not charge Pa because he liked him. I think Pa amused and entertained him and brought him clients, lots of clients—Armenians trying to smuggle money and jewelry out of Egypt.

Mr. Inkjian asked me to give him all the jewelry that I wanted to smuggle out. He then told me that a young Muslim *fellah* would come up the gangplank of our boat, look for me, and hand me the jewelry in some manner or other.

I looked at him doubtfully.

"Don't worry, it will happen," he said.

How could I not worry? The jewelry was worth a lot of money, and a young urchin would be entrusted with it? He could run away with it, for God's sake. But I guess Mr. Inkjian had frightened the bejesus out of this boy.

The day of our departure came. We boarded the boat with our umpteen pieces of luggage. Security for goings and comings up the gangplank was not very tight—not strict at all. I stayed on deck looking at people in the harbor, trying to find this young boy. There were many around, begging for money. What if he did not show up? What if he got caught while embarking on the boat? What if he was not allowed to get on the boat? What if I lost everything? All the "what-ifs" went around my cluttered mind. There would be no recourse if the boy did not show up. I was terrified and impatient.

My parents, my sister, and K's parents were waving at us from the dock and sending kisses. My heart was beating erratically. I thought I would collapse on deck. K did not seem to be worried as much as I was. Well, of course not, it was not his jewelry, although he had given me some of them.

"Relax. He will come," K said. "Mr. Inkjian has his trusted underlings. You know that. He has never yet let anyone down. His reputation would go down the drain if he did. After all, this is one of the ways he makes his living."

I wanted to believe him wholeheartedly, but I was terrified of some unforeseen catastrophe at the last minute.

Finally, I saw a young boy dressed in a not-too-clean *galabeya* running up the gangplank in full view of the control people. Nobody paid any attention to him. They thought he was just another beggar kid asking for some pennies from the voyagers. As soon as he was on deck, he started looking around and asking for "Madame Beggy, Madame Beggy." There is no letter "P" in the Arabic language, and Egyptians have a hard time pronouncing that letter. They tend to substitute it with the letter "B." The ones educated in English and French schools do not have that problem as they have learned the foreign language from childhood.

I was stunned, and I came forward.

"I am Madame Peggy," I told him in Arabic. He handed me a heavy metal box and ran back down the gangplank. None of the ticket controllers was aware of what had just transpired. He had smuggled my jewelry to me on the boat. I was elated. I immediately put the box in my large handbag. My heart almost stopped beating, and I was perspiring profusely. My knees were trembling, but I managed to return to my cabin and was afraid to open the box lest something would be missing. I finally opened it, and all my jewelry was there. I guess this kid was trustworthy after all. His boss had trained him well. I uttered a big sigh of relief.

"Is everything there?" K asked me when he came into the cabin.

I nodded.

"See, there was nothing to worry about. Mr. Inkjian did come through."

We collapsed on the bed.

The three-day boat trip on the Mediterranean was uneventful. All we talked about was our future and how we would manage our life.

We arrived in Napoli.

It reminded me of Egypt—chaotic, dirty, and everybody talking loudly and screaming at the same time. One difference though: the chic streets of Cairo with well-dressed people were lacking in Napoli. People looked like peasants.

We took two taxis to be able to transport our luggage and went to a *pensione*. We just followed one of the screamers at the port offering lodging. We did not know where we would land. We knew nothing.

Two young people on their own in a foreign country with no backing or experience.

The trunks were carried up the stairs by the taxi drivers. There was no elevator in this *pensione*.

I had one look at the room and wanted to cry. It had a queen-size bed, already sunken, a dubious-looking coverlet, and no furniture except for a dresser. The trunks were piled one on top of the other. I hid the jewelry in several pairs of shoes that I unpacked, put the shoes at the bottom of one trunk, and we went walking into town in search of food. I had lost all my appetite in this foreign town away from my family. I could not eat anything. K ate some pasta, and I managed a slice of pizza.

We went to the zoo the next day, and I fed a giraffe. We roamed the city for the next two days, waiting for our boat to come into the harbor.

I was so apprehensive of the uncertain looming future—and we had not even arrived in the States.

What the hell was I doing so far away from home? Leaving the cocoon-like atmosphere of my family? In a strange land, which would get even stranger once we landed in the United States?

I was terrified. I vocalized my misgivings to K, who had his wits together for a twenty-one-year-old guy. He kept reassuring me and telling me that everything would turn out fine in the end. I appreciated K's optimistic attitude and wanted to believe him. We were leaving our roots, our homes to embark on an unknown adventure in an unfamiliar land, where we hardly knew anyone and were not even sure whether we would be able to stay, nor did we have sufficient funds for our subsistence.

We had decided that if we could not make it in North America, we would return home. After all, K would have his job back in his father's photo shop, and I would look for a secretarial position again, and my dreams of becoming a fashion designer in the United States would evaporate for good.

I banished that thought. "Think positive," I kept telling myself.

# CHAPTER XXVI

## United States and Canada

We finally arrived in the States.

We saw the Statue of Liberty. It was awesome. Was this country, the one that I had dreamed of all my life, going to open doors for my own liberty?

We disembarked in New York Harbor, and K's elder brother came and picked us up to take us to his home in Washington, D.C.

Our plan was to stay with his brother for a few days and concoct our plans. They had three kids. There was no separate room for us. K slept on a sofa in the living room, and I shared a bedroom with the three kids. It was awful. Here I was, a married woman, sharing a room with three boisterous kids. On top of all that, I fell sick, very sick.

I developed a fever and a strep throat and stayed in bed without seeing a doctor for a whole week. We had no money for doctors. Luckily, I got better, and we planned our immediate future.

When I got better, we explored the city, the parks. They were so vast and beautiful. The weather was balmy and pleasant. I liked the city in general, but I hated the trashy parts and the trashy people. I never knew they would exist in America. I thought everything would be perfect. It was not what I expected.

I was scared of life, in general. Of life in a strange land.

Our intention was to go to Montreal, get residency, get jobs, and try to get into the States somehow after a few years. We were informed that the Canadian border was extremely easy to cross, that no one checked IDs. The Canadians thought that whoever crossed from the United States must be American.

The plan was that K would go first to look over the terrain and find us a place to stay. He went to Buffalo and had planned to cross the border at night by Greyhound bus. He had gone to a movie and had forgotten the time of the bus's departure, so he rushed, running to catch it. He did get on the bus and sat at the back. Two sinister-looking detectives in hats and dark long coats followed him to the bus, got on, and pointed a gun at him, asking him to show an ID. K was scared to death. Did the detectives know of his intentions to cross into Canada illegally? What on earth was happening? It seemed he matched the description of a criminal seen around town that day. This was his first encounter with a gun. He had heard that Americans often used guns but never thought those would be pointed at him.

After checking his ID, the detectives were apologetic—not too apologetic, it seemed—and got off the bus, leaving one shocked K in the back seat, perspiring through his heavy overcoat.

K crossed the border and went to stay with a couple of Armenian guys he knew from Cairo. They were by no means friends in the true sense of the word, but in a foreign land, people from the same country help one another. They were two brothers who had immigrated and had rented a dinky old tenement house. They were working as pole men with Bell Telephone.

When I finally arrived in Montreal, we rented a bedroom from them. The heating was a gas stove in the middle of the foyer, which was supposed to heat the whole house if you left the doors of the bedrooms open.

Well, there was no way we were going to have sex in a freezing room, so we kept the door open and had no sex. It was quite an uncomfortable situation. We paid them for the room, of course. The major problem was that I did not know how to cook, and the first time I tried to cook rice, I actually made a hole in the pot. It was not a very good quality pot, mind you, a substandard aluminum. From then on, I asked Ma for recipes of all the foods I liked. The letters never arrived on time because there was another war in Egypt—the 1956 Suez Canal War—and the letters were heavily censored.

In October of 1956, a month after we had left Egypt, we read in the news that Israel pushed through the Suez Canal with artillery because their ships had not been allowed to pass since 1950. Two-thirds of the world's oil passed through this canal. The Israelis started a war. They wanted access through the Canal. The French and the English followed suit.

Nasser had nationalized the Suez Canal when he came to power, and the English and the French who had operated it wanted to regain control of it.

The actual troubles had started at the beginning of 1956—that was why we had made plans to leave Egypt as soon as possible—but they were not very indicative of what was about to happen. People did not think there would be a war. We escaped the war in the nick of time; otherwise, we would not have been able to leave the country for at least a few years.

Letters were our only source of news from the family. We numbered them so that we would know their sequence. It was a horrible time for me being cut off from my family. There was no telephone service between Canada and Egypt. The only thing we could do was send telegrams if we wanted immediate news. My sister invented a code to tell me how things really were. I could decipher the code with no problem because she wrote it in another way, not in her usual voice.

In one of my sister's letters, I heard that Hassan, our doorman, had betrayed us during this war. Because of the war, all British and French nationals were deported from Egypt. Jewish people who held French or British passports were also expelled as well as some who were thought to be Zionists or having ties with Israel. Their businesses were confiscated, and they were allowed to leave with only one suitcase and a limited amount of cash.

Ma was British, so was her only living brother, Aram. Hassan, trying to be a hero, told the authorities that Uncle Aram was British, and the government deported him also. The reason Ma was not expelled was because she was married to an Egyptian citizen, my father. In a way, it was a good thing Uncle Aram was expelled because he was an ex-British soldier, released from the army for insubordination. He got a full pension in England. There was nothing he could do in Egypt. He was a pauper, and he would have been homeless. In England, he was taken care of and given lodging, free medical care, and basic accommodation. I pitied him being away from his only family. He wrote to Ma and to me quite often—heart-wrenching letters.

There was nothing we could do.

We did not know the details of what was going on in Egypt, but news trickled through somehow. Nobody was allowed to leave the country on any pretext whatsoever except the ones who were expelled.

My family was constantly on my mind, and subsequently, I had a nervous breakdown, could not sleep, could not eat.

About the fourth day after our arrival, the brothers who worked for Bell Telephone advised me to go and apply for a job there.

"They need people all the time," they said.

"But I have no papers," I said.

"Don't worry, the Canadian system is very lax. You'll get papers once you get a job."

This turned out to be true. I got a job as secretary at Belle Telephone, after taking the required tests. No questions asked. Are you a citizen? Are you a resident? Nothing. They just assumed I was a legal immigrant. The next thing was to get a social security card. That was easy. After getting the job, I got that one too.

We applied for residency papers. The consensus was that we would get them within a year. Wrong assumption. The Hungarian Revolution happened, and Canada saw an influx of Hungarian refugees. The Canadian government concentrated all its efforts to take care of them. I resented this. We were told that we could reside in Canada and work but could not travel anywhere outside the country before getting our legal residency papers.

My job was boring. I was seated among a bunch of secretaries in one huge office space with the supervisor sitting in one corner, handing out the work.

I had a better job in Cairo, but this was no time to complain. At least I was earning a living. I was making $40 a week. K had also found a job with a renowned photographer's outfit, and he was happy. He had retouching skills, and they needed him badly. He retouched negatives. It was a tedious but artistic work. He also photographed people.

The girls in my office were super friendly. It was their first encounter with someone from the faraway desert land of Bedouins and camels—Egypt. They were surprised I could speak English and work in that language and that I also knew French. They adopted me and asked me asinine questions.

"Do you have paved streets?"

"Do you have faucets with running water?"

"Do you ride on camels?"

"Only tourists ride on camels at the Pyramids. We do have cars," I replied.

Mouths agape, more questions were asked every day. I got a kick in educating them about the stylish and sophisticated life we led in Egypt, only in Cairo, Alexandria, Port Said, and some of the smaller towns near the Suez Canal, of course. The rest of Egypt was composed of villages where the *fellahs* lived and did the farming, and the streets there were not paved.

They were also astounded at the quality of my clothes. Everything I wore was handmade and chic and of the latest fashion.

One anecdote in Montreal I'll never forget. As I mentioned earlier, these two brothers we lodged with were pole men for Bell Telephone. They worked the nightshift and were often called for phone line malfunction repairs. They told us that they would receive calls from their office during the night for repair assignments. When they arrived at the assignment, most often, a woman would open the door, clad only in a transparent *negligée*. These women feigned a problem with the telephone line just so that a pole man would come, and they would have sex with him. The brothers laughed about the loose morals of the Canadians. They did not oblige these women with any sexual favors though. They preferred to keep their jobs rather than have a quick roll in the hay.

After a couple of months of living with these guys, we moved into our own apartment—a two-bedroom, one bathroom, a kitchen and a balcony, and an enormous walk-in closet. We just bought two beds, a dresser, a sofa for the living room, a Formica kitchen table, and two chairs. K bought himself a desk to do extra retouching at home.

It was quite a problem going to work from where we lived. We took the bus. But sometimes we were really snowed in and could not get to the bus stop. Even the buses would not run. Very rarely did that happen though. Montreal buses were notorious for braving the snow. It was a hassle, but they managed with enormous chains on the tires. We had to walk four blocks to catch a bus and then walk from the bus station to the office in the snow and slush. I was not used to wearing galoshes, which everybody wore. Being very clothes conscious, I found them ugly, not feminine at all. My obsession with femininity refused that I look like a snow plougher. Stylish boots were not yet in fashion.

After a while, I got used to the snow, and I dressed accordingly. Montreal was a beautiful city. We did not explore much though. We kept ourselves around St. Catherine Street and all the streets perpendicular to that. There were some European restaurants that we liked to frequent. And we also did some skating. I was not too good at it. K was better than me.

My first experience with the life of Canadian young women was at Bell Telephone. The French-Canadian girls, the others were not so friendly and outspoken. They talked very freely about sex, unheard of in Cairo, where we whispered among close friends only. I was curious and was all ears. I wanted to learn. I was stunned that they were having sex with their boyfriends. Some were even unfaithful to them by having one-night stands with other men. Amazing.

As I had done in Cairo, after finishing the work I was handed to do, I took out a book and read. I did not dare knit. My supervisor was aghast. She tried to give me more work, but there was none. Being a fast worker, I finished my assignments quickly. After a couple of months, I started looking for a better-paying job, and I found a secretarial position at the Seafarers' Union. When I informed my supervisor at Bell Telephone that I wished to give notice, she proposed to promote me. I declined, however, telling her that the raise I would get was below that of my new job. I was offered $45 a week, but the new job was paying $50. The amount of $5 was a big difference for me.

The big boss at the Seafarers' Union had a pouch on his side. He was a kind but brusque man. What I liked about this job was that they gave us a bowl of New England clam chowder for lunch. The best clam chowder I have ever had, full of clams and less potato.

I made plans to leave that job also after gaining more "Canadian" experience. It was so boring, all about shipping schedules and transportation. Actually, I don't think I have ever had a secretarial job that was interesting. What is so interesting about taking dictation about boring subjects? What is so interesting about typing umpteen copies of a text? Now if I were a secretary to an intelligence outfit— like spy stuff—that would have been different. Being a secretary was a young woman's career in those days, but I had higher aspirations. I had not left Cairo to continue on being a secretary. Would my dreams ever materialize?

Spring in Montreal was not pleasant; all the snow melted and created slush. Summer finally came, and it was hot and humid. We went to the Laurentians on weekends to get away from the heat. Lovely small towns with a lot of charm. We always took Timmy along with us.

The war in Egypt was still waging on, and it worried me constantly. We corresponded with family and friends nonstop. The letters were censored. I wanted to telephone to hear their voices, but it was impossible.

My next job was at Saguenay Shipping. It was more interesting because I was infatuated with my boss. He was of Irish origin, not very tall, with intense blue eyes—Irish eyes. He was quite knowledgeable about the world unlike other Canadians. It seemed to me that Canadians were so cut off from the rest of the world that they knew nothing about history or geography, but the guy I worked for was different. When he found out I was Armenian, he made a comment. I was impressed.

"Armenia was the first nation that adopted Christianity," he said one day, and we discussed a little history.

I was astonished at his knowledge and, from then on, I had a secret crush on him. Here I was, a married woman with roving eyes. I should never have been married.

There was a male coworker, an uncouth slob, seated at a desk next to me, who would throw the phone book at me whenever I asked for it to look up an address. We had to check addresses of clients. The Montreal phone book was quite a heavy one, and I was annoyed at his behavior, so I started throwing the book back at him when he asked for it. He realized his mistake when the book landed on his papers, which got strewn all around. He corrected his comportment after that.

One of the things I noticed in Montreal was that people were not well dressed. The women wore synthetic ready-made clothes because they did not know how to sew, nor were they interested. Most women knew how to sew in Egypt. We did not have synthetic yarn in Egypt. In Montreal, it was the trend to wear Ban-Lon sweaters. (Funny thing is that my second husband, an American, had a Ban-Lon manufacturing plant in a suburb of Rome in the 1960s.) The men wore suits that were badly tailored. There was no ready-to-wear in Cairo in those days. Maybe a few very expensive boutiques would import women's clothes from France and Italy. Everything was sewn by hand by expert tailors for men and by seamstresses for women, copied from top designer fashions illustrated in European magazines. Some fabrics were imported from Europe, but generally, Egyptian cotton was of excellent quality. I still wear a pink dress I made from Egyptian cotton in 1956 just before getting married—part of my trousseau. I remember Ma advising me against buying that fabric because the white polka dots were not woven but stained on the fabric. Well, after several years and several washings, the fabric is still intact.

I used to show up for work dressed in my hand-tailored clothes, and my coworkers thought I was sophisticated and wealthy. We did not have any money, but our appearance projected otherwise. I did not think I was sophisticated by all means. It was the norm in Cairo to be well dressed. But hey, they thought it, so I let it be.

My depression did not get better. Yes, I could function at work, but I could hardly eat. It was as though my stomach was blocked. I kept losing weight. Not wishing to alarm my parents, I did not mention my depression in my letters. I did not go to a doctor either.

One day K came home, found me in bed, almost in tears. I had not gone to work that day because I had not heard from my family for over a week and was worried about the war.

"Look what I brought you," he said and took out a kitten from his vest. "I picked it up from the SPCA."

It was the cutest kitten ever, with a tail bigger than his body. A fluffy long-haired gray cat. I later found out that he was a Maine coon.

"Why did you do that for?" I asked. "I can hardly take care of myself. How on earth will I ever be able to take care of an animal?"

Actually, that was the best medicine for me. Being obliged to take care of the cat, I forgot all about my depression, and gradually, it subsided. No pills, no doctors. These were not the days of Xanax and Prozac. I started to eat better and sleep better. The cat was a rambunctious one. He was adorable and kept me on my toes.

My energy returned, and I thought of taking a correspondence course in patternmaking as my dream was still focused to be a fashion designer in Manhattan. I had already started designing and sewing for my friends at work. I would charge them $10 a day, excluding the fabric, which I sold to them from the stash I had brought over from Cairo. Beautiful brocades to make evening dresses.

My cooking also improved with the recipes I received from Ma. We ate out a lot though as food was cheap. We would go to a steakhouse and get a huge rib steak served on a wooden board for $1.50 with fries.

What a difference of temperature between Egypt and Canada. Instead of the *khamsin* (the desert sandstorm) as it is called, we had snowstorms. The weather was very agreeable in Cairo except for the sandstorms. The summers were hot but not humid. We used to have a *khamsin* episode once a year. The very fine sand would seep through closed windows and was all over the furniture, our clothes, and even in our eyes and nostrils. The maid would be busy all week cleaning up the sand from all over the house. We had to wash some of the clothes also.

The first time we went dancing in Montreal, K and I were so disappointed. It was a dance hall. Here I was, dressed in a brocade sheath that I had sewn myself and K in his suit and tie. Everyone was wearing Ban-Lon sweaters, T-shirts, casual pants or jeans, and no dancing shoes. It was so different from the Cairo atmosphere of a real nightclub, where people were dressed to their teeth. Finally, after much looking around, we found a hotel that had a proper nightclub with a good band. That was where we went every Saturday evening. Dancing was our manna.

After a few months, some relatives of K managed to come to Canada and moved in with us. We needed to save money on rent. A couple with a small child. Bad decision. What a calamity that was. I did not get along with the woman, K's busybody, bossy cousin. And the child was a nuisance. There was a lot of tension, and we decided to move out. We moved into a one-bedroom apartment in the same area, close to a bus stop.

At this point, I was getting along very well with K. Not many fights, and he was helpful in the household chores as he had promised he would be. It was happy times for us. I did not "love" him, but I liked being with him. That was an improvement. We took a short vacation in the Laurentians one summer. The hotel was situated on a lake, and we swam in the cool waters. What a difference between the Mediterranean and the lake. We enjoyed it a lot. Our first vacation since we had left Egypt.

Around this time, I heard that Tyrone Power was coming to Montreal for a play. He was one of my favorite actors. We bought tickets for the event. I wanted absolutely to meet him after the performance. I did not think it would be feasible as I was sure many people would have the same idea. What I did was to find out which hotel he was staying at. There were only two or three top-class hotels in Montreal then, so it was easy to find out. I just called one hotel and asked for him by name. I was told he was not staying there. So, I called the second hotel on my list, and bam, he was staying there. I did not ask to speak to him. I wouldn't know what to say. Instead, I wrote him a letter—what a childish letter it was. I still have it. I told him I was a fan from Egypt and was sorry that he did not come to Egypt in 1947 for the filming of *King of the Khyber Rifles* because of the cholera epidemic. And then I asked him to call me at home and inform me if it would be okay for me to visit him after his performance.

Surprise, surprise, a couple of days later, his manager called me at home and told me to come to the back after the performance and raise my hand, announcing my presence by name. My heart was in a flutter. My letter had done the trick. I couldn't believe my ears. Ty's manager had called me! Ty was interested in meeting me! We went to the play and afterward went to the back entrance—there was a crowd. The door opened, and I raised my arm, and with a loud voice, I hollered that I was Peggy. The manager let me in, and K came with me. He wanted to take photos.

Well, we entered Ty's dressing room. He was wearing a pale blue polka-dot dressing gown. He was so handsome, with thick bushy eyebrows and deep brown eyes. He asked me a lot of questions about Egypt. I noticed that there was a photo of Linda Christian on his dressing table. She was his wife then. He did not allow K to take pictures. I wonder what would have transpired had K not been there. Tyrone Power died of a heart attack a year after I met him.

I lost one of my idols.

I did the same thing when Vic Damone came into town. He was booked to sing in a nightclub. I found out the hotel he was staying at and called. I talked to him giving him a spiel and asked whether we could see him after his performance. He invited K and me for a drink. He was a pleasant chap but did not seem too happy. I think it was about the time when Pier Angeli had divorced him. I wonder if he saw the resemblance between Pier and me.

Finally, the war in Egypt ended, and my sister immigrated to Canada legally because she was born in Switzerland. She did not have a Swiss passport though. You were not given nationality in Switzerland just because you were born there. You had to reside twelve years after being born there or six years if you went to school there as a child. In North America, it is where you are born that counts—not who you are or your origin. For instance, if you are born in a wooden hut in Timbuktu, that's who you are, a Timbuktuan, according to American and Canadian laws. It is an absurd law. My parents could not immigrate because they were born in Egypt, although Ma had a British passport.

As I was very close to Judy, I was overjoyed at her arrival. She and I were almost like twins but not in looks. She was dark with an olive skin and taller than me. I finally had someone from my family with me.

Judy slept on the couch in the living room. She found a job immediately, and we settled down as best we could. It is not easy for a young married couple to be sharing an apartment with a family member, although this was regularly done in Egypt, where people rarely lived alone. Grandmothers and grandfathers lived with the family. Luckily, Judy got along well with K. She felt lonely without a boyfriend, though. She had left her Egyptian boyfriend behind. He was a Muslim and a lieutenant in the army, and in those days, Christians did not marry Muslims. Later on, there were some mixed marriages. Ma thought that Judy, being in Montreal, would meet other fellows and forget her first love. Judy showed me a picture of him. He was a handsome guy, with a mustache and slanting green eyes.

We passed the time in the evenings playing backgammon or cards. We had no TV and did not intend getting one. We did not have the money to buy one, so our main entertainment was going to the movies. And we wrote long letters to family and friends, sending our pictures in the snow, always including Timmy.

# CHAPTER XXVII

## A Great Calamity

A calamity struck after a few months of Judy's arrival. She developed a cough, and as it was lingering, we went to a lung specialist I picked out from the Yellow Pages. We had no family doctor in Montreal. We had never been sick to need one. We did not even have health insurance. I don't know if it existed then. I don't remember. In any case, in Egypt we did not have any insurance. The doctors charged you according to your standard of living. The doctor we consulted in Montreal diagnosed that it was tuberculosis. The sky fell on top of our heads. TB? Are you kidding? He reassured us that most of the white race had TB germs in their bodies, which sometimes manifested themselves when one had a weak immune system but more often not. He also said that almost all Eskimos had TB. Some reassurance that was. He gave her a great quantity of pills to swallow and also wanted to check me out. X-rays of my lungs were taken, and it became apparent, from the image of a very old scar on one of my lungs, that I had had TB when I was young. I already knew this because I had taken X-rays for my U.S. visa and that problem had been cleared away.

We were in a dilemma. There was no question that Judy would continue working in Montreal while having TB. We therefore decided that she should go back to Cairo and be treated there in her family atmosphere. We had an excellent family doctor there, an Italian who had taken care of Ma and my grandmother in the past. We did not tell Ma the reason of Judy's return. She would have been in hysterics thinking that Judy was on her deathbed. Judy just wrote to her that she did not like Montreal and preferred to return to Egypt. I wrote to the doctor and asked him to contact Ma and transmit the news to her gently.

After Judy left Montreal, K and I resumed our normal lives, and things were going rather well. At this time, we had a number of friends—Canadians, British, French, and Egyptians. There was only a sprinkling of Armenians in Montreal. They arrived in masses in the 1960s, mostly from Egypt, where the political situation got worse, and it was difficult for non-Muslims to get jobs. The reason for this being that office work, up to that time, was done in English and in French—no Arabic had been needed. But the new government insisted that people learn Arabic and work in Arabic. Egypt was little by little losing its international flavor much to the dismay of the European ethnic minorities.

K and I went on weekends with our friends to Lake Champlain in the United States. We were not supposed to go out of Canada until we obtained our residence permits. We had no visas to enter the United States either, but we pretended we were Canadians. The border guards did not ask for IDs; they asked for our names. How silly of them but convenient for us. We, therefore, put on a French-Canadian accent and gave phony names. Our car had a Canadian license plate, so we passed through the border without a problem. Coming back to Canada was no problem either. We would have gotten our residence permits much sooner had the Hungarian Revolution not taken place. Because of the massive Hungarian refugees, our application was being delayed. Bummer. The Hungarians had priority. Damn them! We were taking a big risk but we were young, fearless, and foolish. We did not get caught.

A few months after Judy's departure, K and I began to fight again. He was being unreasonable at small things, details of which I do not remember. I felt in a bind. I had started having some feelings toward Les, my Irish boss, and was curious to find out how far it would go. He had made it a point to meet me for coffee after coming off the bus in the mornings. I was never one for the phrase "till death do us part," not at twenty-one anyway. Are you kidding me? I could not imagine not having feelings for other men. I considered it unnatural.

"I think we should separate for a while and take a break from each other," I ventured to utter one day after a bitter argument with K about something trivial. It was always something trivial.

K looked at me, his jaw dropped, and he was mute. Obviously, he did not expect this outburst from me.

He finally came up with, "Are you joking?"

"No, I'm not. We are fighting every day, so let's try for a separation. No big deal. After a year, we could make a decision whether we would like to continue this marriage."

"Is that why you did not want to have children? So you can ask for a separation?"

"Don't be silly. It has not entered my mind to have children. We don't earn enough, and I don't see myself cooped up at home all day long taking care of child and a household while you go to work. I want to continue working also. You knew this when you married me. I am not the housewife type, and we are too young to have children anyway," I retorted. "I want to have a life first. We are not in Egypt. We would not be able to afford any help, and my parents are not here to help me out."

We came to an agreement to live apart. I sent our cat, Timmy, to Cairo by plane. There were no jets then, and I don't know how this cat survived the plane ride and arrived in Cairo safe and sound. My friends thought I was crazy and that I should have given the cat away. No way. Timmy was like a child to me, and I adored him, and I could not possibly think of giving him away. He was used to Judy, and I was confident that my parents would take good care of him.

When my family picked him up at the airport, they noticed a sign put on his cage: "Tiger, beware." I suppose people had tried to touch him, and he had hissed at them violently. Poor Timmy, he was no tiger. He was the most gentle cat, ever. I was so relieved that he had a safe journey. Judy wrote to me, saying that he made himself at home immediately and got along with Mickey, our Siamese cat.

# CHAPTER XXVIII

## Life without a Husband

When K and I moved out of our apartment, I rented a room in a house owned by an older woman, who was a neighbor of Mrs. Mira, the childhood friend of Ma whose husband had been my boss at Sun Life Insurance in Cairo. It was a tiny room, the tiniest room I have ever seen—a bed, a dresser, and a cupboard, nothing else. Some of my stuff was stored in Mrs. Mira's basement. Mrs. Mira offered that I eat with them in the evenings and on the weekends. I accepted the offer by paying her my share. I liked being with them. They had a good family atmosphere and had a daughter and a son. She was Jewish, and he was Catholic of Maltese origin, and they had been deported from Egypt at the outcome of the 1956 war as they held British passports. Before that, he had been excommunicated from the Catholic church for marrying a Jewish woman.

Now I was finally free to accept dates from Les. We went out now and again, and sometimes we ended the evening in his apartment to make out. He was an excellent kisser, but that was all we did. He did not make moves for anything further. Actually, I was surprised, but he was a gentleman, and I guess he felt I was not ready.

I had two girlfriends from work with whom I went out to bars to socialize. It was such a new thing for me to date guys, especially having been with one man, the only man, for six years.

One evening, while listening to some music in a bar, we met a couple of guys from Yorkshire, England, and the older one, Rick, fell for me. He was much older than I was. He had served with the British Army in Cairo during the war and was fascinated with my background. I was flattered, but I did not fall for him. He was just fun to be with and had a great sense of caustic British humor.

I met quite a few guys during the time of my separation, but they were all unimportant. I was just having a good time, going to movies and parties. Nothing more. The only one I took seriously was Les, but we were not advancing in our relationship. I think he was being cautious. As for me, I was not the type to jump on him. We continued our half-assed romance.

"Do you intend to get a divorce?" he asked me one day after a lengthy session on the couch.

"I guess so, but I don't know when and how. I might get one in Egypt if and when I go back on vacation."

"When would that be?"

"When I get my official Canadian residency papers."

"Are you looking forward to it?"

"The Canadian residency papers or my divorce?"

We both laughed then.

"I am more interested in the divorce," he said.

That was the end of the conversation. Well, it was one step forward. I surmised that he had plans vis-à-vis ME!

I wanted to change jobs again, but first, my desire was to revisit Egypt and see my family. I was so homesick. I had saved enough money by then and decided to leave my job and take an extended vacation as soon as I got my official residence permit. Jobs were easy to find in Montreal—no worries in that domain.

It was the beginning of summer of 1959. Judy had recovered from her TB and had a prestigious job working at NAMRU, the American Naval Medical Research Unit, where they did scientific experiments on monkeys. Her boss seemed to be her man friend, a guy much older than she was. Judy seemed to be attracted to older guys, and I wondered whether it was because she craved a father figure.

Our father was so young. He was not the patriarch type at all. I don't ever remember him using harsh words in the house. He never even sanctioned us.

# CHAPTER XXIX

## Return to Cairo

I finally got my official Canadian residency papers. It had taken three years to process.

I was overjoyed. This was a big burden off my back. I was now free to travel out of the country. Of course, my first destination was going to be Egypt. I was so homesick and craved my family. We had been separated for three long years. I was also curious to find out how Cairo had changed since I had left in 1956.

I bought a return ticket as I planned to return to Montreal after my trip.

Being overexcited on the airplane was an understatement. I could not even doze off thinking of my homecoming. I made a stopover in Rome and spent the night in a hotel. At the airport, I realized I did not have my gold chain with a cross, my *porte-bonheur*. I remembered I had left it on the bed while taking a shower. I called the hotel and asked them to ask the chambermaid but had little hope of its recovery. My suspicion was right. My cross had disappeared. The chambermaid must have pocketed it. I wondered how she lived with the sin of stealing, being a Catholic. I was furious. It was a cross given to me by my parents when I was ten, and I always wore it around my neck and took it off only when bathing.

I finally arrived at Cairo airport, which, in fact, is in Heliopolis. All my family was there to greet me. What a heartfelt reunion it was. I cried of joy when I saw all of them. The minute I stepped off the plane, I was confronted with the relentless Egyptian sun and was surrounded with the long-forgotten smell of home. While riding home by cab from the airport, I could almost smell the jasmines from the gardens of the villas.

My parents had not changed much, and Judy was the same with a more confident air about her. And my cats, they welcomed me too. They had not forgotten me. I hugged them all and would not let them go. The taxi took us to our building, and I was greeted by all the shop owners adjacent to it. I felt so much at home as though I had never been away. Tears welled in my eyes and trickled down my cheeks. They all greeted me with big smiles.

I was so tired from the flight and did not know what to do first, whether to go to bed or yak all morning. Ma came to the rescue and gave me a belladonna pill to make me relax and tucked me in bed. I slept the sleep of angles and, upon waking up, a feast was ready for me in the dining room. All that homemade food. I was in heaven.

I had my own bedroom now, no longer sharing one with Judy. I got the bedroom with the closet that had the three-pane mirror, where I scrutinized the shape of my nose. I looked at it again now and was satisfied with it. I went from room to room to see what had changed. Not much. I sat in the north-side balcony in the evenings and looked at the people strolling by, going to the metro station. The tattered couch was still in its place in the south-side balcony, and I enjoyed taking naps, listening to the chirping of the birds. Often, Timmy and Mickey would join me on the couch.

Life was great. We were all together again.

During my days in Cairo, I realized that people still had great social lives, and I certainly intended to benefit from it. This was going to be an "all play" vacation, something I needed badly.

Would I be able to leave my family behind again and return to the cold of Montreal?

First thing I did was become a temporary member of the Heliolido Sporting Club in Heliopolis. When I was living there, we could not afford the membership fee at this club, but now I could with Canadian dollars in my pocket. I loved swimming and went swimming every day in their Olympic-size pool.

One day I was alone in the swimming pool except for one guy at the other end. He swam toward me and introduced himself. His name was José and he was a Christian Palestinian. He was the son of one of the owners of the King David Hotel in Jerusalem, which was bombed by the Zionist paramilitary group during the Israeli Independence war in 1946. His parents had died, but he had managed to escape with the help of family members and came to Egypt. He had quite a story to tell. I was fascinated by the story of Palestine.

"You are new here," he said.

"Yes, I am in Helio (short for Heliopolis) for the summer only. I am visiting from Montreal," I replied.

He then invited me to lunch, and we became friends. He wanted to be more than a friend, but I did not go along with it. I was not attracted to him physically. He was not my type. He was short, and his face did not exude sensuality. His blue eyes were cold. He introduced me to his group of friends. They were Lebanese, Syrians, and Palestinians, no Armenians. Finally, I was in the foreign crowd of Cairo. We had good times together at parties, lots of parties. I quite fancied a Copt graduate student who was planning to go to Miami to study medicine. He was the water-skiing champion of Egypt, good-looking fellow, and he knew it. I would have loved to have a fling with him, but common sense prevailed, and I did not follow through with my impulses. It would have been short-lived and meaningless.

My sister introduced me to her crowd, and I met quite a few other male specimens. They were all so eager to go out with a girl who had lived in Montreal. Also, having been married, they thought I would be easily beddable and would have no qualms.

Wrong.

Finally, I was meeting foreign men, some eligible bachelors. I just flirted with them but smothered their hopes of getting to "know" me better. The situation in Egypt was uncertain, and I did not wish to indulge in some hopeless romance with no future. People were making plans to leave Egypt, to immigrate to Canada or Australia, two countries that easily accepted immigrants from Egypt. They asked me a lot of questions about Montreal.

Life was extremely enjoyable for me living at home, not having to work, just making myself pretty, meeting old friends, going to parties, and socializing. However, because of the uncertainty of the political situation, I did not intend to stay on in Cairo. My plan was that I would return to Montreal, make every effort to get into the United States and bring my family over.

I visited all my old haunts—the elementary school, the social club, and the sports club. I also went to the Pyramids and the zoo. I loved having lunch in the tea garden there. The main dish was *macaroni au four* (macaroni in the oven), not as good as Ma's, but it was acceptable.

Luckily, we did not have one of these *khamsins* that summer. The gods were with me. I got used to the hot weather again and roamed the elegant streets of Cairo, always after sundown, when a gentle breeze would swish the tree branches. It did not rain either that summer. What luck.

One day there was a big group of us at the swimming pool. I met an Armenian acquaintance who had just broken off with her Egyptian Muslim man friend. Good-looking woman. She was divorced and was free to date. I was introduced to her ex-boyfriend, and I liked him. His name was Nabil, and he was really handsome, dark and foreboding, oozing power, the macho type. We conversed about this and that. He was a lieutenant colonel in the army. That was the time of the Egyptian military being in power, and most of the high-ranking officers in the army were playboys. They were impeccably dressed in well-tailored suits and had good manners toward women. They had Christian girlfriends, Lebanese and Syrians mostly. Muslim girls were not in the dating game.

A few days later, the doorbell rang, and I came face-to-face with Nabil, dressed in a pale blue crisp cotton shirt open to show some chest hair and a gold medallion hanging around his neck. I was taken aback.

"What are you doing here?" I asked him.

"I came to ask your mother if I could take you out to lunch at the sporting club," he replied with a charming grin.

"How did you find out my address?"

"Easy, just asked a few friends at the club. Would you like to go out to lunch with me?"

"Come in and wait in the hall. I'll go tell my mother," I replied, feeling a little giddy.

I went into the kitchen, where Ma was cooking, and told her I was going out with Nabil for lunch.

"Are you crazy?" asked Ma.

"Why? What's wrong?"

"He is the ex-boyfriend of one of your old friends. That's why," she said.

"So what? He is an ex, not a present boyfriend."

"It is just not done. What will people think?"

Again, the same phrase "what will people think." I was sick and tired of hearing this phrase all the time before getting married, and here I was, hearing it again.

"I am going," I said, gathering up my things, and went out with Nabil for lunch at the club. We went out a couple of times after that, but I did not succumb to his charms. He was tempting, I must say. I was adamant not to have any relationship in Egypt as I had decided to return to Montreal, much as I loved my life here now in Cairo. I knew the *dolce vita* atmosphere would not last; things were changing too fast.

"Don't you want to stay here with us and not return to Montreal?" Ma asked me one day.

"No, I want to go back. Although I know there are plenty of job opportunities for me here, I can't see myself restarting in Cairo. Yes, it is a safe place, the social life is still fabulous, but for how long? People are going away in droves. Things will change rapidly."

Rick and I were corresponding, him telling me how much he missed me. I did not miss him in the least because I didn't really consider him as being my boyfriend. He thought he was. One day I got a letter from him telling me that he was now seeing Trudy, one of my best friends. I was not surprised. I had not shown any particular interest in him. I was glad he understood my feelings without me spelling them out for him. And I was also glad that he took up with Trudy. I thought they were quite suitable for each other. They both liked to drink till the wee hours of the morning.

Departure time came again—too soon, after three months of paradise.

It was a tear-jerking moment, with Ma telling me she did not know when she would see me again with the situation being so uncertain in Egypt, now that the military was in power. Judy was waiting for me to move to the United States so that she would also immigrate to the States to join me. She was happy at her work, with her social life and with her boss being her man friend. She liked him a lot, and I don't know why she did not want to pursue her relationship. Being married to an American with an important and prestigious job in Egypt was the next best thing to leaving Egypt and going to the United States. But then Judy always followed in my footsteps.

Pa's situation was the same. Good one day, bad the next. I vowed to bring them over to the States if and when I landed over there one day. I had not forgotten my dream. It was constantly on my mind.

# CHAPTER XXX

## Return to Montreal

A few days after my return to Montreal, K called me up and invited me out to dinner. I was not surprised. We had kept up a friendly relationship since our separation, and he knew I had gone to Egypt. He was hungry for up-to-date news. I had not seen him in over six months. I prettied myself up, and off I went. It felt like I was going on a date with a new guy. He complimented me profusely on my looks, and I enjoyed the dinner. We talked and laughed a lot. Toward the end of the dinner, he took my hands in his and, looking straight into my eyes, asked me if I would like to get back with him. I was not expecting this proposal. I had suggested a year of separation, and I was not prepared to give an answer. The year had not yet passed, and I had just returned to Montreal, and Les wanted to see me. I was envisaging getting seriously back with Les. But now I had a choice: K or Les. I looked at him and realized that I really liked him more now, after having gone out with a few men who did not really take my fancy as long-time partners. Also, Les was the unknown, foreign element. I had a long way to go before feeling comfortable with him.

Therefore, I said yes, and we kissed, and it was thrilling again. I thought I had made the right decision. Restarting with K kindled some of the initial attraction I had toward him.

Maybe that was the answer to everyday married life, separate for a while and then get back together and start all over again.

I called Les and felt embarrassed telling him that I had returned to my husband. He was disappointed.

Letter writing to my family continued. Ten pages back and forth. They were also surprised at my decision of going back to K.

K and I moved to a condo in the town of Mount Royal, where we could take the train to the main station in Montreal. This facilitated our lives because we did not have to walk in the snow and take buses. My workplace was in the building of the train station. All I had to do was take an elevator. The bank, the post office, the cleaners were all in the same building, so were a couple of eating places.

My next job was with ICAO, the International Civil Aviation Organization, an affiliated agency of the UN. They offered six weeks' vacation time a year and various other benefits. I was a secretary again, taking dictation and transcribing. Boring. My officemates were fun though. We kept wondering whether our boss was gay. He was shy and did not look straight into your eyes. The girls I worked with, French Canadians from wealthy families, were outrageous. They had steady boyfriends but went on one-night stands with American businessmen who visited Montreal on weekends. I was astounded. I asked questions. The answers somehow made sense.

"We are still young. Why not have more fun?" they said.

"What if your boyfriends find out?" I asked.

"Nah, no chance, we cover for each other."

K and I resumed our lives, and we still went dancing once a week. K now had a more prestigious job. The funny thing is that, as a photographer, he often took wedding pictures, and more often than not, the bride happened to be pregnant. Therefore, the photo shoots had to exclude the waist down portion of the bride. This never happened in Egypt. Brides were never pregnant because they did not indulge in sexual activities before the wedding. They fooled around, but it stopped at the crucial moment. I only knew of one girl who went all the way with her boyfriend. She got pregnant, had an abortion, but ended up getting married to him.

Astonishingly, some Catholic priests happened to have mistresses, and K was invited to their homes to take photos of them together with their women friends but without their priestly garbs. This shocked us to no end, and we were amused at the morality that reigned in the province of Catholic Quebec. What kind of religiousness was that? I even had a girlfriend whose sister was the mistress of a Catholic priest.

All this talk at the office about fooling around with other men made me curious. I had not been unfaithful to K. Yes, I had gone out with other guys during our separation period, but nothing had expired. Just kissing, nothing further. Was I destined to sleep with only man throughout my life? That was not a destiny I cherished. I thought I should at least have one sexual experience for comparison purposes.

One evening, we were invited to a party at a friend's house and met a few new people. A tall Spaniard was one of them. He had come with his gorgeous German girlfriend, a model. The dance music was fabulous. I got up and danced the *paso doble* and *flamenco* with K, showing off our talent. I got the Spaniard's attention, his name was Juan, and he asked me to dance with him a couple of times.

"You dance the Spanish dances very well," he said. "How come?"

"I have always loved dancing, especially to Latin music and the rock and roll," I told him.

Then he asked for my phone number.

"I am married, Juan," I said.

"And so?"

"What do you mean and so? I can't go out with you, that's what, and you have a girlfriend."

"And so?" he repeated with a grin. He was trying to work his charms on me. I was not fooled.

I had told him that I went to art history classes at McGill University on Wednesday evening and found out that he was a student in civil engineering at the same university.

"I'll pick you up from your class and take you home," he said.

I just looked at him hesitantly and then agreed.

Why did I agree? I agreed because I wanted some spice. I was not thinking of being unfaithful. After all, he was only going to walk me to the train station. I saw no harm in that. A little flirtation, I thought, would be good for me.

True to his word, Juan was waiting for me at the exit on Wednesday evening. As we were walking and chatting, we passed by a building, and he stopped in front of it.

"A friend of mine lives here," he said. "Let's go up and say hello."

"Okay," I said, not seeing anything wrong in that.

We went up on the elevator, came to an apartment door, and instead of Juan ringing the doorbell, he took out a key from his pocket and opened the door. I looked at him, puzzled.

"My friend has given me the key," he said.

"Where is he?" I asked.

"He'll be here shortly."

I just followed him inside the apartment.

"Do you want to have something to drink?" he asked.

"No, I can't stay long. My husband will wonder why I am late," I said lamely.

He then started kissing me. I resisted. I did not particularly like his kissing style, all tongue and saliva, and I drew away from him. It all felt wrong. I should have curtailed my curiosity. I was not prepared for this.

He got hold of my arm and threw me on the bed. He was a big fellow and quite determined. I resisted and fought him off with difficulty, but I managed to do so and stood up.

"What on earth are you doing? You're such a bastard. I hate you," I said.

It all felt so awkward. What was I thinking following Juan to this apartment? I picked up my coat and handbag and walked toward the door without saying another word. Juan turned out to be a slobbering Spaniard with no manners. All my initial attraction toward him vanished.

"I am so sorry," he said. "You can't imagine how irresistible you are."

I still did not say anything and just walked out the door. He followed me, being apologetic all the time as we were walking.

"Leave me alone!" I barked at him.

"Say you'll forgive me," he insisted.

"Never."

At the train station, he wanted to give me a peck on the cheek, but I pushed him away.

"Will I see you again?" he asked.

"Definitely not."

He still kept apologizing and kept repeating that he could not help himself. I did not wish to hear anything more.

I could not sleep that night lying next to K. I was so ashamed of myself for having fallen into such a trap. Was I so stupid? Or just plain dumb? Days went by, and I saw Juan again the week after, at the exit of my art class.

"I'll just walk you over to the train station," he said. "I don't want you to think badly of me."

"I am not thinking of you at all," I replied. "Please stop harassing me."

Nevertheless, he walked me to the station in silence, and that was that.

My relationship with K improved after that incident. My experience with Juan was so bad that I was happy being with K. I was also glad that it had not gone all the way.

My eyes and mind stopped roving for a while.

One day I met a Belgian guy near the elevators in ICAO. He was from Geneva and in Montreal on business. He invited me for a coffee downstairs at the train station. Why did I accept? Because I liked the attention of men. I realized then that I was not made to be married. I was too young and impulsive and still had a roving eye. Biblical verses regarding infidelity came popping into my mind.

What did I really want out of life? Did I really want to stay married? Marriage should be a serious commitment, and I don't think I had been ready for that.

The guy's name was Norbert. He was interesting and amusing and wanted to take me out while he was in Montreal. I told him I was married. He was also married. I refused his advances. Nothing good would come out of it. He told me to look him up if I ever came to Geneva.

What a far-fetched idea.

I took up painting in Montreal, which had been my passion since I was a child in Egypt. The living room was used as my studio. Looking out the window at the abundant snow outside, I painted imaginary abstract landscapes drenched in sunlight. A gallery on Crescent Street agreed to exhibit my paintings, and I was thrilled. My very first solo exhibition. I invited all my friends to the opening, and I managed to make a few sales. I hated parting with my canvases, though. It was the first time, and I was attached to them.

The year before, I had taken part in a group exhibition and had been awarded an honorary mention for a totally abstract oil painting. I still have that one and will never sell it. The funny thing was that at first, I had submitted a nude painting to this group show. It got rejected because "children would attend the exhibition, and nudity was not permitted," I was told.

I suppose these children had never been to Europe or seen the Sistine Chapel with all the nudes on the ceiling or the nude statues in the streets of arty Italian cities.

# CHAPTER XXXI

## Boston

At this time, K was putting a lot of effort to find a job in the United States. We were getting along very well, thank God. He applied at a renowned photographer's firm in Boston and got accepted. They liked the photos he had sent them. Before they could bring him over with a special work visa, they had to first advertise for an associate all over the United States for six months. That was the law. Then they pretended no applicant matched their requirements and offered the job to K. We were elated that we would finally go to the United States—both of us had dreamed about it in Egypt, and it was finally happening.

What a journey it had been—from Cairo to Montreal, which we considered as a stepping-stone to the United States—five years in the cold, slush, snow and unfamiliar surroundings, which we adapted to quite quickly. Different culture, different people, different customs.

My impossible dream had come through. Next step was Manhattan. That was where my future lay. To be a designer in Manhattan, the most vibrant city in the United States. I had dreamed about this all my life, and I had prayed.

Yes, I do believe in prayer.

We moved to Boston.

We found Boston to be an unfriendly city. We were both sociable animals, but we did not make any friends except for one couple—she was French and he was American from from Paris—whom we met accidentally at a red light stop. We were both in our cars. From then on, we were inseparable.

We used to roam the streets of Cambridge at nights to look for entertainment, and we were shocked to see young people sprawled on the floor of buildings, almost unconscious, drugged to the core. We were told they were outsiders, not Harvard students. Drugs were à la mode among the university students, so who could tell the difference between outsiders and Harvard students? We were never tempted to use any. We did not need to get high; we were already high.

I scoured the Yellow Pages for design houses, and I found one—the House of Bianchi. I asked K's fellow workers whether they had heard of them. In fact, they had. It was a high fashion firm run by two Italian sisters. They were specialized in high-end bridal and bridesmaid gowns. I had no experience in formal designing, nor had I gone to design school, but I had designed dresses for friends and family back in Egypt, and I had designed my own wedding dress. I had also taken a patternmaking course by correspondence in Montreal.

I made an appointment and went to apply for the job, dressed in one of my own designs—a beige suit with a silk coral-colored blouse. The reception hall was quite classy. I was received by the two sisters seated behind an ornate desk. They were ordinary-looking women, rather homely. I was asked to sit, and they interviewed me.

"I have studied fashion design and worked in Paris with *Chloe et Cie*," I said, inventing a bridal design house. This was not the age of the internet and there was no way of checking. My heart was racing, but I kept a stoic demeanor. They believed me but were still hesitating.

"If you would try me out for a week without pay, I would be willing to show you what I can do," I said.

"We cannot hire you without pay, but we'll give you a minimum wage and try you out for a week" was their reply. "When can you start?"

"Any time you wish."

"Can you come in tomorrow then? And bring your own tools."

I was thrilled, and my heart was aflutter. I had my first designing job at last. I was extremely confident that I could do the job satisfactorily.

My co-designers were two gay men, and they adopted me quite enthusiastically.

I was given a 4' x 10' table and was told to start making patterns with a hard, plastic material. I went over to the gay guys and asked them how things were done in the United States, pretending that I had another way of doing patterns, which, in fact, I did not. They gladly showed me, and off I was on my way, creating wedding dresses for the House of Bianchi. The Bianchi sisters were satisfied with my work, and they raised my salary after a week as they had promised they would.

I was now a full-fledged designer for the House of Bianchi, designing wedding and bridesmaid dresses.

The funny thing is that one of the gay guys liked one of my paintings, a nude woman (who looked like me), and wanted to buy it. I wondered why a gay guy would buy a painting of a nude woman. Did he by any chance have bisexual feelings? He paid a down payment and took it home. A couple of weeks later, he came back and apologetically returned it, and I gave him back his money. Maybe his partner objected to his choice.

The House of Bianchi had clients from all over the Eastern United States.

After a few successes of my designs being sold to their clients, I got brazen and decided to design an A-line wedding dress. I wanted to get away from the bouffant skirts with umpteen crinolines and intricately designed bodices with puffed-up sleeves. I created a simple, slimline, elegant model with no extra trimmings. I chose a beautiful ornate fabric, which in itself enhanced the dress. There was no need for added beading or frills. The sisters liked it but were hesitant to present it to their clients, thinking the latter would see too much of a difference compared with their regular designs.

Then they had a bright idea.

The day came to show their collection to the buyers in their studio showroom. They asked me to model my own two creations.

"What?" I asked.

"You are a size 8, and we are sure you can model your designs better than a regular model," the sisters said.

"If you say so," was all I could utter and was thrilled at the prospect. After all, I knew how to act like a model as I had posed for my husband regularly. I was not shy. I had my hair cascading over one shoulder and walked the gangplank of the showroom, confidently showing my two designs. They got a lot of applause and praise, and it was a success. After that venture, I was free to design as I saw fit. My creations appeared in *Bazaar* and *Vogue* but not under my own name, of course. The House of Bianchi got the credit. I was a little disappointed, but that was how things were in the design world.

# CHAPTER XXXII

## Manhattan

We stayed in Boston for six months only. K was transferred with the same photo company to Manhattan—our dream city. I was focused on getting ahead as a designer. It was easy for me to get designing jobs, the market being full of them, but I had to be clever. I was sometimes asked to leave my portfolio when I applied for a position "for a better look," but I always refused, knowing what would happen. They would copy my models and then tell me I did not get the job.

We rented an apartment in West New York—which is in New Jersey—overlooking the fabulous skyline of Manhattan that turned to gold at dusk. Excellent transportation into Manhattan. A bus in front of the condo every five minutes, stuffed to the brim. A short walk from the bus station at Port Authority to Seventh Avenue, where most of the designing houses were located.

Manhattan had its peculiar smell. It was charged with energy, and I could almost feel the electricity in the air. I vowed to make it in this high-powered city.

I worked as designer for sports clothes, town apparel, cocktail gowns, even bathing suits, where I also had to model one once—step in a bathtub to make sure it was not transparent and did not show nipples or fanny.

I did not particularly like any of the jobs. The owners were small-time manufacturers who used my talents and then let me go. One wife got jealous that her husband was paying too much attention to me. Another place just used me to do the pattern of a special kind of sleeve. Yet another place was so dusty that I developed a sinus problem, and when I complained, I was fired. I did not care, though, for design jobs were easy to find.

I applied to one job for town apparel; the owner was Jewish. He had one look at my sophisticated designs and said, "Can you design less sophisticated clothes? Most of my clients are Jewish, and they like whorish clothes." I was appalled at this remark and did not like him at all. He seemed to have little regard for women.

"Sorry, I can't do that," I told him, and I did not accept the job. Designing whorish clothes? My reputation would plummet big time.

Finally, I found a good position with a cocktail dress designer. His name was Philip Hulitar. He was a gentleman. I enjoyed my job. I liked designing elegant evening dresses with fancy fabrics. That was my forte. My designing space was a cubicle with no window. I used one of the big tables in the sewing room to cut my patterns.

Philip called me into his office after a couple of months.

"Peggy, I am going into hospital for an operation and, as I will be absent, I would like you to keep an eye on Tom, the purchasing manager. I think he is cheating and invoicing me for more fabric than is actually being used."

"How can I do that, Philip? I have no access to his files," I said.

"Try and do it discreetly," he insisted.

How could I possibly do that? Tom was a cocky older guy who thought he was the boss when Philip went to the hospital. A week later, he fired me because he got wise into what I was doing, going in and out of his office, measuring fabrics, and so forth. I could not complain to Philip. He was still in the hospital.

Our life in New York was all work. No social life. We did not know anybody. The only enjoyment we had was to go to a nightclub called Chateau Madrid. Dancing was still our passion. We danced to Cuban bands—musicians who had escaped from Cuba after the revolution. I have not found a better partner than K for dancing. Too bad he passed away early—we had become friends after the divorce.

I liked the museums and galleries in Manhattan and visited them quite often. I was painting frenetically in my spare time and was looking for gallery representation. A difficult task. I also liked walking up and down Fifth Avenue, dressed in trendy outfits and high heels (how stupid of me), and window-shopping. Saks was my favorite store, and I bought some stuff from there. I was making good money and could afford to do so.

We also liked to walk in Central Park but never at night. We were told it was quite dangerous. We did not like Queens, but we liked Brooklyn. It had a certain charm, and of course, we explored Greenwich Village, where the beatniks hung out. I did not particularly care for them.

One of my jobs as a fashion designer was with Ann Lowe, Jackie Kennedy's wedding dress designer. She was a black woman from the South. She had a small designing studio. Ann was an excellent designer. Her eyesight was failing though, and that was why she hired me and another younger girl. Before that, she was doing all the designing herself. The other girl was only a sketcher. She did not know how to make patterns. When you are designing clothes, you need to know everything: how the fabric yields, how to do a pattern of your sketch. Is it comfortable to wear? Where would the zipper or the buttons be? Everything has to be considered. Ann got rid of the girl and kept me as her principal designer. I learned a lot from Ann. She used to finish the dresses on the inside with lace sewn on the seams. It was an extravaganza. The inside of the dress looked almost as finished as the outside. I then started sewing my own dresses that way. Waste of time, but I enjoyed the challenge and the outcome of the finished product.

Women from all over the United States came to her studio for their bridal, mother of the bride, and bridesmaid dresses. They were such snobby women, so proud of their money and so proud to have their clothes designed by Jackie Kennedy's designer. The rumor was that Jackie had not liked the dress. It was her father-in-law who had ordered it. And she never once mentioned, in any of her ramblings, that it was a black woman who had designed it. She was so much taken in by Oleg Cassini and French designers.

I was happy working there, almost my own boss, but the pay was not enough.

I told Ann that I would be looking for another job because I needed more money, and I knew she could not afford to pay me more.

"Peggy, I have an idea," she said one day. "Why don't you take over my business? I can't continue alone. I am getting too old, and my eyesight is failing. You're just the right person. You've got a head on your shoulders, and my clients love your designs."

I was flattered, but I could see a huge drawback.

"Ann, I would love to do that, but I can't work with your seamstresses. (They were all black women.) No matter how hard I try, there is reverse discrimination toward me. They don't like following my instructions. You know me well, Ann, I am not bossy. If I took over your business, I would have to fire them all and employ new people who would listen to me."

"That would be too bad, Peggy. You see, they are all relatives and rely on me for their livelihood. I can't let them go."

She was saddened, but I could not help it. The matter was decided. There was no deal.

# CHAPTER XXXIII

## Ma and Judy in New York

Finally, in spring 1962, Ma and Judy made all the arrangements to come to the United States. Ma would come on a tourist visa. As she had a British passport, this was easy. Judy would come as an immigrant as she was born in Switzerland, and the Swiss quota was wide open. Pa would not be able to come, not yet—he was Egyptian born. No exit visa was granted from Egypt if the United States did not accept Egyptians as tourists. We had to find a way and soon. His situation was not brilliant in Egypt. He was teaching at the Armenian elementary school and doing the accounting of the social club, but he earned peanuts.

I had the bright idea of meeting Ma and Judy in Cannes to take the transatlantic ship with them to New York. I flew to Paris and reconnected with Aram and his wife. They showed me all the important Parisian sights. It was heaven to be in Paris, eat European food, and hear decent French spoken. I particularly enjoyed strolling around the left bank and visiting art galleries. I sat in outdoor cafés, sipping *une demie* (a glass of beer, as they called it in France), watching the people walk by.

After a few days in Paris, I took the train to Cannes to wait for their arrival. It was the first time I was seeing Cannes, and I was excited, sitting in a café at the harbor, impatiently waiting for them to disembark. I ordered a *café au lait* and watched the people. Café society. I watched the yachts in the harbor and imagined myself on one of them. I had a sudden yearning to live and work in Europe but told myself to stop daydreaming and jumping all over the planet. I had to focus. Part of my family was coming to New York, and that was what I should be concentrating on.

We had taken a decision. We were going to live in New York. *"Un point, c'est tout"* (meaning full stop, and that's that).

Carrying my heavy suitcase (no wheels on suitcases at that time), I went to meet them at the docks. I had tears in my eyes when I embraced them. Tears of joy. They were extremely tired because of everything they had to handle in Cairo, selling the furniture and dealing with other stuff. We took a porter to take us to our ship.

We were traveling cabin class. We had separate cabins. For dinner, we were seated at the purser's table in the dining room. I wore one of my handmade cocktail dresses on the first evening. A few years back, Pa had gotten some material when he was doing one of the rooms of King Farouk's Abdeen Palace—a *bois de rose* silk taffeta fabric with fancy tassels, which I had transformed into a cocktail dress with a shawl garnished with the dangling tassels of the curtains. I sold this dress to the Museum of Art and History in Geneva, together with some of Ma's ballroom dresses, much later.

I danced a few times with some guys seated at our table. Nothing to rave about. Ordinary guys. I always wanted to meet the extra-ordinary. But where?

The big surprise was that Anthony Quinn was on the same boat, in first class.

One day I was swimming in the swimming pool of the cabin class, and he was watching me from the deck above. The purser came and told me that Anthony Quinn was inviting me to the first-class swimming pool. I was astounded and flattered. I did not particularly like him as a man, but hey, he was a famous actor, and he wanted to meet me. I agreed, and taking Judy along, we went upstairs. We set by the pool and chatted. Then he invited me for cocktails and the movies that evening. There was always a movie every night on the boat. I declined because I guessed where this was heading to, and I did not want to complicate my life. I certainly did not want to take up with an actor. They had egos as huge as ocean liners.

The funny thing is that a year later, I met him at my dentist's office in Manhattan. He was with a young woman, who was all over him. He recognized me and winked. I just smiled.

We arrived in New York Harbor. Great commotion.

K met us, and we drove to our apartment in New Jersey. Ma and Judy took over our second bedroom, which I was using as my painting studio. I don't know how they fit in that small room with all the suitcases they had brought over. Luckily, we had a good-size walk-in closet in the hall. There was only one bathroom. They were surprised that there was no balcony and that all the windows were screened. It was so different from our apartment in Heliopolis, where we enjoyed large balconies and all windows were wide open all the time.

We later learned that Pa had given up our apartment and was sleeping in one of the dressing rooms at the social club. Pa could make himself comfortable wherever he was. He had been extremely wealthy, and now he was poor. It absolutely did not matter to him. He made the most of it. He adapted without complaints to every circumstance. That was what I admired in him. He never gave up hope that life would change for the better one day.

We contacted a friend of his from the U.S. Army, who was living in Upstate New York, for a work visa for Pa. He was delighted to oblige. He said he owned two resort hotels and would like to hire Pa as the manager of one. It would take time, though, to do all the formalities.

Judy soon found a prominent secretarial position at the Rockefeller Foundation a week after her arrival, and we were settled as comfortably as we could. K got along with my family. Ma did all the food shopping and the cooking. Finally, I was tasting Ma's cooking again.

Then the cats arrived. Pa sent them over with Scandinavian airlines, each in a separate basket. I don't know how these poor cats survived the long flight. We were so deliriously happy to have them with us again. They adjusted to their new life in New York quite quickly. The apartment was one-third the size of our Heliopolis apartment and had no balconies. The poor cats, they were cooped up all day long.

And I found a new job with a sports clothes manufacturer on Seventh Avenue. As I said earlier, designing jobs were easy to find in Manhattan in the 1960s.

Judy and I would meet for lunch—the short period that we had—in some hamburger joint on Seventh Avenue. We were always asked to vacate the premises as soon as we had finished eating because there was a line of hungry people outside, waiting to get in. We hated to be rushed and would order another beverage just to keep our seats.

Manhattan in the summer was unbearable. The apartment had no air-conditioning, and we did not sleep well at nights. We bought a couple of fans and made do.

Ruth, the top designer in my new job, had a female Siamese cat, and when she found out that I had a male one that had not been neutered, she suggested that we bring them together for mating purposes. The rule was that the male went to the female's abode. I took Mickey over there. After a few days, on a weekend, she called me.

"Peggy, you'll have to come and take back your cat. He bit me badly."

I was aghast. "What happened?"

"Actually, it is my fault. I interfered while they were mating, but I can't keep him. Has he been vaccinated against rabies?"

"Yes, of course," I said. After the Alice incident in Heliopolis, we had had Mickey vaccinated pronto.

What was wrong with these women? One plays with his testicles, the other interferes while he is trying to copulate. Don't they know any better? Anyway, Ruth had to go and get a tetanus shot at a clinic, and I picked up Mickey. Too bad, I would have loved to have kittens by Mickey. Ruth did not report this to the authorities, and Mickey did not have to go to quarantine like in Cairo. That was a big relief.

I don't know why I preferred the company of Ma and Judy to that of K at this time in my life. We were quarreling again. In hindsight, I was at fault somehow. I was just not affectionate toward K because I was no longer in love with him. I didn't make any effort to keep this marriage going. I was too much of a free spirit and did not like the "married" state. We were just too young to be married. Marriage was a lot of work and needed commitment, and I just did not have any.

One day K got mad over something. I don't remember what. We had a fight. A serious fight. Not about my family, that I know. He liked them and appreciated everything Ma did for the family—shopping and cooking and looking after the house. Judy was not a problem and did not bother him at all.

"I think we should separate for a while. I will go and live on my own," he said one day after a big quarrel.

"Go," I said and was surprised at my outburst. It was one of the rare times that I had shouted at him. Whatever he said or did got on my nerves lately. I was glad that he took the initiative.

Vague plans were lurking at the back of my head, making me antsy and, suddenly I had an urge to go to Europe, to travel and see new horizons and meet new people—new men.

Off he went with his clothes, the stereo, and the car. I did not need a car in New York anyway.

I continued working in the design field on Seventh Avenue.

Winter soon set in, and it was hell going to work. After arriving at the Port Authority terminal, I had to walk a few blocks in the piercing wind and the sleet. The money was good, but life was not so good. Lack of friends and entertainment was taking a toll on us. We had wanted to be in America, and here we were. Not so rosy after all.

After my initial attraction for Manhattan, I found it overwhelming with all the skyscrapers and people rushing in and out of the subway and almost trampling you to death if you happened to go in the opposite direction.

A mutual friend of ours, who had arrived from Egypt recently, started asking me out when he found out that K and I were separated. It was Arty. K did not know he had designs on me. He was Armenian and the ping-pong champion of Egypt. He had taught me how to play ping-pong at the social club when I was fifteen. He started paying me quite a bit of attention. I was rather disoriented not having a husband, and I accepted his discreet advances. I dated him a few times, and he then asked me to marry him after I would get a divorce from K. He asked me to move to L.A. with him, where he intended to take up residence and start his own business. Los Angeles sounded appealing, but I didn't accept his proposal because I didn't love him. I was looking for romance and excitement. I was not going to jump into another relationship, especially a loveless one.

My desire to go to Europe and working there started to come to the forefront of my vision.

To make more money, I went into the designing business for myself. I was interviewed by a fashion house who liked my designs and suggested that I go freelance. This meant I would be given carte blanche to choose fabrics from a certain fabric wholesaler, buy the fabrics at their expense, manufacture a size 8 dress, and sell it to them. I was a size 8 then, so I modeled it to fit me. The going rate for this kind of work was $60 a dress, excluding the fabric and any trimming. They would then take the dress apart, have patterns made in several sizes, and sell them to retailers. This was excellent pay because I could make up a dress in one day with the help of Ma. I did about five dresses a week. As a designer, I earned $150 a week. I now had two jobs and was able to save money for my European trip that was looming ahead.

# CHAPTER XXXIV

## Separation Papers from K

Friends advised me that before making plans for a European trip, I should hire a lawyer to file legal separation papers from K. It had to be a New Jersey lawyer because my residence was in that state. I don't remember how I found one.

His name was Frank with an Italian last name, which I will not divulge here because his attorney wife is still alive.

When I called to ask for an appointment, I was informed that the custom was for the lawyer to come to the home to interview the client. I found that rather strange, but I accepted.

"I suppose he wants to see how we live," said Ma, "to charge you accordingly."

On the designated day, our doorbell rang.

Frank and a woman, whom he introduced as his partner, came in. Much later, I found out that she was his wife, also a lawyer and working with him.

I told them the whole story, and she noted it down. He gave me an appointment to meet him in a restaurant the following week to discuss things further.

Why not his office?

I met him. We talked.

A slight depression had taken hold of me. I was again without a husband. Not that I yearned for K, but I was so used to him and his moods. Frank saw the state I was in and he suggested that I leave the designing field for a while, as it seemed to be rather stressful for me, and work for the NYU law school as a secretary. That job would not require my full, undivided attention. No creativity was involved, therefore no stress. He also told me that the woman who did the hiring of secretaries at the law school was very old-fashioned. He had graduated from that law school, and he knew her personally.

"You should dress very prim and proper, put stockings on, and wear white gloves. That will impress her, and you'll get hired," he advised me.

Bizarre, I thought, but those were the days when women wore gloves. I had about eleven pairs, winter and summer ones.

"All the law students will go bananas over you," he added.

I went for the interview and was hired. I guess my not crossing my legs and wearing stockings and white gloves did the trick. The salary was half that of a designer's, but it was easy work. I shared an office with a girl around my age, who was a natural redhead. I was a phony one. Patricia is still my friend after well over fifty years.

Patricia and I started a side business going. We typed theses for the law students. There were no computers then, and the students were not proficient in typing. I also "hired" my sister, and she, in turn, "hired" her coworkers, and we had a lucrative business going during office hours. We had ample time. It did not interfere with our work.

Frank then asked to see me a third time.

He warned me not to accept dates from anyone. "Just in case your husband has you followed, then he will have the advantage over you, and will accuse you of adultery and you'll not get a penny from him. You can only be seen in public with me because I am your lawyer."

I listened to him. I had the faint suspicion he was coming on to me. I must admit that I was attracted to him. He was not handsome, but he exuded strength and power and had a very convincing way of talking. Meekly, I agreed to everything he said and we filed the separation papers.

Now I was free to date.

One day a law student asked me out for a date. I agreed. His name was Simon.

"I'll come and pick you up from Jersey," he said.

The date was supposed to be the next day. Frank called me in the morning of that day and asked to see me to discuss more details. I found that rather strange. How many times was I supposed to meet my lawyer? And to discuss what? I thought we had finalized the matter of the separation.

He picked me and we went to a bar this time.

We walked to his car after having had a couple of drinks. I thought he was going to take me home, but instead, he drove to a motel, and when I refused to get out of the car, he almost carried me to the room. I could not create a fuss just outside the motel. I followed him unwillingly. Well, I thought, I could always refuse his advances once inside the room and demand that he takes me home.

That did not happen.

I don't know what had come over me. Why did I not object? I was in a zombielike trance, just following the leader. I am trying to think back but can't come up with a valid answer. I must have been taken in by his masculine charms and his way of taking charge.

I didn't like the session in the motel one bit. Extremely disappointing performance on his part. I was hoping for romance and I got sex. Stupid me. What was I thinking of? Also, I didn't particularly care for his sexual innuendoes. He made plans to see me in a couple of days, but I made up my mind to keep him on only as my lawyer and no more drinks, dinners, or motel business. Any feelings of admiration I had for him evaporated into thin air during this motel interlude. I did not tell him of my plans, not yet. No use antagonizing him before getting home safe and sound.

While driving me home, he told me that he would not charge me for the divorce proceedings. How could he? He had slept with the client. If it were ever come to light, he would be breaching the rules and would be disbarred.

Ma reprimanded me when I got home. "Simon was here, and he waited for you for over an hour. It seems you had a date with him. What happened? Why did you not show up?"

"I forgot," I replied, feeling ashamed.

"How can you forget? Did Frank hypnotize you? What will Simon think of you? He looks like a decent chap. How are you going to explain things to him?"

"I don't know."

The next day, I went to work, and Simon came over to my office and asked me what had happened. I gave him a lame excuse, and I don't know whether he believed me. He asked me out again, and this time I was home when he came to pick me up. He was a decent guy, but he did not arouse any sparks in me. Simon was a one-time date.

Frank called me and invited me for a drink to discuss "more stuff" as he put it. But this time I had my wits with me, and I did not agree to meet him. He cajoled me, but I did not budge.

For the next several days, he called and called, but I still refused to see him. He did not understand why, and I did not tell him the reason. I just told him that I was busy or that I was sick. I had come to my senses. I did not like him and did not feel like pursuing a horizontal relationship with him.

A bill arrived one day in the mailbox. It was from his law firm. The stupid fool had billed me for his services. I picked up the phone and asked to speak with him. He would not come to the phone, feigning a meeting.

"You tell him," I told the secretary, "that if he ever dares send me a bill again, I will denounce him to the New Jersey Bar Association. You can also tell him that I am firing him as my lawyer. I will take care of my own divorce proceedings. I don't need him."

The secretary just said that she would transmit the message. I don't know what she thought of me or him or whether the wife was also aware of his shenanigans; she shared the same office space.

That was the end of Frank, or so I thought.

He never contacted me again by phone or otherwise, and I threw the bill in the wastebasket.

Judy and I often went to NYU for lectures and stuff and hung around there. We met a few Egyptian students and became friends. We went out in a group. One philosophy student took a liking to Judy and a math student, a liking to me. He was such a sweet guy. Poor soul, he fell for me and wrote me love poems. Not wishing to hurt his feelings, I had a difficult time rejecting his advances. I did so gently but firmly.

Another student, also a Muslim, a more brazen one, pursued me more aggressively. I was very careful in my relationship with him. No smooching. Egyptian guys think a girl is too forward if she succumbs and then he has no respect for her. Such narrow-mindedness. He even proposed marriage so that he would become more intimate with me. He was an intelligent fellow and came from a good family, but he just was not my type. I could never be with a guy who had a rather restrictive mentality concerning the female sex. Middle Eastern men tend to be this way.

After six months, the trial separation was over, and K and I were summoned to court to determine whether we really wanted to go through with the divorce.

Lo and behold, Frank was in the courtroom.

I went up to him.

"I thought I had made it clear to you that you were fired and that I didn't need you for this hearing," I said, looking straight at his downcast eyes.

"I know, I know, but I have to finish the work I started. I will not bill you, don't worry. I would also like to talk to your mother, by the way," he said.

Ma and Judy had accompanied me to the courthouse. Frank took us aside and told us how the procedure would go and advised me on replies to certain questions I would be asked by the judge.

I listened to him without uttering a word.

I really pitied K that day. His lawyer, a mousy older guy, was nothing compared to Frank, who was eloquent and exuded strength and was master of the proceedings, making a case out of nothing. I must admit he was imposing.

When K was asked whether he would like to go back to being my husband, he meekly answered, "if she wants me to."

When I was asked the same question, I replied in the negative while in the meantime thinking maybe I should go back to him, but my senses got the better of me. I wanted to be free, did I not? What was I thinking? I had already had one separation two years ago. Now this was the second one. How many separations did I need to determine whether I wanted a future with K? The problem was that I was so used to him. After all, I had been with him for eleven years. There was nothing basically wrong with him. It was just me. I wanted to be free from marital ties or any ties for that matter. I thought I was too young to be bogged down. I wanted to have an adventurous life before settling down.

The court proceedings were finally over, and I never heard from Frank again.

Good riddance.

# CHAPTER XXXV

## Single Life in Manhattan

Life in Manhattan was boring. It was all work. Judy and I had drawn up a budget and found out that at the end of the week, after paying for everything, we were left with $1 each. Not even enough for a movie.

One social event brightened our lives. Charles Aznavour was scheduled to give a concert at Carnegie Hall. I adored Aznavour. He was an Armenian singer/composer from France and had a raspy voice. He sang soulful melodies. At the beginning of his career, he was rejected as a singer because of his voice, but later on, he got a lot of notoriety being the composer of Edit Piaf's songs. In fact, he wrote the lyrics of songs for most of the major singers in France. He was the son of Armenians who had escaped the Turkish Genocide and had come to Marseilles. He was a tiny guy with deep-set dark brown, bedroom eyes. He was also a good actor and played in a few French films.

Ma, Judy, and I went to the concert. The tickets were rather expensive. The hall was full to the brim, with French-speaking people and Armenians from New York and New Jersey. I noticed that K was there also. He was alone. I nodded and gave him a perfunctory smile. He nodded back but did not smile. I suppose he was still angry with me for not accepting him back as my husband.

It was an exciting evening. Aznavour's songs gave me goose pimples all over my body. There was so much energy and charisma emanating from such a diminutive guy. He sang from the heart.

During intermission, Judy and I walked the corridors and met some Moroccan dignitaries, TV personalities, journalists, and a high-ranking minister from the government. They were super friendly and invited us out the next evening. The minister took a liking to us and invited us to return to Morocco with them and spend a week in Morocco with all expenses paid. We were tempted to take him up on the deal but could not possibly take time off from work. And also, I was not inclined to take up a relationship with the minister. I sensed that was coming next. No man is going to invite me somewhere, all expenses paid, and not expect something in return.

During their stay in Manhattan, we often went out with the Moroccans on dinner dates—nothing else. The minister and I became close—but not too close—because we had a lot in common. I liked him. He was also an artist and had an extremely interesting personality. He was married to a French woman, I was told by one of the journalists.

"I can find you a good job in Morocco if you come back with us," he suggested once when we were at dinner with a few of his friends.

"Thanks, but I can't leave my family behind," was my reply. I had no inclination whatever to take up with a married man or work in Morocco. I suspected, or rather I knew, what he was thinking—to keep me as a mistress in Rabat. The prospect did not appeal to me in the least. A relationship with this guy would go nowhere, but nevertheless, I just went along for the ride while he was in New York because it was exciting and fun. I made sure never to be alone with him. We were always with his entourage and Judy. I became quite friendly with the journalists also, and they told me a lot of gossip about him.

We had a Swiss neighbor in our building. The way I found out he was Swiss was because he brandished the Swiss flag outside his window. His name was Bruno. He was a young, jovial fellow. I met him in the elevator one day, and we talked in the lobby. I invited him for coffee at our place and introduced him to Ma and Judy.

We talked about Switzerland. I then told him about my jobs at the garment center and at NYU and about my discontent.

"Why don't you go and work in Geneva?" he asked me. "You have the languages. You could find a good job in one of the international organizations. That's a good solution for you since you are not happy with your jobs in New York," he added.

"Yeah, that is an idea, but I would like to do something in the design field, and unfortunately, there are no prospects in Switzerland, except in St. Gallen, but there, they only make lace and embroidery," I replied, "and I'm not into that."

"So, take some time off from designing and explore Europe. You'll like it. Switzerland is close to most major cities in Europe, and you can even explore them on weekends."

Bruno was quite persuasive in depicting the fabulous life I would have in Switzerland.

A yearning to go to Europe sparked up in me again. I thought it over and tried to come up with different scenarios. I then remembered the guy I had met in ICAO in Montreal who worked for one of the UN agencies in Geneva. He had told me the same thing. We had corresponded intermittently, and he had asked me to look him up if ever I would go to Geneva one day.

In New York, Arty was still around, pressuring me to marry him and go to Los Angeles and get a family going and eventually find a designing job over there.

"Arty, I like you a lot, but I cannot envisage another marriage right now. As for children, that is in the distant future. I just got out of one marriage, and I need some space. I think I am going to Europe and apply for a job there. I cannot settle down now. Sorry."

"Okay, if you don't make it there, you can always come to L.A. I'll be there waiting for you."

"Please don't do that. I don't wish to commit myself to anyone just yet."

Arty went to Los Angeles after a heart-wrenching goodbye. I felt sorry for the guy. He was a nice guy, kind and dependable, and would make a good husband to someone, but he was not for me. He would remind me too much of my past in Egypt and my life with K.

We corresponded.

"What have you decided to do with your life?" Ma asked me when she saw me deep in thought one day, scribbling on a piece of paper at breakfast.

"I have made up my mind. I will go to Europe," I told her.

"Are you out of your mind? You have no money, and you don't know anyone there. What the hell are you going to do? You wanted to go to the U.S. all your life and become a fashion designer. You came and became one. You brought us to the U.S. Obviously, you had plans of staying here. Your sister had an excellent job with the Americans in Cairo. She has a good job here with the Rockefeller Foundation. And now you want to leave the U.S. What about us? Have you thought about us? We can't afford to live here by ourselves once you are gone. You are like a grasshopper or some crazy chicken without a head. And have you thought about the cats?"

"I can make a good living here as a designer, but life is too hectic. I have worked my ass off in the designing field. It is good money, but it is work, work, work. No time off to enjoy anything. As for being a secretary, forget it. I can't make ends meet here, and I hate being a secretary anyway. Arty wants me to go to L.A. and marry him, but I can't possibly do that either. I am not in love with him. I have to try Europe. What's wrong with that?"

"He is a good guy, you've known him forever, and you can also have a designing job in L.A.," Ma said. She liked Arty.

"Ma, stop it. I want to go to Europe, and I don't want to marry anyone yet. I am too young. I want to meet new people and have adventures."

Ma and Judy listened to me intently.

"Bruno says that in Geneva, people have two-hour lunches, and Paris and Rome are not too far away for weekend trips. I do want to try Europe. I know two people there, the guy I met in Montreal and a friend of Arty's. He gave me the telephone number of his best friend from Lebanon, who is now working in Geneva as a photographer. I will try and get a job at the United Nations or one of the international organizations as a secretary to start with," I told Ma. "I don't mind being a secretary in Geneva. The pay is better than in New York, with a lot of time off. Once I get a job, I can bring you guys over, and Judy will also find a job with an international organization. And the cats will come with you."

"Just because you know two guys there, you think this is a bonanza? For all you know, this guy you met in Montreal is married. It was four years ago, remember? And who the hell is Arty's friend?" asked Ma. "And how are you going to manage with so little money?"

Her objections went on and on. Judy agreed with her.

"I am almost sure I can make it in Switzerland, and then we'll be together again. If I don't make it, I'll come back, and we can all go to California. I can start a new life over there. At least the weather is better than in New York, and people are more laid back."

"What? Are you going to marry Arty if you go to California?" asked Judy.

"No, of course not. I have not decided that far ahead yet. When the time comes, I'll think of something."

I always had a plan B.

Ma and Judy looked at me apprehensively. Ma shook her head, but she could not deter me from my plans. I had made up my mind.

"You have always been a rebel and continue on being so. I hope you will be able to settle down one day," she said.

A friend of mine from the law school, Dede, another secretary, also manifested a desire to go to Europe. I pondered for a few days and came up with a plan.

Dede and I would buy chartered tickets and spend two or three weeks in Europe—mostly in Switzerland and in Italy. My plan was to apply to all the UN agencies in Geneva and then go to Rome for some fun and apply also at FAO (the Food and Agricultural Organization).

Dede just agreed to everything I had planned. She was a blind follower. She had never been out of the country. I was being fatalistic and quite impetuous, and I can't deny I was not scared to death about my venture and the uncertain future ahead. No prospective job, no money in the bank, and no husband to fall back on and, on top of all that, I had a family who relied on me.

But was it not what I had wanted all along? To be free and independent?

I knew life was full of surprises, and I could not predict the future. I was just damn curious to find out what was in store for me on the other side of the Atlantic. I was still young, and anything could happen.

There was a new world on my horizon, waiting to be discovered.

# NOTE FROM THE AUTHOR

Most of my memoir has been reconstructed from my diaries, which I have kept since age twelve. I would never have remembered all the details of my narrative had it not been for the diaries. I also kept all the letters written to me by friends, boyfriends, and family since 1950 and copies of some of my letters to them. They are most interesting and eventful. It took me weeks to read all the collection. It was also easy to remember my early life as I have numerous albums full of photos since I was born.

Another collection that helped me revive my memory was our old black-and-white movie reels from the 1930s. I hauled them from Cairo to Montreal, from there to Boston and New York, then to Geneva, and then finally to the United States again. I am branded "the hoarder" by my husband and two sons. Yes, I am a hoarder. But that has kept me from getting bored, ever.

I feel that I have lived five distinct lives: my early life in Cairo; my married life in Montreal; my careers in Boston and Manhattan; my adventurous, artistic life in Geneva; and finally, my settled life in the United States, which is not without excitement.

It has been rather difficult to write about my true feelings about the people and events in my life as I felt that I was baring myself to criticism. However, I managed to do so, and I feel strong enough to withstand any negative comments.

CPSIA information can be obtained
at www.ICGtesting.com
Printed in the USA
BVHW030519150721
611947BV00006B/95

9 781664 133815